Baker → Rebuilding the house of I_j.

Cohen → beginnings of Deepness → Diversity

Goodblatt → Rabbinic Instruction

... Heges → Greek Impurities

Hezser

Lightstone → Rhetoric of the B+

Saba:

P.87 → Next
114 — motivations

→ ...

The Mind
of the Talmud

THE MIND
OF THE TALMUD

*An Intellectual History
of the Bavli*

DAVID KRAEMER

New York   Oxford
OXFORD UNIVERSITY PRESS
1990

Oxford University Press

Oxford   New York   Toronto
Delhi   Bombay   Calcutta   Madras   Karachi
Petaling Jaya   Singapore   Hong Kong   Tokyo
Nairobi   Dar es Salaam   Cape Town
Melbourne   Auckland

and associated companies in
Berlin   Ibadan

Copyright © 1990 by David Kraemer

Published by Oxford University Press, Inc.,
198 Madison Avenue, New York, New York 10016-4314

Oxford is a registered trademark of Oxford University Press

Library of Congress Cataloging-in-Publication Data
Kraemer, David Charles.
The mind of the Talmud : an intellectual history of the Bavli /
David Kraemer.
p.   cm.
Includes bibliographical references.
ISBN 0-19-506290-6
1. Talmud—History.   2. Jewish law—Interpretation and
construction.   I. Title.
BM501.K72   1990
296.1'2506—dc20   89-22953   CIP

4 6 8 9 7 5 3

Printed in the United States of America
on acid-free paper

To Susan, who, through her insistence
that scholarship have meaning,
taught me to write this book

Preface

THE LINE OF INQUIRY from which this work emerges began with my
doctoral dissertation, written at the Jewish Theological Seminary under
the guidance of Prof. David Halivni. At that time I catalogued the forms
of preserved amoraic traditions in the Babylonian Talmud, primarily in
order to ascertain whether, and to what extent, the sages of the Talmud
(the amoraim) preserved argumentation. It was Halivni's thesis then, as
now, that the amoraim were not generally concerned with argumentation,
and that the wealth of argumentation found in the Talmud is preserved as
a consequence of the interest in such material that developed among the
authors of the later, unattributed Talmud text. My conclusions showed
that amoraic publication was primarily apodictic and brief, but that middle
amoraic generations appeared to show at least a nascent interest in argumentation. Accordingly, I supported Halivni's views generally, albeit with
some important reservations.

There were, I have come to recognize, two serious flaws in my earlier
work. First, at that time I did not account for the methodological critiques
and refinements suggested in the work of Jacob Neusner. As will become
apparent, I have attempted to confront these issues directly in the chapters
that follow. More important, and going beyond the redactional ramifications, in my earlier work I did not inquire into the meanings of amoraic
and Talmudic literary style. This is the primary focus of the present work.

The conclusions of my earliest investigation, though somewhat supplemented, are found in the sections of chapter 2 on the first, second, and
third amoraic periods. The balance of this work is largely new. Naturally,

I have not, in the present context, repeated many of the details of my earlier research; for those details I direct the reader to my dissertation, "Stylistic Characteristics of Amoraic Literature." The latter is quite technical and is primarily of interest only to specialists in the field. In the present work I have sought to avoid such technicality as much as possible.

However, it has not always been possible to avoid technical discussions. I hope such discussions will be of interest to my colleagues in the field of rabbinics. But I have directed this book to other audiences as well, particularly to those interested in the history of religion and of ideas. Such readers might be unnecessarily frustrated by sections in which there is considerable textual analysis, but I advise them not to be intimidated by such obstacles; the synthetic analyses and conclusions are accessible without a technical understanding.

Accordingly, the reader should be aware of the following divisions in the text. Chapter 1 lays an essential foundation for all subsequent chapters. The second through fourth sections of chapter 2 are somewhat technical, and their analysis (contained in the last section of the same chapter) can be understood without undue concern for details. Similarly, since the "Evidence" section of chapter 3 primarily consists of textual analysis, the more general reader might be better served by turning directly to the conclusions of the same chapter. The first section of chapter 4 is likewise technical, but it is important for a proper understanding of the Talmudic form as a whole, so I would encourage the reader to try to steer a path through it. Finally, chapters 5–7 contain my most important contribution, so the reader who is interested in the theoretical implications of this work is directed to these chapters in particular.

For the reader with little or no experience in the field of Talmud and rabbinics, I have sought to avoid, as much as possible, the use of Hebrew or Aramaic terms. Naturally, such terms cannot be avoided entirely, but where it has been necessary to employ them I have made sure that at their first appearance they are accompanied by a translation or explanation. I have also included a glossary of such terms for ready reference. In addition, the reader may also find useful a table of Talmudic tractates and commonly used abbreviations.

The questions I have asked in this work originated in my exchanges with several parties. The formative influence is that of Prof. David Halivni, who directed my dissertation research and whose subsequent insights and challenges have been invaluable. I continue to be immensely grateful for his kind and thoughtful support. Second, I have learned a great deal from the writings of Jacob Neusner, who frames arguments that I often find compelling and persuasive, and whose influence, reflected in many of the questions I have raised, will be evident to all. He is, without his personal avowal, my second teacher, and I look forward to his future critical comments. Last, and in many ways most important, I have learned much from the questions raised by many of my students, who have refused to permit a lazy presentation of facts and have always insisted that I address the question "what does it all mean?" I have also been prompted to ask this question by another source and in this connection I draw the reader's attention to the dedication of this book.

There are many other parties to whom I must express my gratitude. My colleague and dear friend Prof. Baruch Bokser read the first draft of the manuscript and suggested many essential improvements and corrections. Another colleague and old friend, Dr. Alvin Sandberg, also read the whole manuscript and suggested many improvements, both stylistic and substantive. Profs. Neil Gillman and Henry Morgenbesser read the last chapter and offered essential critical refinements. And, not least of all, an anonymous reader for Oxford University Press left many comments in the margins of my first draft manuscript that led to important improvements. Without the wisdom of these individuals this work would have been very different.

I thank Prof. Shamma Friedman for making available to me references in the Yerushalmi from his computer database. Due to the lack of a complete concordance to that work, I would not have been able to conduct comprehensive examinations of certain questions without his help. Thanks also to Prof. David Roskies, who suggested the title for this book. Finally, I must acknowledge my debt to Prof. Reuven Kimelman, whose analysis of the text at Eruvin 13b suggested to me several fruitful analytical possibilities. A number of my interpretations of that important text emerged from my reflections on his comments.

The editors and other staff members at Oxford University Press have maintained high editorial standards and provided professional support throughout this project. Carole Schwager did a meticulous job of copyediting the manuscript. Henry Krawitz, who also assisted me with my earlier book, *The Jewish Family: Metaphor and Memory,* is especially to be thanked; he is a superb editor and a kind human being. I have been fortunate to work with him.

New York   D.K.
September 1989

Contents

Glossary

Amora (pl. amoraim)   The named sages whose opinions are recorded in the two talmuds; things that pertain to the period of the amoraim are called amoraic

Baraita (pl. baraitot)   Traditions of purportedly tannaitic origin that were not, however, included in the Mishnah; baraitot are found in the two talmuds as well as in specific tannaitic collections, such as the Tosefta or the Midrashei Halakha

Halakha   Rabbinic law

Mekhilta   The Midrash Halakha to the book of Exodus

Midrash Halakha   A tannaitic exegesis of the books Exodus, Leviticus, Numbers, and Deuteronomy

Mishnah   The first document to emerge from early rabbinic Judaism, completed by about the year 200 C.E.; apparently (though not definitely) a legal code, arranged by topic, and divided into six "orders" (Heb. *sedarim*) and further into tractates (Heb. *masekhtot*)

Seder (pl. sedarim)   A major topical division of the Mishnah

Sifra   Midrash Halakha to the book of Leviticus

Sifrei   Midrash Halakha to the books of Numbers and Deuteronomy

Stam (or stamma; pl. stammaim)   Literally, "anonymous" or "unattributed"; used in this study with two meanings: (1) the unattributed compositional level of the Bavli text, or (2) the authors of the unattributed Bavli text

Sugya (pl. sugyot)   A self-contained, sustained deliberation in the Talmud

Tanna (pl. tannaim)   Used in this study primarily to mean (1) a rabbinic sage of the period of the Mishnah, with recognized superior authority within the rabbinic system, but also (2) an official repeater of rabbinic traditions; things that pertain to the period of the tannaim are called tannaitic

Tosefta   A collection of baraitot that relate as a commentary to the Mishnah; traditions included in the Tosefta purport to be tannaitic, but the document is clearly redacted subsequent to the Mishnah

Tractate (Heb. *masekhet*)   The basic topical division of the Mishnah and, consequently, of the talmuds

Yerushalmi   The Talmud of the Land of Israel; also known as the Jerusalem or Palestinian Talmud

Abbreviations

Arakh.	Arakhin	**Men.**	Menahot
A. Z.	Avodah Zarah	**M. K.**	Mo'ed Katan
b.	Babylonian Talmud	**Naz.**	Nazir
B. B.	Baba Batra	**Ned.**	Nedarim
Bekh.	Bekhorot	**Neg.**	Negaim
Ber.	Berakhot	**Nid.**	Niddah
Bez.	Bezah	**Pes.**	Pesahim
B. M.	Baba Mezia	**R. H.**	Rosh Hashanah
B. Q.	Baba Qamma	**San.**	Sanhedrin
Eruv.	Eruvin	**Shab.**	Shabbat
Git.	Gittin	**Shev.**	Shevuot
Hag.	Hagigah	**Sot.**	Sotah
Hor.	Horayot	**Suk.**	Sukkah
Hul.	Hullin	**Taan.**	Taanit
Ker.	Keritot	**Tem.**	Temurah
Ket.	Ketubot	**y.**	Talmud Yerushalmi
Kid.	Kiddushin	**Yom.**	Yoma
m.	Mishnah	**Yev.**	Yevamot
Mak.	Makkot	**Zev.**	Zevahim
Meg.	Megillah		

The Mind
of the Talmud

Introduction

THIS BOOK IS MEANT TO BE a particular kind of history of the Babylonian Talmud (the Bavli). It is, first, a literary history. It traces the development of the literary forms and conventions by which rabbinic sages in third- through sixth-century Sasanian Iran (which Jews still referred to as Babylonia) recorded their opinions and rulings. What motivates this examination is the assumption—spelled out at length in chapter 1—that literary conventions are reflections of ideological choices and that by tracing the history of literary developments we can say something of the history of ideas. This is also, therefore, intended as an intellectual history of the Jews who produced the Bavli. It will not, to be sure, be a comprehensive intellectual history; it will, instead, be a history of the ideologies that are embodied in the very form, structure, and methods of the single most comprehensive record to emerge from classical Babylonian Jewry.

Because this is an intellectual history, the analyses and explanations proposed will naturally exhibit a particular bias. But I do not mean to suggest, by this bias, that these explanations are the only ones that may reasonably account for the literary features that I describe and analyze. There are surely numerous influences—literary, social, political, religious, and intellectual—that affected the shape of this Talmud in its various historical stages, and these all must be considered in their proper place. Still, the Bavli is, in my opinion, primarily an intellectual opus of interest for its theoretical elaboration of the law of God and of the rabbis—in combination with many related issues that are not strictly legal—and, for this reason, the particular concerns of intellectual history are of

3

first-order import when discussing this document. This perspective may not be comprehensive, but it is, at the very least, one essential part of an explanation of why the traditions of the Babylonian rabbis took the forms that they did. It is the history of the ideologies of the literary forms recorded in the Bavli, therefore, that I will seek to highlight and clarify.

Of course, it is evident even from what I have already said that I believe that this sort of history can be written. I do, in fact, believe that in the pages of the Bavli we have access not only to the final document but also to the various stages that led to its creation. As many readers know, this is presently a disputed claim,[1] but I will defend it at length in the chapters that follow. Suffice it to say that I am confident that I can demonstrate that opinions attributed to amoraim (as the sages of the Bavli and Yerushalmi were called; sing. amora) accurately reflect the period of the sage to which they are attributed. This does not mean that we can know that a certain statement was made by that particular sage, or even that the precise content accurately represents a view that was current in the circle of that sage. We can, however, know, at the very least, that certain forms of expression were typical in certain generations, and, given additional data, we can even say that it is likely that the essence of a certain opinion was held in the circle of disciples of a particular sage. Since this work is a history of literary forms as ideological expressions, we do have access to the sort of information needed to write such a history.

This book joins a recent profusion of studies, both scholarly and popular, on the Bavli and other literary documents that emerged from rabbinic Judaism during its formative stages (first to sixth centuries).[2] Many of these studies have been directed to scholars with a unique interest in rabbinic texts, but others, most notably those of Jacob Neusner, have claimed that the Bavli (and other rabbinic works) should be of interest to the broader intellectual world as well. In my opinion, this view is a correct one, and I should like to articulate my own understanding of why this is the case.

The Bavli is, as I have said, the most comprehensive of all documents produced by rabbinic Jews in late antiquity. Having come to closure, most likely, some time in the sixth century,[3] its pages represent an enormous range of interests. It includes commentaries on the Mishnah and related texts, exegeses of scripture, and independent deliberations on legal and religious matters. Its discussions are both practical and theoretical, seeming to admit no limit to the topics it might pursue. Admittedly a text of immense difficulty, it is also one which, by means of careful editorial planning and manipulation, is extremely seductive.

Being the most comprehensive record of the rabbinic community in Sasanian Iran, the Bavli offers unrivaled evidence as to the nature of that community. The Bavli embodies its thoughts and its emotions, its practices and its variety. Serving as a record of at least a segment of what was then the most ancient continually populated Jewish community on earth (having first come to that territory in the Babylonian exile of 586 B.C.E.), the Bavli is of unique interest as a source for the history of Judaism. It is, after all, the document through which a segment of that community chose to express itself at length, and it is through its pages, therefore, that we may gain access to the particular assumptions and ideologies of those who composed it. Moreover, it is a document of the exile—one which seeks to adapt a document of the land of Israel, the Mishnah, to foreign surroundings. In this respect, the Bavli offers insight into the development and survival of a religion away from its formative home. It is of interest, therefore, not merely to historians of Judaism but also to historians of religion in general.

The Bavli is of interest to historians of Judaism and religion in another way as well. The Bavli became the authoritative legal source for medieval Judaism. It was on the basis of its opinions that Judaism was defined from the Moslem conquest to the dawn of the modern age and, for some, even to the present day. Hence the Bavli is an essential source for the history of later Judaism, in obvious and sometimes not so obvious ways. For example, the history of the politics of the Bavli and its supporters in their competition with the partisans of the Yerushalmi for ascendancy in Judaism is a well-known chapter in the study of Judaism during the so-called Geonic period—the period of Islamic primacy in the territories where most Jews lived, between the seventh and eleventh centuries. Most have ascribed the triumph of the Bavli to primarily political factors that, by all accounts, were certainly significant. Few, on the other hand, have considered what in the nature of the Bavli itself may have played a role in its success.[4] Why was the Bavli's influence so pervasive? What in its form and method caused it to speak so directly to the hearts of rabbinic leaders in communities that were so scattered and so different? In the lessons that it taught, what was so "right" for Jews living so much later than the centuries during which it had been conceived?

The Bavli is of interest also beyond the study of Judaism and religion. As a legal document the Bavli is unique in the ancient world, for it claims to record not merely the law itself but, more important, the process by which the law came to be formed. Although close reading of the text will reveal that the deliberations that presumably represent this process are in fact subsequent to the laws that they treat, these deliberations do represent someone's claim concerning the nature of the process. At the very least they demonstrate that the process was considered important, an assessment that is by no means universal in either the ancient or modern world. Moreover, if these deliberations were composed in relative chronological proximity to the conclusions that they accompany—and my view is that this is the case in a noteworthy minority of instances[5]—then they may in fact embody something of the reasoning by which certain opinions in the law came to be produced. Be that as it may, even the majority of cases that were composed only much later, to serve as speculative "re-creations" of the formative process and of the reasoning that informed that process, represent an original chapter in the history of law. Only the authors of the Yerushalmi before had recognized the potential value and impact of the legal process and saw fit to record it, and the Yerushalmi's record parallels that of the Bavli in neither comprehensiveness nor elaborateness. The ideology of the law is here, in a unique and most explicit way, for all the world to see.

But I will argue that in significant respects the Bavli is not a legal document at all but a work of religious philosophy. What is outstanding about the deliberations that the Bavli records is that they so often avoid any conclusion; more often than not they prefer to support competing views rather than deciding in favor of one view or the other. What is the meaning of this preference? Why would a presumably legal document see fit to avoid decisions in the law? Furthermore, what characterizes the Bavli perhaps more than any other feature is the incessant questioning with which it approaches its subjects. "Everything" requires a reason. "Everything" is accompanied by justification or clarification. Everything, in fact, is the potential target of question or objection. How might such an approach be explained?

To begin with, this method represents a not so subtle challenge to authority. The authority of the text being analyzed—the Mishnah or scripture, for example—was not sufficient justification for a law. Often, other justifications were necessary. Questioning opened up alternatives that were not originally apparent. The search for the source of a given law often revealed rival opinions that subsequently became legitimate subjects for investigation. Furthermore, as suggested earlier, once alternatives were proposed, often no determination regarding the preferred alternative was made. The Mishnah had declared the law with a limited number of options. Certainly, with a few rules of thumb ("the law follows the majority") it could have been employed in practice. Not so in the case of the Bavli. The Bavli opened up options. It could allow for no immediate practical application at all.

What motivated such a posture? I will argue that the form of the Bavli embodies a recognition that truth, divine in origin, is on the human level indeterminable. For this reason, at least in part,[6] the Bavli considers alternative approaches to the truth but methodically seeks to avoid privileging one over another. The Bavli challenges authority because, in the end, it argues that we have no direct access to ultimate authority. We have only human approaches to truth and they are all, of necessity, merely relative.

In consideration of this thesis, the Bavli is a document of interest not only in the history of religion, but also in the history of ideas in general. As we will see in the final chapter, the premodern world—and the world of antiquity in particular—generally assumed that the truth, either religious or rationalistic, could be identified. The Bavli may be one of the earliest and certainly one of the most comprehensive documents in which this assumption is challenged.

This conclusion, to be defended at length in the chapters that follow, will be surprising (perhaps even "counterintuitive") to many students of postclassical Judaism. In the medieval age, legal decisors and the communities that admitted their authority declared the law, on the basis of the Bavli, with great definitiveness. There is certainly little indication in the halakhic codes that they produced that "truth" is uncertain. On the contrary, these works appear to speak, for the most part, with absolute certainty.[7] And there is little doubt that the communities for which they were authoritative understood this to be the case. The law was observed, in its precise detail, because it was "God's *true* law." As divine command, interpreted and enunciated by authorities who had direct access to the "chain of tradition," this law was as good and true as if spoken by God Godself.

But the reader should keep in mind that the chapters that follow are not concerned with the way the Bavli was understood and employed by later Jews. They related to the Bavli in their own ways, for their own reasons, but not because theirs was the best or most correct understanding of the source document in its own context. Rather, they shaped and reinterpreted the Bavli to fit their own circumstances much as the Bavli had shaped and reinterpreted earlier traditions to speak to the needs of its community. So the later understanding does not (necessarily) tell us much about the earlier tradition at all. For such an understanding we must address the source document directly, on its own terms. The thesis that I described emerges on the basis of such an approach.

Moreover, the counterintuitive nature of this conclusion (the indeterminability of truth in the Bavli) will disappear when one recalls the audience that the Bavli assumes. The Bavli is composed by rabbinic scholars for rabbinic students and scholars. Its deliberations are elaborate and difficult and they demand extensive preparation and probably lengthy discipleship. These are not discussions that are directed at Jews in general, or even at literate but untutored Jews. They are designed for individuals who are willing to undertake specialized training, and they are directed at the larger community of male Jews only in their capacity as potential scholars—as an expression of the rabbinic ideal that all male Jews might become *talmidei ḥakhamim* (students of sages).

It is precisely such an elite, sophisticated community that can tolerate the indeterminacy that I claim the Bavli represents. Such a community can admit the gap between divine revelation and human understanding and not be debilitated by the tension inherent in practice that is at best an imperfect application of the divine will. This is not to say that all members of such a community would subscribe to such a position, or that they would think this view instructive beyond this community. But if we recognize this to be the nature of the audience that the Bavli addresses, it will not be nearly so startling to conclude that the Bavli embodies a relationship to divine truth that is both subtle and sophisticated. It is in this context that the thesis presented in this book must be considered.

1

On Writing an Intellectual History of the Bavli

The Meaning of Literary Forms

As I SUGGESTED in the introduction, what follows is intended to be an intellectual (or ideological) history of a literary document—the Bavli. The premise that justifies combining "literary" with "ideological" is simply this: given the fact that a variety of forms are always theoretically available to an author—though practical constraints might limit the choices that are genuinely available—the selection of a particular form to express one's ideas must be understood to be a value judgment (even if the pragmatic choice is made), an expression of ideology.

On one level, the assumption that the choice of a literary form is meaningful is self-evident. It is on the basis of this assumption that many works of literary analysis and criticism have proceeded;[1] the insights that they yield support the commonsense correctness of the assumption as a whole. Nevertheless, it is essential, due to its centrality in what follows, to consider why and in what ways such an approach is justified.

Literary expression, whatever its form or purpose, is a social act.[2] Through such expression an author seeks to communicate ideas to a reader, thereby creating a relationship of sorts. Of course, if the author intends to communicate convincingly, that is, for ideas to be considered and valued, the author must communicate in a manner that will be understood. This requires that the author identify the intended audience and express ideas through conventions that are likely to be effective with such an audience.

The conventions that are available for such communication will be determined by the precise nature of an author's subject and intended audience, and by virtue of these considerations the options available to the author can be either limited or many. If, for example, a lawyer seeks to communicate regarding a subject in the law with other lawyers, her options will generally be limited to established journals. In contrast, if an author wishes to share his views of romantic love with contemporary Americans at large, he might choose to communicate these views through fiction or nonfiction, prose or poetry, comedy or drama (to name only some of the options). In either case, once the variety of options is identified, then the choice of a particular option can be understood as meaningful.

This is true regardless of the number of options. Even if the society of lawyers imagines that there is only one manner to communicate with other lawyers—in respected journals—the choice to abide by that limitation is significant. It assumes, to begin with, that the conventions established by such journals are to be respected. It assumes, furthermore, that there is good reason to accept the authority of such journals and not seek alternatives, even if this would mean the establishment of a new, perhaps more radical, organ of expression. Most obviously, it reflects the desire of the author to be included in the legal establishment, for even dissent will, in the pages of such a vehicle, have to be expressed with great caution and through the use of accepted forms.

The choice of a form for literary expression is perhaps even more meaningful when numerous options are available. Taking our other example, if an author chooses to speak of romantic love in a novel, he might thereby demonstrate his desire to reach a rather wide, but not necessarily sophisticated audience. Should he instead express his views in a nonfictional study or through poetry rather than prose, he might, in so doing, express his judgment that only more sophisticated audiences merit his efforts. Of course, he could also illustrate his opinions in a dramatic presentation or write a journalistic commentary for a popular periodical. Any of these choices would be the product of certain evaluations and, in light of the alternatives, would reveal something about the ideologies of the author.

One excellent illustration of this approach is Leo Strauss's work on Plato's dialogues. Stating his thesis most directly, Strauss writes: "One cannot understand Plato's teaching as he meant it if one does not know what the Platonic dialogue is. One cannot separate the understanding of Plato's teaching from the understanding of the form in which it is presented . . . to begin with one must even pay greater attention to the 'form' than to the 'substance' since the meaning of the 'substance' depends on the 'form.' ''[3] Plato's dialogues are not philosophical treatises in any conventional sense. At no point does Plato speak for himself, and the multiplicity of spokesmen for various views often serves to confuse rather than clarify the issue. This is in particular true because Plato's preferred spokesman, Socrates, typically refutes the views of others without suggesting alternatives of his own. How do these factors of form affect our understanding of the substance of the dialogues?

The fact that Plato always uses spokesmen, Strauss argues, means that "we cannot know from [the dialogues] what Plato thought."[4] "Plato conceals himself completely in his dialogues. . . . [He] conceals his opinions."[5] He conceals these opinions, as I said, in the mouths of multiple spokesmen, this being intended, Strauss believes, to overcome the basic shortcomings of writing in the first place. The problem with writing—unlike speaking—is that you cannot choose your audience and tailor your argument appropriately. To eliminate this difficulty, Plato spoke through various individuals and "so contrived as to say different things to different people."[6] At the same time, even though many of the dialogues address similar issues, "Plato's work consists of many dialogues because it imitates the manyness, the variety, the heterogeneity of being."[7]

These meanings emerge from the variety of features that characterize the Platonic form—not from the content of the dialogues as such—and it is impossible, therefore (as far as Strauss is concerned), to quote this or that view from the dialogues and represent it as Plato's own.[8] Any claim for Plato's own opinion must be preceded by a study of context and dramatic development and even then conclusions should be stated with caution.[9]

The application of this method to a rabbinic text can be most effectively illustrated by reference to several recent treatments of the Mishnah. Briefly, the Mishnah is a text that bears little resemblance to any Jewish document that preceded it. The Mishnah expresses judgments on the law, generally through illustrative cases, in a terse, sometimes elliptical language. It either speaks on its own behalf, in an anonymous "voice of the author," or presents views in the names of rabbinic authorities who flourished in the late first or second century. Sometimes it records dissenting views, but often not. It rarely quotes scripture, though to one who knows scripture well implicit reference is far more frequent. Despite the fact that it took shape in history, subsequent to events (the destruction of the Temple and several wars with Rome) that must have shaken Jews residing in the land of Israel to the depths of their beings, it generally takes no explicit notice of these events, unwilling to admit that much of what it prescribes has no context in which to be executed. Finally, it speaks in a Hebrew that has no precise literary precedent, either in the Hebrew Bible or elsewhere.

In *Midrash, Mishnah, and Gemara: The Jewish Predilection for Justified Law,*[10] David Weiss Halivni assumes that the Mishnaic form represents primarily a pragmatic choice of its authors. He does so because, in his opinion, the Mishnah is, in recognition of the larger Jewish context, an aberration. Jews, he argues, had from their very beginnings seen fit to justify their laws, and not to state them as mere categorical assertions. This was true even in the Torah where, though the authority of the lawgiver (God) would presumably have been sufficient, laws are often accompanied by justificatory motive clauses.[11] Jewish literature in the late second Temple period—the period to which Halivni attributes the early midrashim—was also grounded in reasons ("this law must be obeyed because it is implicit in this scriptural verse"), and this would again be the case in the talmudim of Palestine and Babylonia. This being the "natural" Jewish preference, why, then, did the Mishnah differ?

The first reason according to Halivni, is the development at around the beginning of the common era of "complex midrash," a midrashic form of immense sophistication that in Halivni's view began at the time of Hillel. Because of its great difficulty and complexity, this sort of midrash was no longer a reasonable vessel in which to transmit the presumably vast body of rabbinic oral law. An alternative, more straightforward and easier to memorize, was needed.

Shortly after this innovation the Temple of Jerusalem was destroyed, the war with Rome was lost, and Jews in Palestine were faced with a serious threat to their survival. They could seek protection and stability in the law, but for that to be effective, it would be necessary to redesign the manner in which the law was kept; it had to be easily accessible. These factors together called for a form that was comprehensible and easy to memorize. The solution was the Mishnaic form.[12]

In Halivni's view, then, the ideology of the Mishnah—allowing pragmatism to win out over predilection—was the value of survival. The form itself is, in some sense, to be despised; because Jews had always preferred justification, the Mishnah should ideally have been combined with midrash.[13] But if we admit that the form is an aberration, and recognize that alternatives ought to have been preferred, it becomes clear that the

Mishnah's manner of expression embodies the value of survival. Even mere pragmatism is not valueless.

The most comprehensive analysis of the Mishnah's form and meaning is contained in Jacob Neusner's *Judaism: The Evidence of the Mishnah.*[14] For our purposes, we will limit our discussion to the several characteristics of Mishnaic expression that Neusner considers most meaningful.

The first feature that Neusner emphasizes is the Mishnah's relationship/ nonrelationship to scripture. He notes the puzzling fact that although the Mishnah rarely refers to scripture explicitly, it exhibits three widely divergent relationships to scripture. According to Neusner's reading of the Mishnah, some texts merely restate the laws of scripture, others relate to scripture in a selective fashion, and still others stand in complete isolation from it. What is to be made of this variety?

Neusner understands this variety of relationships as an indication that whereas to "the philosophers of the Mishnah . . . all of Scripture is authoritative . . . only some of Scripture is relevant."[15] In other words, though the rabbis of the Mishnah considered scripture the ultimate source of authority, they did not allow it to dictate the precise religious or legal program that they were to pursue. The questions and problems that informed their agenda were, rather, wholly their own and, in this sense, *their* authority—independent of scripture—was most significant.

What makes this particular analysis striking is the fact that Neusner assumes a different Jewish literary history than does Halivni. Neusner does not believe that midrash preceded, and therefore set the context for, Mishnah. He denies this possibility because the redacted works in which these presumably early midrashim are included all postdate the Mishnah. In view of what he believes to be the lack of evidence that the midrashic traditions themselves long antedated the documents in which they are included, Neusner deems it unjustified to claim that the midrashic form is more ancient. In his opinion, the Mishnah must be compared with other literary precedents, well known in the history of ancient Jewish literature, and his comparison of options taken illuminates Neusner's whole discussion.

Neusner details at length[16] the fact that nearly all Jewish texts in the centuries preceding the Mishnah had defined themselves in explicit relation to scripture. They either imitated the models of scripture literally, as in the Genesis Apocryphon or 2 Baruch, or they commented on it, as in the various *pesher* texts of Qumran. What none of them did on the surface—as, for the most part, the Mishnah did—was to ignore it.

Therefore, the choice of the Mishnah's authors is entirely innovative and without precedent, and it clearly demands interpretation. Whether Neusner's specific interpretation is correct, or whether, for example, the redactional and linguistic independence of the Mishnah merely reflects its desire to express its evaluation that scripture has now been *closed*[17] and that new forms henceforth had to be employed, is immaterial. What is important is the recognition that these choices are significant and that an interpretation of them is appropriate and necessary.

A second characteristic of the Mishnah that Neusner emphasizes is its "striking continuity" with the priestly code (what others call "P").[18] Its concerns are overwhelmingly those of the priestly code, and its perspective is frequently that of the priests or Levites. Again, what is to be made of this?

Neusner, to begin with, attributes this redactional choice to the group within which the Mishnah originated, a group which, like the authors of the Qumran scrolls, sought to extend the restrictions of priestly purity to lay people. These "were people who wished to act at home as if they were in the Temple"[19] because, in their estimation, the whole nation of Israel was a nation of priests, and it was in the midst of this people that the tabernacle and, therefore, the divine presence resided.

Priestly separation, in Neusner's view, had another purpose. In the vast ocean of pagan Rome, it was often difficult for small peoples to maintain their distinct identities. Hellenization of the Near East had been accompanied by the opening of borders and the breaking down of barriers. How, in such an environment, were the Jewish people to remain distinct?

The Mishnah's answer, Neusner claims, is in the walls constructed by the priestly system. Cult is most concerned with defining the holy and the profane, the pure and the impure, what is in and what is out. That is why the Mishnah absorbs this system so completely; the distinctions now insisted on by the Mishnah, following the model of the priestly code, would permit Israel to remain distinct.[20]

A third, more formal and strictly literary feature of the Mishnah that Neusner takes to be meaningful is the grammatical and syntactical forms of the Mishnaic language.[21] He agrees with Halivni that the Mishnah is designed to be memorized, that its forms are mnemonic. But in Neusner's analysis the mnemonic design of the Mishnah is not to be found in the recurrence of words or superficial patterns; it is to be found, rather, in the recurrence of deep grammatical and syntactical relationships. The mnemonic patterns are subtle and abstract, not explicit or tangible. Since the goal—to facilitate memorization—could have been accomplished in either of these ways (and perhaps even more effectively in the way that was not taken), the decision to speak in recurrent, deep-set patterns must be explained.

According to Neusner, the language of the Mishnah serves to "create a world of discourse quite separate from the concrete realities of a given time, place, or society. The exceedingly limited repertoire of grammatical patterns by which all things on all matters are said gives symbolic expression to the notion that beneath the accidents of life are a few comprehensive relationships. Unchanging and enduring patterns lie deep in the inner structure of reality."[22] In other words, patterns of expression mirror patterns of thought, and the assumptions of an author and his society find expression in the literature that they produce.

The point of the foregoing review is not to endorse or defend the excellence of a particular interpretation. A variety of interpretations might legitimately be considered, each with its individual insight and contribution. What is crucial, however, is the recognition that such interpretations are grounded in a secure assumption: in a variety of ways, the literary choices that an author makes, preferring a certain sort of language with certain formal patterns of expression, choosing a certain overall redactional design, making one set of demands of the reader and not making others, grounding a text in history or ignoring history entirely—all of these speak just as eloquently about an author's views as does the explicit content of the text that he composes. "Mere" formal choices of this sort must be made even before an author embarks upon stating his thesis. They are priorities in the true sense, and it is therefore here that an author's valuative judgments must begin.

So, too, by approaching the Bavli with these questions and sensitivities will we be able to witness firsthand the values and ideologies that shaped that project as a whole. We will transcend the limitations of individual units and approach the values that are mirrored in the overall structure of the literature. We will be able to describe how one form of Judaism in sixth-century Babylonia, as reflected in the Bavli, differed from the Judaisms that preceded it. And, if I am correct in claiming that we do have access to the history that gave way to this end product, we will be able to describe how it came to be what it is. We will write the history of the development of a certain set of ideologies that shaped, most profoundly, the Judaism of the ensuing fourteen centuries.

The Bavli: A Preliminary Description

We must begin with a preliminary description of the choices that the authors of the Bavli made. To a greater or lesser extent, the Bavli is unlike any Jewish document that preceded it. First, to state the obvious: it in no way resembles any of the numerous forms that came to constitute Hebrew scripture. This is perhaps not surprising, since rabbinic sages many centuries before had already decided that biblical forms were no longer to be replicated. But other Jews, at or around the time of the Mishnah, did continue to employ forms of biblical expression (2 Baruch, 4 Ezra, Matthew, and some of the other gospels). It is therefore noteworthy that the Bavli affirmed this decision.

More surprising is the fact that the Bavli does not resemble the texts that those rabbinic "founding fathers" did choose to produce. The Bavli, with its abundance of questioning, challenge, and dialogue, is wholly dissimilar from either the Mishnah or Tosefta, both of which spoke in the form described previously, being brief and to the point, tolerating differences of opinion, but with rare exception (rarer in the Mishnah than in the Tosefta) ignoring the dialogues that such differences generated. It is also unlike the earlier midrashim, which, though rich in a formal "give and take," rarely record dialogues (actual or purported), and do not, like the Bavli, explicitly identify and evaluate a variety of authoritative sources. In addition, all of these predecessors speak in a limited variety of forms of Mishnaic Hebrew—a language whose use was at least severely restricted at the time these documents were promulgated.[23] The Bavli, on the other hand, speaks in eastern Aramaic, the language of the people at large.

The differences between the Bavli and the Yerushalmi, the document with which it superficially has the most in common, are more difficult to identify. In some ways the choices made by the authors of the Yerushalmi and Bavli were nearly identical. In an obvious way, both of these texts are commentaries on the Mishnah. Both discuss the meaning and application of the laws of the Mishnah, and both do so in the spoken language of their day—eastern and western Aramaic. Both attribute opinions to named amoraic authorities and other identified sources, but both also have an anonymous "voice of the Talmud" that speaks with great frequency. And perhaps most significantly, both are built around argumentation—the deliberations that themselves constitute the "Talmudic" form.

Despite all that they have in common, there are also many noteworthy differences. One of the best reviews of these differences remains Zechariah Frankel's *Mevo ha-Yerushalmi (Introduction to the Yerushalmi).*[24] Among the differences that Frankel notes are the following:[25]

1. As a general observation, the Bavli is far more verbose than the Yerushalmi. This tendency is expressed in a number of specific ways, including the likeliness of the Bavli to pursue matters in far greater length than the Yerushalmi.

2. The Yerushalmi will raise questions or objections and never supply an answer to them. This phenomenon is so common that a student of the Yerushalmi need not be particularly advanced to be familiar with it. In contrast, such an absence is extremely rare in the Bavli.

3. The Bavli is generally more independent and even "radical" in the treatment of its sources than the Yerushalmi. This trait is expressed, for example, in the Bavli's willingness to suggest that there is a gap in the Mishnaic text and to propose what needs to be added; the Yerushalmi will not make such a suggestion. In addition, the Bavli's explication of scripture is far more creative than the Yerushalmi's. In its extreme, this includes suggestions by the Bavli that the biblical text be rewritten in forms that Hebrew grammar will not accept (see pp. 152–53).

4. The Yerushalmi generally limits the number of objections and solutions that it will permit in a given sequence to a mere few steps. The Bavli's discussions, on the other hand, will commonly continue for several pages.

The difference in the length of deliberations in the two documents, which Frankel takes to be the most pronounced difference, causes him to observe that the Yerushalmi resembles not the completed Bavli, but more the deliberations of the later generations of amoraic sages, particularly Abbaye and Rava.[26] This may be explained, in part, by the fact that the Yerushalmi is generally more directly concerned with the halakha (the legal ruling itself), whereas the Bavli seems to pursue deliberations for their own sake.[27] Whether or not this is the case—and I will argue in a later chapter that it is—what is noteworthy about Frankel's evaluation is his suggestion that what distinguishes the Bavli from the Yerushalmi is the unattributed portions of each. This will be a crucial factor in later chapters.

Frankel's observation that the Bavli tends to admit lengthy deliberations to a far greater extent than the Yerushalmi is stunningly confirmed by reference to recent translations of parallel Bavli and Yerushalmi tractates by Neusner and his colleagues. These translations divide the gemara text into units of discourse, that is, sustained discussions of a single limited issue, and then further into individual steps of deliberation. Comparing the total number of units of discourse in several of the same tractates of the two talmudim, we find the following:

Tractate	Yerushalmi	Bavli
Beẓah	168	260
Sotah	319	411
Sukkah	139	237
Sanhedrin	322	909

Since units of discourse represent the variety of different ways that a gemara is willing to approach and examine issues raised by the Mishnah or in combination with the Mishnah, these figures mean that the Bavli is generally willing to consider a far broader spectrum of issues and to allow one issue to lead to another with less inhibition. This sample, moreover, is likely to be representative of the whole, because it includes Bavli tractates that mostly limit themselves to the legal issues at hand (Beẓah and Sukkah) as well as less typical tractates that admit large bodies of text that address scripture independently of Mishnah (Sotah and Sanhedrin).[28]

A comparison of the smaller divisions in these translations confirms that treatment of individual issues also tends to go on at greater length in the Bavli. Comparing the length (in number of individual steps of deliberation) of units of discourse in the first chapters of Bavli and Yerushalmi Beẓah and Sotah, we find the following:

Units of Discourse	Yerushalmi	Bavli
Beẓah		
Total units	50	119
Average length	7.5	11.3
Longest unit	25	68
Sotah		
Total units	57	141
Average length	8.5	8.6
Longest unit	22	55

Again, the total number of units, that is, the variety of approaches that are pursued, is more numerous in the Bavli than in the Yerushalmi. In Beẓah, chapter 1, the average length of the individual deliberations is far longer, though in Sotah it is only slightly so. What is noteworthy about the number in Sotah is that many individual treatments are very short. Averaging over such a large sample, we would expect the average length to be drawn down, as is in fact the case. But the number of individual lengthy deliberations is still significant enough to maintain an average that is larger than that in the Yerushalmi. This observation is reinforced in the third figure, from which it becomes apparent that certain Bavli discussions go on at considerable length—far longer than is likely in the Yerushalmi. In fact, whereas the length of units of discourse in the Bavli often reaches double digits (or, in this case, double characters, i.e., longer than twenty-six steps), the sample from the Yerushalmi never does (in the Bavli it occurs a total of fourteen times). An examination of the available translations to the other tractates clearly confirms this tendency.[29]

To Frankel's description of the differences between the Bavli and the Yerushalmi we will later add many, but for the present it suffices to note that in comparison with the Yerushalmi (the text to which it is most similar), the Bavli makes choices that render it unique. It is the meaning of these choices that I will attempt to define.

Of course, if the form represented in the Bavli had been modeled after some non-Jewish document, that would be of particular interest. The fact that the Bavli took shape in the same centuries and place as the Zoroastrian holy canon, the Zend Avesta, and came to completion at more or less the same time as the grand compilation of classical Roman law under Justinian has invited comparison of the Bavli with these works. Is it possible, it is asked, that the formation of these works influenced the shape and history of the Bavli? Whether or not there was influence, there is certainly no evidence of it. The Bavli resembles neither the Zend Avesta nor the code of Justinian.

The surviving portion of the Zend Avesta is a compilation of several different forms. The Vendidad is primarily the purported record of a dialogue between Zarathustra (Zoroaster) and his God Ahura Mazda, "beneficent Spirit, maker of the material world, Thou Holy One," concerning a variety of legal matters, but especially questions of purity. In both form and spirit, this text is far closer to Leviticus than it is to the Talmud. The Gathas record, in verse, a variety of inspired proclamations by Zoroaster, either directed to Ahura Mazda or purporting to transmit the message of

Ahura Mazda to the believers. Finally, the Yashts are a series of hymns to various divinities. Major portions of the Avesta are used in Zoroastrian ritual and their form attests to this fact. Thus in form, function, and content there is virtually no significant parallel between this scripture and the Talmudic tradition.[30]

So, too, there is no meaningful parallel with the great encyclopedia of classical Roman law. Those who suggest a comparison relate the Bavli to Justinian's digest, a compilation of thousands of fragments taken from the writings of the Roman jurists of the first to fourth centuries. The major difference between these two works—a difference too significant to ignore—is that whereas the Bavli speaks most often in its own voice, a voice which dominates the voices of the sources that it quotes, Justinian's digest purportedly records only the voice of others. Every text in it is identified by author and title of original source, and though it is replete with the alterations and interpolations of its compilers, it everywhere gives the impression of being copied from the original.[31] Hence it is a catalogue of sources of the law and not, like the Bavli, a self-admitted source of the law itself.[32]

The Bavli's Sources:
On the Reliability of Attributions

One characteristic of the Bavli that will profoundly affect the nature of the history in this book is its claim to record a variety of sources. Aside from its own voice, the Bavli claims to quote from and deliberate on the Mishnah (the only such claim that we can affirm definitively and without debate), baraitot (texts attributed to the same authorities as the Mishnah, which, however, the author of the Mishnah chose not to include in his work), and amoraic opinions. Particularly if the latter claim can be affirmed, we will have access through the pages of the Bavli not only to its final stage, but also to the several stages that ultimately yielded the final document. We will not be restricted to describing a final product, one that can be taken to be reliable evidence only of the sixth century; instead, we will be able to trace a path through the intermediary centuries, beginning with the first generation after the completion of the Mishnah and including all of the generations to follow. But this is possible, again, only if the "history" that the Bavli claims to record can be relied upon. How might such reliability be substantiated?

The question that we ask is really this: why should the words that the Bavli attributes to a given individual be considered any more reliable (as an accurate "historical" record) than those attributed by the Bible to Abraham or by Plato to Socrates?[33] More often than not in world literature, the views placed in the mouths of even confirmed historical figures have been the inventions of the author of the work; why should the Bavli be different? Attributions as such are clearly insufficient. There are many reasons other than the truth why a document's authors might want to make such claims. For these claims to be considered reliable evidence of the times they purportedly represent, an independent test of their reliability must be proposed.

To begin with, for claims of this sort to have any credibility there must be evidence of a means by which a statement could have been transmitted from its purported author to the document in which it is finally recorded. If, for example, we know that the author of the document had access to correspondence or some other record, there will be reason to consider the possibility that the claim of that author might be reliable. Or if we have evidence of an established system of oral transmission and preservation, then, again, we may explore the possibility that traditions recorded in a later text represent earlier expressions. In other words, if the authors of the Bavli had immediate access to the words of the amoraim that they claim to quote, a prima facie case that the sources recorded in the Bavli could be reliable is established.

The Bavli claims that its tradition is oral, relying on the activities of a class of "professional" repeaters, who would memorize the opinions of rabbinic authorities and repeat them, as necessary, for study or for transmission.[34] The internal evidence of the activity of these repeaters is powerful, and in theory, in any case, the existence of such repeaters would explain how the opinions of third-century sages survived in oral form until the fifth or sixth century. Again in theory, the availability of such a means might explain how the authors of the final document had access to material that originated long before them.

But precisely because so much is at stake for the Bavli (and the rest of rabbinic tradition) in claiming that these repeaters existed and operated in this way, we must be cautious not to claim too much on the basis of such evidence. It is reasonable, given what we know, to believe that traditions were in fact transmitted by such repeaters, but in the absence of far more convincing tests, our awareness of this system allows us to draw no conclusions regarding the reliability of individual traditions. Yes, we know how the final document *might* have had access to earlier opinions, but we have no idea whether the opinions that it purportedly quotes were actually passed down in this way. Other means of confirmation are necessary.

In several different works, Jacob Neusner proposes a variety of tests that might confirm the reliability of the source claims in the Bavli and elsewhere. Two of these, in particular, are applicable to amoraic sources found in the Bavli.

The first, found in *The Rabbinic Traditions About the Pharisees Before 70,* suggests that if a tradition preserved in a rabbinic text was also to be found in a text "entirely external to the rabbinic tradition," then that tradition would be deemed "verified."[35] Clearly, if such a text were truly external, that is, not dependent on the rabbinic source in which the tradition is first quoted, then it would be necessary to posit a common source for both the rabbinic and the external source. This common source, it seems reasonable, is the individual to whom it is attributed or, at the very least, the circle of his disciples.

The general sense of this proposed "verification test" is unimpeachably correct, but with an important revision. For this test to yield positive results, it is not necessary, in fact, that the "external" text be entirely external to rabbinic tradition. What must be sought, rather, is a text that cannot be dependent on the text being questioned and one that it too cannot depend on. Two demonstrably independent texts obviously require a common source and, where such a source is not actually known to us— such as when both the Bavli and Yerushalmi quote a Mishnah (we would have been able to confirm the Mishnah as a source independent of the two later works)—we will have to posit a reasonable urtext. It is therefore independence, but not externality, that is necessary here.

For the Bavli, the independent text that may serve such a function is the Yerushalmi. Obviously the Yerushalmi could not have been dependent on the Bavli; the latter document was composed after the former and came to closure as much as two centuries later. The Bavli, also, did not use the Yerushalmi as a source. This, to my knowledge, is the virtually undisputed opinion of contemporary scholarship.[36] Common sources (aside from the Mishnah) in the Bavli and the Yerushalmi are nearly always quoted with differences, from minor to major ones, and there is no evidence that such sources in the Bavli are in any way influenced by the earlier document. This is true in larger matters as well. The expository programs of each are entirely independent, allowing both for different paths of inquiry and for frequently differing (and even contradictory) halakhic conclusions. These differences are so striking that they move Neusner to write: "The Bavli and the Yerushalmi assuredly stand autonomous from one another."[37]

If these two documents are independent and if, as noted, they often quote common traditions, then each may be used to verify such traditions in the other. More to the point, the Yerushalmi's quoting an amoraic tradition that is recorded in the Bavli forces us to conclude that the tradition originates, at least, in the circle of disciples of the sage to whom the tradition is attributed. To begin with, neither of these documents could have known the tradition from the other. There is also no known common third source for amoraic traditions (such as an earlier compendium of amoraic sayings), nor is one ever alluded to. The only reasonable alternative is to suppose that the tradition originated in the circle of the named authority and from there was received into the literature of the two great centers of rabbinic study. Common quotation will, in such cases, yield verification.

The second possible source of verification, which Neusner discusses in *Judaism in Society*, examines traditions for superficial but characteristic modes of expression that in their variety might testify to the fact that a final, all-shaping editorial hand did not eliminate what was unique in the sources that it employed. According to Neusner: *"If . . . we knew that there was a characteristic mode of formulating ideas, always particular to one authority or school, and never utilized by some other authority or school, we should have a solid, because superficial, criterion for sorting out valid from invalid attributions"*[38] The point is that if traditions of a particular sage or school of sages are characterized by some superficial feature, they will have to be deemed reliable because these patterns must first be "uncovered" (through statistical analysis of forms) and, not being immediately evident to the eye of even a discerning reader, there is no suspicion that they are the fruit of the pen of a final author. If such an author intended to shape texts to communicate his individual message, he would have done so in a way that was obvious to the reader. No purpose would be served by hiding such messages; the author benefits only if the forms that he chooses effectively communicate to all. Furthermore, if superficial characteristics continue to distinguish bodies of tradition one from the other, we must conclude that no final editorial hand eliminated what was unique in its source traditions. No author would invent traditions that consistently and gratuitously use different, but otherwise undistinguished, voices of expression. If such voices are discovered, therefore, they may be said to affirm the presumptive reliability of the traditions in which they are present.

But if we are correct in assessing the way in which such a test is meaningful, then the precise formulation suggested previously will require revision. If these "characteristic modes of formulating ideas" turn out to be "always particular to one authority or school and never utilized by some other authority or school," then for this very reason they will have to be considered suspect. Such exclusivity could too easily be the product of an author who seeks to create a unique characterization for a particular authority or school. Characteristic modes of expression tend to create stereotyped expectations,[39] and under such circumstances what might not have been present originally in a tradition might later be borrowed from elsewhere to assure that expectations are not disappointed. This being so, traditions that are too consistently characteristic should, for that very reason, be deemed suspect.

On the contrary, it is precisely those features that are not immediately evident that will be most convincing in this context. If characteristics that are hidden to all but a comprehensive and detailed examination are in the end discovered, then such characteristics will, in fact, verify the presumptive reliability of the traditions so characterized. Accordingly, hidden features of this sort ought not be exclusive; being exclusive they are less likely to be hidden. What should be preferred, instead, is the presence of patterns that characterize an individual or a school or a generation by virtue of their statistical likelihood. Broad but significant statistical differences would offer persuasive evidence of the reliability of the group of traditions which they characterize precisely because these differences were hidden even, apparently, to the author of the final document. He did not detect these differences and he could not, therefore, have eliminated them. When differences of this nature remain it is apparent that the sources have preserved something of their original character.

Admittedly, because of the nature of this test, its procedures are circular. The only way to discover whether such patterns exist is by grouping together the traditions attributed to one individual or group and comparing them with the collected traditions of another individual or group. We must therefore begin by presuming reliability—but only until we have ascertained whether such a presumption is sound. If no distinguishing statistical characteristics are discernible, the test will have failed and the groupings must, for historical purposes, be disregarded. But if such patterns are discernible, then the groupings with which they are associated must be deemed valid, and the attributions that identify these groups must be presumed reliable.[40]

Chapter 2 will prove that literary patterns of this nature do distinguish generations of amoraim. Since it is generations of sages, but not individuals, that are so distinguished, the verification that will be achieved will extend only to the level of the generation, not to particular individuals. Still, this can be the basis for the sort of history that I have proposed. Because traditions attributed to a certain sage are likely to accurately reflect a view that was held in or near to his generation, the history of the development of rabbinic expression, generation by generation, may confidently be written. Moreover, since it is the mode of expression itself that concerns us in this history and not the specific content of particular traditions, then everything necessary is accessible. The conclusions that this history draws will, by definition, be based on distinguishing modes of expression, characteristic of large numbers of individual traditions. It is unimportant, for such a study, whether a given tradition is reliable; it is only important that a body of traditions may be deemed representative, and this is precisely what this test can confidently confirm.

Under certain circumstances it may even be possible to verify individual traditions.[41] But it is unnecessary in this case for us to demand that much. This will be, as I described, a history of ideas—ideas that reside in literary expression itself—and for such a purpose, access is needed to only an individual generation or generations. From time to time I will employ, by way of demonstration, the actual content of amoraic traditions, but only as evidence of views that were held in a generation, and only to the extent that they reflect opinions or ideologies that are supported by the formal characteristics of the literary product. At this level, the evidence may be considered reliable.

We may proceed, on this basis, to a description of the history of amoraic literary development. It is the sages of third- to fifth-century Babylonia to whom we now turn.

2

A History of
Amoraic Literary Expression

A LITERARY HISTORY OF amoraic traditions must begin with a delineation of the criteria by which that corpus can be described. What features are salient in such a history?

Because the text that immediately precedes the amoraim, both chronologically and logically, is the Mishnah (and perhaps its related texts, such as the Tosefta), the question that most obviously stands before us is the extent to which amoraic traditions resemble that document. Stated simply, how ''Mishnaic'' are amoraic traditions?

The most outstanding features that characterize the Mishnah were reviewed in chapter 1. The Mishnah, as noted, is brief and succinct. Are amoraic traditions written in the same way or do they instead express themselves through lengthy, discursive exposition? The Mishnah most often declares law. Do amoraic traditions do the same or do they, in contrast, concern themselves with argumentation and process? Do amoraic traditions, like the Mishnah, speak on their own terms, assuming their own authority, or does their authority seem to reside elsewhere? Do they think it necessary to offer reasons for the laws that they address? The Mishnah asserts it own authority through its general willingness to omit references to scripture. Do amoraic traditions speak in similar isolation or do they, instead, often quote scripture? Do they quote other authoritative sources? Finally, and in some ways most obviously, do they, like the Mishnah, speak in Hebrew or do they tend to favor Aramaic?

The answers to these questions will allow us to determine the stylistic relationship of amoraic traditions and the Mishnah. Having done so, we will be in a position to compare the amoraic corpus to the Mishnah in even more significant ways. One of the things that most essentially defines the Mishnah is its overall independence of other texts. Clearly, the presence or absence of such independence in amoraic traditions would be meaningful. One way that these traditions might state their relationship to the Mishnah is in the degree to which their style diverges from its literary model. Would it, in fact, be correct to speak of literary dependence or of divergence? Similarly, we must also consider the functional relationship between amoraic traditions and other texts. Do these traditions legislate on their own terms, as does the Mishnah, or do they prefer, instead, to comment on earlier texts? Do they claim to speak in a "community" of other texts or are they essentially independent?

When we inquire into the stylistic relationship of amoraic traditions to the Mishnah, on the one end, we at the same time obviously anticipate the option that will emerge at the other end of this development, in the completed Bavli. When we know the degree to which amoraic traditions diverge from the Mishnaic precedent, we will, in the same instant, define how closely these traditions approach the final Talmudic form. This determination is crucial in this history for obvious reasons. But there is at least one other rabbinic model that is relevant here. Presumably, the form of the Midrash Halakha was already known during this period. This form too may have suggested a model for expression; was this the case? To answer this question we must more than merely ask the extent to which scripture is employed in amoraic traditions; of greater concern is *the way that scripture is employed*. Are verses quoted as simple proof texts, for example, or are they combined to form elaborate and often technical comments on the way scripture comes to mean what the rabbis take it to mean? These midrashim also typically speak in a series of questions and answers which do not, however, appear to represent different voices. Is this also the case in amoraic discussions, or is amoraic dialogue intended to convey a more literal, true-to-life impression?

Although it may be necessary to express these questions by means of either/or contrasts, they need not have similarly categorical answers. In fact, we will find that all generations record some combination of this variety of styles. What is more crucial in fashioning an answer, then, is describing the precise combination in any given generation and the relative shifts in the combination as the generations proceed. The history of this literature is one of degrees, and it will be in the predominance of one preferred style over another and the affinity of those styles with other texts, both prior and subsequent, that meaning will be found.

The developments described in this chapter will follow the conventional division of amoraim (up to the generation of R. Ashi) into six generations.[1] The following list indicates the major sages associated with each generation:

- first generation (early to mid third century)—Rav, Samuel
- second generation (mid to late third century)—R. Judah, R. Huna
- third generation (late third to early fourth century)—R. Sheshet, R. Ḥisda, R. Naḥman, R. Yosef, Rabba
- fourth generation (mid fourth century)—Abbaye, Rava
- fifth generation (late fourth century)—R. Pappa
- sixth generation (early fifth century)—R. Ashi

Though each generation might be composed of a relatively large number of sages, most of the traditions in each generation are attributed to the small number of teachers listed. Because the traditions of these sages comprise the majority of amoraic statements in their generations, this history is restricted, for the most part, to traditions that bear their names. The traditions of those whose names appear less frequently might not be typified by the same characteristics,[2] but the smaller number of total traditions in their names means that statistical descriptions of their product would be less reliable and less representative. Furthermore, because it is the product of the generation as a whole that we are concerned with, the corpus of traditions associated with the most prolific teachers of each age will most nearly represent the whole. Finally, both R. Yoḥanan and Resh Laqish, Palestinian sages of the first generation (though more nearly contemporary with the second Babylonian generation), are widely represented in the Bavli, and so a consideration of amoraic traditions in that document must account for their record too.

Several further words of definition and clarification are necessary before this literary history is begun. First, in describing the characteristics of the traditions of each generation, I will employ several terms by way of a shorthand, generally in pairs of corresponding opposites. In each instance, I will remark upon the degree to which traditions of a given sage or generation are brief or argumentational. Brief traditions are those that simply state an opinion or ruling in law. They may literally be quite brief, or they may be somewhat longer; they are distinguished by the fact that they are neither deliberative nor dialogical. They are often independent or, when they interpret an earlier text, they may require a referent. But, crucially, they are always, at least potentially, the end of a process; they either state the law in a self-sufficient way or record an interpretation that may itself stand as the final comment. Because of this brevity and relative independence, such traditions are more or less similar to the Mishnah. Argumentational traditions, on the other hand, are either explicit, direct objections or deliberative, dialogical sequences (which I will count as one tradition and then describe the length). Argumentation of this sort is obviously highly unusual in the Mishnah, and so such traditions will reflect relative distance from the Mishnaic purpose and style.

Brief traditions will also be characterized by the degree to which they are either halakhic or interpretive. Halakhic traditions declare the law, and their concern is neither reasons nor justification. In contrast, interpretive traditions clarify or justify the texts upon which they comment, and they often employ formulas that explicitly declare their interpretive intent. The former type are obviously closer in kind to the Mishnah, which speaks with an uncompromising self-confidence, rarely offering either reason or justification. The latter type, while still employing the brief form of the Mishnah, has clearly departed from it in terms of general purpose.

This distinction between halakhic and interpretive, where interpretation might easily be thought to be identical with commentary, should not become the source of confusion. Some readers are familiar with two works of Baruch M. Bokser: *Samuel's Commentary on the Mishnah. Part One: Mishnayot in the Order of Zera'im* and *Post Mishnaic Judaism in Transition: Samuel on Berakhot and the Beginnings of Gemara*. In both of those books, Bokser concludes that the product of the first-generation sage Samuel was primarily a commentary on the Mishnah. I will, however, argue that relatively few of Samuel's traditions are interpretive. These two claims are not contradictory.

Bokser's primary concern in his study is the overall relationship of Samuel's traditions to the Mishnah. This means that not only traditions that actually interpret the Mishnah in whole or in part, but also those that address or supplement the legal agenda of the Mishnah, or respond to it, in fact, in any discernible way, are counted by Bokser as being part of Samuel's Mishnah commentary. By defining commentary this broadly, Bokser's overall argument is convincing, and his conclusions are useful for describing the functional relationship between the traditions of early amoraim (as represented by Samuel) and the Mishnah.

But my concerns, as should be clear from the previous chapter, are different from Bokser's. This literary history addresses the question of the similarity (or absence thereof) in form and purpose of amoraic traditions to those of the Mishnah. This means that even if the apparent purpose of a given tradition is to supplement the legal agenda defined in the Mishnah, this tradition may still not be commentary, or, as I prefer, interpretive. If a tradition states halakha, even if its law apparently responds directly to the Mishnah, it will be considered here as halakhic. Only if a tradition is manifestly interpretive, in form as well as by consideration of purpose, will it be counted as such.

In fact, if we examine Bokser's categories with an eye for this distinction, we will find that a good portion of Samuel's commentary is nevertheless not interpretive. Two of Bokser's categories, which he calls related rulings and additional cases, enunciate halakhic rulings in precisely the same fashion as the Mishnah itself. Although these rulings might extend the legal agenda first described in the Mishnah, they are in no direct sense interpretive. Even the category that he calls decisions, which does depend directly on the primary Mishnaic text, nevertheless employs a form that is used on occasion in the Mishnah.[3] Its primary purpose, in any case, is obviously not interpretation. Since the Mishnah generally prescribes law, and rarely comments, explains, or justifies, these traditions may be said to replicate the Mishnah more closely than interpretive traditions. In our understanding the categories in this way, it turns out, in the case of Samuel, that at least 63 percent of the counted traditions are halakhic.[4] Furthermore, if we evaluate the other traditions by means of their ability to make a clear halakhic statement independently (regardless of their relation otherwise to the Mishnah), then the total number of halakhic traditions will increase still more. The picture that emerges from this reassessment of categories will support my conclusions quite closely.

The First Amoraic Period

By all measures, the traditions of the major sages of the first amoraic generation in Babylonia (Rav and Samuel) closely resemble the Mishnah. The vast majority of their traditions are brief declarations of opinion or law, independent and without elaboration. In contrast, the number of argumentational sequences in which these sages are involved is extremely small and the ratio of brief traditions to argumentational/dialogical traditions is nearly 22 to 1 (see p. 57 of my doctoral dissertation).[5]

The majority of the brief traditions are halakhic, outnumbering interpretive traditions by approximately two to one (pp. 49 and 56). Many of these traditions replicate the style of the Mishnah exactly, and in the absence of amoraic attributions they might easily be mistaken for Mishnaic texts. This is particularly so since the great majority of these traditions are recorded in Mishnaic Hebrew (the ratio of Hebrew over Aramaic for Rav being 4.56 to 1 and for Samuel being 4.88 to 1).[6]

While halakhic traditions resemble the Mishnah most closely, the Mishnaic imprint is not restricted to these traditions alone; a notable minority of interpretive cases nevertheless preserve the brief formulation that typifies the Mishnah (p. 51). In this way they combine the Mishnaic precedent with an interpretive tendency that, in light of its rarity in the Mishnah, is innovative. The nature of these interpretations is varied, including explanations of words or phrases, identification of the authors of anonymous statements in the Mishnah, and other responses to perceived gaps or omissions in the Mishnah (pp. 51–52). Such comments are frequently preceded by formulaic words or phrases as "they taught this only with respect to," "what are we dealing with here?" and "this is what is being said" (p. 52).

Traditions attributed to these sages also do not quote or comment upon verses of scripture with any frequency (pp. 53 and 56). Those traditions that do so comment are often extremely short and straightforward, generally doing little more than identifying the scriptural source for a given law. There are rare exceptions that are longer or more elaborate, but they are extremely unusual and do not affect our description of the whole.

The only departures in this generation from the stylistic precedent established by the Mishnah are the presence of a sizable minority of interpretive traditions and also of a notable minority of argumentational/dialogical traditions. Still, in relative terms, the number of argumentational traditions attributed to Rav and Samuel is extremely small [154; in contrast, the combined number of their brief traditions is 3,338 (p. 57)], and most of these argumentational sequences are only one or two steps long. Long sequences that involve Rav and Samuel are extremely rare.[7] Again, in view of the degree to which the traditions of these sages replicate the style and purpose of the Mishnah, the extreme rarity of argumentation in this generation is no surprise.

The traditions attributed to the major sages of the second generation in Babylonia (R. Judah and R. Huna) are by these measures essentially identical with those of the first generation. This is true both in the predominance of brief over argumentational traditions and in the predominance of halakhic traditions among the brief. Again, the argumentational sequences are, on the whole, extremely short (pp. 62–64).

Outstanding in this generation, and without precedent in the previous, is the great number of cases in which R. Judah is recorded as having

acted as a tradent for the teachings of Rav and Samuel. This form is
extremely rare in the Mishnah. But its presence here is not evidence of
an emerging distance from the Mishnaic model. On the contrary, it is a
clear indication of R. Judah's commitment to the Mishnaic form, for it
is only brief traditions that, according to this record, he deems worthy of
repeating. In combination with the character of the larger body of traditions attributed to these sages, again what stands out is the remarkable
extent to which the early amoraic production maintained its fidelity to the
Mishnaic precedent.

   R. Yohanan and, to a far lesser extent, Resh Laqish, are the primary
spokespersons of Palestinian Rabbinism in the decades contemporary with
these Babylonian generations. According to the record of the Bavli, the
nature of the traditions of these sages is, in many respects, highly similar
to that of their Babylonian counterparts. Again, brief traditions far out-
number argumentational traditions (by a ratio of approximately 12 to 1),
and argumentational sequences tend to be only a few steps in length (pp.
69–72). In addition, according to the record of R. Yohanan, the brief
traditions are overwhelmingly in Hebrew, utilizing Hebrew above Aramaic by a ratio of 5.78 to 1.

   On the other hand, certain aspects of the record of these sages distinguish them from their Babylonian contemporaries and, correspondingly,
from the Mishnaic model. To begin with, many more of the brief traditions are interpretive (though the majority are still halakhic). In addition,
R. Yohanan quotes and comments on scripture far more frequently, and
the forms that such comments employ are sometimes far more elaborate
than those recorded in the names of his Babylonian counterparts. For
example, on several occasions he connects the opinions of two or more
authorities by suggesting that they interpreted the same scriptural verse,
but with different results. He also comments on the meaning of the proximity of two different subjects in scripture *(smikhut),* using this phenomenon as a source for generating law, and in a few instances he derives
rulings from the use of the same biblical term in different contexts *(gez-
erah shava).*[8]

   Also apparently distinguishing the record of these sages is the willingness ascribed to Resh Laqish to object, on at least two occasions, to an
earlier authority on the basis of logic alone and without the support of a
recognized authoritative text (p. 73). Objections from earlier authoritative
texts, introduced by the Aramaic term *eitivei* are present already, in small
numbers, in the first generation. But a widespread willingness to render
objections with the support of nothing but one's reason (introduced by

the term *matkif la* will not be present until the next generation. In light of this, these traditions attributed to Resh Laqish are noteworthy. However, there are in any case only two explicit instances of such objections, and these do not, therefore, require a revised description of the corpus as a whole.

Similarly, the deceptively abundant record of objections marked by *eitivei* that involve R. Yoḥanan and Resh Laqish should be discounted. If the argumentational sequences that employ this form were genuine, they would significantly affect the shape of the corpus of traditions attributed to these men. But such sequences are sometimes patently fictitious, often constructed around literary formulas that render them suspect, and, with only one or two exceptions, never paralleled in the Yerushalmi—a highly surprising absence in view of the fact that this is where such traditions should presumably have originated and that other traditions are often recorded in similar forms in both documents. It is therefore reasonable to conclude that nearly all such sequences are later Babylonian inventions and are thus irrelevant to the present stage of the Bavli's literary history (pp. 182–92).

On the whole, then, the traditions of these sages can be seen as preferring the literary model of the Mishnah. An increasing preference for interpretation should be noted, but this preference will not fully transform the amoraic product until the following generation. It affirms the conclusion that the purpose of this literature is, using Bokser's broadly defined term, commentary. But overall, the characteristics of these traditions are still closer to the Mishnaic precedent than they are distant from it.

The fact that the source of this information about R. Yoḥanan and Resh Laqish is the Bavli and not the Yerushalmi—the document produced in the land where these masters taught—does not invalidate the picture that these data present. To begin with, the information that I have accumulated from the Yerushalmi confirms the patterns suggested in the Bavli. For example, of all major sages whose traditions in the Bavli I have examined with regard to language of expression (including Rav, Samuel, Yoḥanan, Rabba, Yosef, Abbaye, Rava, Pappa, and Ashi), the traditions of Yoḥanan are the most predominantly Hebrew (5.78 to 1 over Aramaic; the closest to this proportion are Rav and Samuel, whose ratios are 4.56 to 1 and 4.88 to 1). The Yerushalmi's record of Yoḥanan's traditions also shows an extremely high preponderance of Hebrew over Aramaic (4.6 to 1). Two factors could account for the difference between the precise records: the effect of the memory of the messengers who transported Yoḥanan traditions to Babylonia or the stereotyped expectation that a Palestinian sage would express himself in Hebrew (after the model of the Palestinian Mishnah). What is more crucial for present purposes is the fact that the picture of both the Bavli and the Yerushalmi is one in which Yoḥanan's traditions are recorded overwhelmingly in Hebrew. This suggests that the earlier corpus of Yoḥanan traditions was not completely molded to accord with the standards of the Babylonian context.

Further support of this conclusion is the Yerushalmi's recording of relatively few argumentational sequences that are attributed to R. Yoḥanan and Resh Laqish (or to any other sages, for that matter). As noted previously, according to the Bavli's record, the tendency in the traditions of these sages for brief expression is extremely high. Though I have not conducted a precise counting in the Yerushalmi, other information leads me to believe that this tendency according to its record is even more extreme. Seeking lengthier argumentation (three steps or more) attributed to any amoraic sages in the Yerushalmi, I found that in all of Seder Zeraʿim and tractates Shabbat, Eruvin, and Pesaḥim of Seder Moʿed there were only forty argumentational sequences that persisted for this many steps. In the course of my search, I was also left with the distinct impression that amoraic argumentation of any length was relatively rare in the Yerushalmi. At the same time, of course, brief traditions number in the thousands in these same texts. It is reasonable to believe, therefore, that this broad picture is also true of the traditions of Yoḥanan and Resh Laqish and that the record of the Yerushalmi in this regard is very similar to that of the Bavli.

Even if this were not true, however, the value of the Bavli record in the present context would not be invalidated, for even if the preceding discoveries represent the Bavli's own (re)formulation of Palestinian traditions, we would still have to ask when this formulation took place. Since the characteristics of this corpus are so generally similar to those of contemporary Babylonian traditions, and because they are so obviously different from the traditions of following generations, as we shall see, we can conclude that this formulation is not the product of the Bavli's final authors. If it were, we would expect it to conform to some final convention of formulation. Rather, given the similarity of these traditions to apparently contemporary traditions, it is likely that any (re)formulation was done at this very same time, that is, before the third Babylonian amoraic generation. Since it is the history of this period and place that we seek, the traditions of these Palestinian sages, as recorded in the Bavli, may be taken to be representative.

The Second Amoraic Period

The traditions of sages of the third Babylonian generation, R. Sheshet, R. Hisda, R. Nahman, R. Yosef, and Rabba, are significantly different from the traditions of their predecessors. The production of these sages embodies a shift from the Mishnaic form to other, more innovative ones. Traditions of this generation often include explicitly self-conscious statements. There is concern for reasons and justification. There is a somewhat greater number of argumentational sequences. Overall, there is a sense that the nature of the enterprise is changing.

To be more precise, the predominance of brief traditions over argumentation in this generation, although still large (3.5 to 1), is far smaller than had been the case previously (pp. 80–81). In fact, in the case of Rabba and R. Yosef, who stand at the end of this generation, the proportion approaches 1 to 1. Also shifting, by the evidence of these sages, is the preference for halakhic over interpretive traditions. For R. Nahman, in the earlier part of this generation, halakha still predominates, but in the latter part of this period interpretive traditions are strongly preferred (p. 81). In addition, the preferred language of formulation is no longer obviously Hebrew. For Rabba, Hebrew still predominates over Aramaic, but only slightly (1.22 to 1); for Yosef, Aramaic is now preferred by a slight margin (1.54 to 1 Aramaic over Hebrew, counting through Seder Nezikin).

Brief traditions in this generation exhibit sensibilities that were not noticeable before. These sages will, for example, justify earlier opinions by suggesting their source (p. 81). Also present are explicit references to the dictates of reason and statements that employ reason in explicit self-justification (p. 82). Even implicit objections are not infrequently present in traditions of this form (p. 83).

Of even greater note is attention to argumentation, both earlier and contemporary. This includes comments on earlier argumentation and records of the argumentational process that led to certain conclusions (pp. 85–86). Some instances are striking. For example, on several occasions Rabba remarks: "We object to our tradition . . . but this is not valid [as an objection]" (p. 87). This is but one of many expressions of the recognition that more than the final product is important.

In terms of its use of scripture, this generation also departs from earlier standards. It employs more creative exegetical methods. These include derivations from presumed extraneous terms in the text (*ribui*) and assumed equations of different topics by scripture (*heqesh*) (p. 89). Some of these cases are quite complex and lengthy, and these cases, as well as others, approach the sophisticated style and methodology of the halakhic midrashim.[9]

Distinguishing the traditions of this generation from those of the prior most profoundly is the body of argumentation attributed to these sages. All of the developing sensibilities noted in the brief traditions are present also in the argumentation. This includes self-awareness and appreciation for process that, on some occasions, leads to the explicit repetition of one's own or another's argumentation. These recollections might be quite elaborate; for example, we find recorded at Sukkah 17a–b: "Rabba[10] said: 'I found the sages of the house of Rav, who sat and said . . . and I said to them . . . and they said to me . . . and I said to them . . . and they said to me: If this is so, then according to you also, who said . . . and I said to them: What is the case? It is fine for me, for I said . . . but for you, who said . . .' " Such repetitions do not appear in earlier generations.

More than any other phenomenon, the most outstanding innovation of this generation is the presence of frequent objections based on reason alone (*matkif la*) (p. 94). Earlier, objections had generally required the support of an authoritative text, either a verse of scripture or, more frequently, a Mishnah or baraita. Presumably,[11] an amora could not differ with one tannaitic source without the support of another tannaitic source (with the occasional exception of the earliest amoraim,[12]) and so such texts were the ideal source of objections. But the confidence to object based on one's own logic alone was something else again.

The presence of such objections is all the more noteworthy given the explicit evidence that sages of this generation were aware of the qualitative difference between these two sources of authority. At Zevahim 96b, Rami b. Hama asks R. Isaac b. Judah why he had abandoned his scholarly companionship for that of R. Sheshet. R. Isaac responds that when he would address an inquiry to Rami he would respond using his own reasoning, and his answer could therefore easily be refuted by a baraita. R. Sheshet, on the other hand, used to base his answers on baraitot, and so even if a contradictory baraita was found, his answer might still stand. An exchange ensues in which the truth of this claim is demonstrated.

Clearly, for these sages the authority of reason is secondary, as shown by the unwillingness in earlier generations to rely on reason alone. Thus the willingness to employ reason independently beginning in the third generation must be recognized as an innovative and bold move. It is a move, of course, that distances these sages from the Mishnaic precedent and brings them closer to the form that would eventually be the Bavli.

Beyond such specifics, the most innovative shift in this generation is both the increased amount and the greater length of argumentation in general. Many more such exchanges are three or more steps in length (pp. 92–93), and some are extraordinarily complex. Again, by all measures the corpus of traditions of these third-generation sages breaks new ground.

The fourth generation, represented by Abbaye and Rava, carries trends that were initiated in the previous generation to their natural creative conclusions. This is true of all the matters discussed thus far.

In this generation the majority of brief traditions are explanatory, and simple halakhic statements are relatively fewer, the predominance of brief traditions over argumentation being now considerably less than two to one (pp. 109–10). In fact, if one considers the sheer literary quantity of these types, as opposed to the total number of instances of such types—counting even many-step argumentation as only one instance, as we have done thus far—then the quantities of brief and argumentational traditions are close indeed. The total number of brief traditions attributed to Abbaye and Rava is approximately 2,125. If one includes as brief those traditions that are followed by a single argumentational response (which I counted as one-step argumentation), then this number will be slightly higher. But if each responsive step of an argumentational sequence is counted, then the number of argumentational statements attributed to these sages is approximately 1,800. If one includes in this counting those steps attributed to contemporaries of these sages, this number will of course be higher (at least 2,800, by my count), and the relative quantities of brief and argumentational traditions will be that much closer (with argumentation, perhaps, even predominating). In addition, the shift in the preferred language of record continues in this generation as well; the traditions of Rava prefer Aramaic over Hebrew by a ratio of 1.18 to 1 (counting through Seder Nashim) and those of Abbaye have the same preference by a ratio of 1.79 to 1.

Self-awareness, attention to reasons and justification, and concern for argumentation in general are even more prevalent in this generation. Illustrative of this tendency is the tradition of Abbaye at Niddah 24b, where he remarks: "It should be learned from this [baraita, quoted immediately preceding] that a scholar who states an opinion should also say its reason, for when it is recalled to him he will remember [the correct version of his opinion]." The lesson that Abbaye derives is implied in the earlier tannaitic text (the baraita), but this only strengthens the importance of Abbaye's statement; others presumably could have made the point explicit earlier but did not. For Abbaye it is important to declare the necessity for reasons unambiguously. The same sensitivity is evident in the statement attributed to Rava at Eruvin 8b, where he is shown to comment, "I will state my own reason and I will [also] state their reason." Not only does this statement continue the attention to justification first seen in the previous generation, but it does so in a reciprocal fashion. Attention to all opinions, in this manner, is typical of the Bavli later, and this therefore represents another step taken on the road from the Mishnaic to the Talmudic form.

Also illustrative of the triumph of such sensibilities is the frequent reference by these sages to argumentation and its procedures to the extent that, in a few instances, they explicitly preserve the argumentation of others. There had also been some instances of such preservation in the third generation, but these sages seem to assume the centrality of argumentation with greater confidence.

There are many ways that this centrality is manifest. First there is the very large number of argumentational sequences attributed to Abbaye and Rava (1,366), a number that far exceeds anything before it. In contrast, and reflecting, I think, a diminished interest in simple brief traditions, these sages rarely act as tradents for the traditions of earlier masters. Abbaye does so on only a handful of occasions, and Rava does so, in any significant number (48), only for R. Naḥman. Furthermore, the argumentational sequences that are preserved are frequently of considerable length (pp. 123ff.).

The confidence that is reflected in the occasional willingness of these sages to preserve the argumentation of others is made (virtually) explicit in two cases in which Abbaye formulates brief traditions that comment on argumentation. At Gittin 25a–b, Abbaye comments: "He asks him regarding a matter in which the outcome depends upon the will of others, and he [in turn] answers him from a case in which the outcome depends upon his own will, and [the last sage] objects to him from a case in which the outcome depends upon the will of others." This translation, while accurate, misrepresents the original tradition, which makes the same points in very few words. Represented more accurately, this tradition would look something like this: "He asks him X, and he answers him Y, and he then objects to him X." The tradition is formulated tightly and concisely. So, too, is a similar sort of comment at Baba Mezia 56a (see my analysis of these texts, pp. 216–20).

I emphasize the brevity and careful formulation of these traditions because of what these features imply regarding their referents. The brief form that these traditions assume is the form of amoraic publication, that is, when the intent was to assure the preservation of given opinions, they would be formulated in this fashion. When such brief traditions were interpretive (as these two are), they clearly assumed the prior, stable preservation of the texts upon which they were commenting. It was possible to formulate interpretations of the Mishnah only because the Mishnah was a published text. It became reasonable to compose interpretations of amoraic opinions (in noteworthy numbers first in the third and fourth generations) only when such traditions were already preserved with confidence. Similarly, traditions of this sort referring to argumentation could reasonably have been composed only when the argumentation itself had been confidently preserved. At the very least, these traditions represent the estimation of Abbaye (or of whoever put these words in his mouth) that argumentation was being preserved by contemporary sages. (We shall return to this important point in the next chapter.) Of course, they also represent the increasing ascendance of argumentation at this time. This ascendance is without precedent in earlier amoraic generations.

Finally, the use of scripture during this generation exhibits a clearly innovative tendency. In addition to the several exegetical devices employed in earlier traditions, other, more sophisticated methods are (re)introduced at this time as well.[13] These include, in particular, the construction of general categories from specific scriptural examples (*binyan av*) derivation from the specification of details that would otherwise have been understood from a general scriptural rule, and derivation from cases that legislate from the general to the specific (*khlal u-frat*). In summation, all characteristics of the product of this generation distance it further from earlier conventions and draw it that much closer to the breakthrough that would be the Talmud.

The Third Amoraic Period

Developments over the course of the next two amoraic generations are extremely modest. Comparing traditions attributed to R. Pappa and R. Ashi, of the fifth and sixth generations respectively, with those of Abbaye and Rava, we will find that in all significant respects the development of amoraic forms has already run its full course. Only details will be added in this later era.

R. Pappa is less prolific than most of his predecessors whom we have been discussing. Nevertheless, his is the major contribution in this generation. The corpus associated with his name is, with respect to the factors that have been crucial in this history, less than spectacular.

The ratio of brief to argumentational traditions associated with R. Pappa is approximately 2.4 to 1. Among his argumentational traditions, well over half (188 out of 288) include only one responsive step, reinforcing the impression that Pappa's traditions prefer brevity overall. Only in the matter of language of expression, where Pappa's traditions prefer Aramaic to Hebrew by a ratio of 2.09 to 1, does his product extend, statistically, the trends that had begun earlier.

But this is not to say that Pappa's traditions represent a stylistic retreat. Like the latter third and the fourth generations, Pappa's brief traditions are most often interpretive [418 out of 690 (p. 139)]. Like Rava earlier, Pappa sees fit to explain both his own opinions and those of his disputants. Self-awareness and concern for process are also widely evident. The latter concern is present, in particular, in Pappa's willingness to admit, with respect to earlier traditions upon which he is commenting, that "this [opinion] of R. so-and-so was not stated explicitly, but was logically deduced"; this observation is found in his name more often than in the name of any other sage.

R. Pappa also exhibits concern for argumentation, though generally in quite modest ways. He similarly sees fit to quote earlier argumentation on several occasions. With respect to argumentation, only two features characterizing R. Pappa's product are noteworthy. First, Pappa is recorded as having objected to earlier opinions on the basis of his own independent logic a total of forty-one times. This number is exceeded only by R. Yosef (forty-five) and later by R. Ashi (forty-seven). Second, on three occasions, R. Pappa repeats sophisticated analyses—two of which are quite lengthy—that are introduced by the term *havei ba* (translated roughly as "he raised a question or discussion"). These analyses are in both form and content typical of the product of the later anonymous Talmudic author. While this form is also present in the previous generation, its presence here is testimony to the willingness of R. Pappa (or those who composed his traditions) to employ even the most innovative of amoraic forms.

What has been said of R. Pappa may, as a general description, be correctly applied also to R. Ashi. Aside from sheer numbers of contributions, where Ashi is far more prolific than Pappa, no significant phenomena distinguish the product of R. Ashi from that of the elder master.

Like the several previous generations, the traditions of R. Ashi tend far more to be argumentational than had been the case in the early amoraic period. The predominance of brief over argumentational traditions is only 1.4 to 1; if the actual literary quantity of the traditions is considered, the predominance of brief traditions will be wiped out entirely. In addition, the brief traditions themselves are overwhelmingly interpretive. Like R. Pappa earlier, and in almost precisely the same ratio (now 2.07 to 1), Ashi's traditions tend to be in Aramaic.

The argumentation of R. Ashi offers little that is new. Many sequences are very brief, but others continue for many steps (p. 146). The brief sequences generally include a single concise statement repeated before R. Ashi, followed by his response. These are significant because this form appears to reflect the desire to record not merely the conclusive statement but also the process. If so, this phenomenon is evidence that the sensibility that process and argumentation are worthy objects of attention and comment continues into this generation from the previous one. Also continuing is the willingness to employ reason as an authoritative source of comment, now in even more profound ways. As noted earlier, objections from reason *(matkif la)* appear more often in the name of R. Ashi than that of any other sage. In addition, Ashi is willing to declare reason to be the serious competitor of scripture; at Yevamot 13a he suggests[14] that where logic could have yielded a particular conclusion, there was no need for scripture to have done so. Earlier in the amoraic period, the priority surely would have been reversed.

The only broad area in which there is noteworthy and apparently innovative creativity is in Ashi's use of scripture. He becomes fully involved in the mechanisms of Midrash Halakha, allowing his own voice to speak in the developing midrashic text. In one instance he challenges a *khlal u-frat,* in another he offers a refutation to a *binyan av* (p. 145). His logical extensions of midrashic dialogue are unparalleled in earlier generations.

The Meaning of the Evidence

With the generation of R. Ashi, we have completed the broad strokes of the literary history of amoraic traditions. If we can be confident in assuming that the traditions in truth reflect the generations from which they purportedly emerge, then we may begin to consider the meaning of this history.

On the basis of the developments described in this chapter, we may indeed conclude that these traditions speak for the generations to which they are assigned. As noted earlier, superficial patterns of expression that characterize the traditions of a particular individual or group and distinguish it from another establish the presumptive reliability of those traditions. Because such superficial patterns are undetectable except by detailed, extensive study, they cannot be the result of artifice. Such patterns therefore allow us to consider the traditions that they characterize as original.

One thing, then, is for certain: no final author of the Bavli flattened all distinctions in his sources to create a single, undistinguished whole. To the contrary, the Bavli retains a multiplicity of formally distinct voices. These distinctions assure us that we may still discern the parties for whom these traditions speak.

But the nature of the distinctions that we have uncovered requires that we admit to the limitations of these conclusions. The characteristics generally distinguish generations but not individuals. What we may speak of with assurance, therefore, is the nature of the literary production of a generation as a whole but not of individuals who comprise that generation. And even speaking of a generation may be overreaching because, as noted, the first two generations were highly similar, as, in different degree, were the third and fourth generations, and then the fifth and sixth. Though it is not necessary, I think, to speak of the third and fourth generations as one—though similar, they are sufficiently distinct—still, to be cautious, it seems reasonable to consider the development of the amoraic literary product in three stages (1) the first and second, and the earliest figures in what we have called the third generation; (2) the latter part of the third and the fourth generations; and (3) the fifth and sixth generations. Examining the developments in these three periods will yield a great deal.

The earliest amoraic generations, we saw, stay remarkably close to the Mishnaic model in their literary expression. Their traditions are overwhelmingly brief, halakhic, and in Hebrew. Some deviations from the Mishnaic form are evident at this stage, but the most noteworthy characteristic of this corpus is the degree to which it seeks to replicate the earlier form.

To make sense of this picture, we must put it in context. Bokser's work, spoken of earlier, shows rather clearly that the Mishnah was at the center of the whole early amoraic enterprise. (Given what we have seen, I think it safe to say that the traditions of Samuel are typical of the whole contemporary corpus in this regard.) The Mishnah established the agenda, to a great extent, for the productive activity to follow, and even the many amoraic traditions of this era that do not actually require the Mishnah for understanding nevertheless do (most often) respond to it. The centrality of the Mishnah was clearly admitted. The Mishnah was the foundation of the Judaism that the amoraim now began to form.

This being so, it seems most reasonable to understand the form of early amoraic traditions, replicating the form of the Mishnah so closely, as an implicit homage to the text that had set the standards. Imitation here may indeed be the sincerest form of flattery. The Mishnah's impact was so profound that it was impossible for the amoraim to avoid it. Nor, of course, did they exhibit much desire to do so.

The most obvious characteristic of early amoraic traditions, on the basis of the evidence examined in this chapter, is their distinct traditionalism, that is, their legal and literary continuity with the central text of the emerging rabbinic canon. What purpose would such a deep continuity serve? The point, I think, is that in continuity was to be found legitimacy. We must recall that by this period the rabbinic movement as a whole had not long been at the center of political power even in Palestine, and in Babylonia it now sought to impose itself on an ancient Jewish community. In seeking to do so, the rabbis required a claim to legitimacy. Why, after all, should a Babylonian Jew accept the authority of these rabbis? In this context, the single document that spoke for the rabbinic movement in a coherent, comprehensive fashion—setting out its program and recording its practices—was the Mishnah. By establishing, without ambiguity, their relation to the Mishnah, these sages stated their claim to authority in the community. They were the carriers of the Mishnah; they were its teachers. Experts in Mishnaic law, they were the parties whom it would empower.[15] Moreover, theirs was the right to interpret it. When the text required clarification, the rabbis provided the expertise; through interpretation they extended its power—and their own as well.

But interpretation as such was not the primary activity of these amoraim. Rather, their most frequent contribution, as we saw, was decisions about or supplements to the law. The first of these activities was another assertion of power within the context of legitimacy that the Mishnah established. The second, supplementation, must be understood to be more than this.

Augmenting the law in the style of the Mishnan did, as noted, pay it homage. The Mishnah pointed the direction, the amoraim merely extended the path to details the Mishnah's system had for some reason not covered. But legislating after the fashion of the Mishnah is an assertion of authority that goes far beyond mere homage. If these rabbis laid claim to the right to extend the Mishnah, they were on some level declaring that their authority was equivalent to Mishnah. As it declared law, so too could they. They were, in this respect, the next "Mishnaic" generation.

This too, moreover, could be the meaning of literary continuity. Imitation of Mishnaic style reflects a refusal to admit, in absolute terms, that what the Mishnah did could never again be done. The fact is that, by the testimony of the literary evidence, the early amoraim continued Mishnah. The gemara recognizes this later, at least, in the case of Rav. Rav, we are told, was considered a tanna, and therefore could dispute the ruling of the Mishnah on the basis of his own authority alone.[16] Many other amoraim, both early and late, also disputed the Mishnah, and though the gemara assumes that such boldness can occur only when an alternative tannaitic text is available for support, the willingness to do so is still an important assertion of power in competition with the Mishnah. Homage, then, is not equivalent to subservience. In fact, the absence of clear stylistic distinctions with relation to the Mishnah in much of early amoraic literature can with equal correctness be interpreted as evidence of the absence, at this stage, of an unambiguously superior Mishnaic authority.

Yet it is not sufficient to recognize that continuity itself may be an assertion of comparable authority. There is an ambiguity in the meaning of such phenomena that requires comment and appreciation. It would be correct to say, in fact, that imitation is both a statement of homage and an assertion of authority; these two alternatives are not mutually exclusive. The dual message of this phenomenon may perhaps best be illustrated by considering the case of works such as the Book of Jubilees. Jubilees, a lengthy elaboration and augmentation of Genesis 1 to Exodus 12, expresses itself in biblical style. Sometimes it incorporates the biblical story verbatim, sometimes it transforms it for its own purposes, and more often it simply supplements the biblical text with material meant to communicate its own message.[17] This book and others like it that consciously and literally employ the biblical idiom obviously grant the authority of the biblical text. But at the same time, by according to themselves the right to replicate the biblical idiom, borrowing its power to empower their own creation, the authors of these works evidently believe that they may share that power. What they seek to write is also bible, and so at the very moment they pay homage to biblical authority they refuse to admit that that authority cannot be extended.

The same duality, I suggest, is embodied in the early amoraic product as it relates to the Mishnah. Submission and competition are both evident in the form of this work. The fact that the primary task of these traditions is supplementation of the Mishnaic program suggests that the former relationship (submission) was the more conscious one. But the latter (competition) cannot be denied and, in a different way, it will become the more obvious thrust of the traditions produced in the following generations.

What I have said to this point is true only to the extent that brief halakhic traditions prevail, as they do in the first two generations. But as the form of traditions shifts more and more to interpretive, and as other even more obvious criteria distance the traditions of middle-period amoraim from the Mishnaic model, the way we understand the relation of these sages to the earlier tradition must shift accordingly.

The most obvious developments in traditions of the third and fourth amoraic generations are the increase in interpretation, the greater preference for Aramaic (as opposed to Mishnaic Hebrew earlier),[18] and the presence of abundant argumentation. All of these features, on the surface, evidence a greater distance between these traditions and the Mishnaic tradition. All therefore reflect a willingness to define new agendas and directions—to establish a new tradition. Granted that this meaning of these developments may not be apparent at first reading—distancing and distinctions could also theoretically be understood to be evidence of undisputed admission of earlier authority—but a closer consideration of the details will confirm the correctness of this reading.

To begin with, interpretation in these traditions generally has one of two purposes: either to define the conditions when a given ruling applies or to seek reasons or justification for an expressed opinion (mere clarification of terms is relatively less common). The definition of conditions is not an innocent interpretive gesture. Nearly all such definitions have immediate halakhic consequences. When a sage reduces the applicability of a Mishnah by means of the very popular formula "they taught this only with respect to . . . ," he may, to a greater or lesser degree, be declaring that the ruling of a Mishnah (or baraita) is no longer accepted. It is possible, in fact, to reduce the conditions to which a ruling pertains to such a degree that the ruling is essentially nullified. In any case, under the guise of interpretation, the amoraim of this period used this and other devices to assert immense prerogative over the Mishnaic law. (Such devices were also used earlier, but far less often.) Interpretation in this mode is not acquiescent but often strongly assertive. Sometimes paying only lip service to earlier authority, such interpretations allowed the amoraim not merely to supplement the law of the Mishnah but actively to transform it.

2   Interpretations that sought reasons or justification had a more subtle but no less profound effect. Since reasons and justifications became important at this time, it is essential to consider why this would be so. Generally speaking, a text of undisputed authority needs no justification.[19] An absolute tyrant may promulgate a law, and that law needs no further support than the authority of the tyrant himself. The fact that reasons are offered already shows that the authority of the law or lawgiver is itself not enough and that additional support is necessary. By the same token, if only one reason or justification accompanies any given law or opinion, then, though absolute authority is not being granted, we would at least have to admit that the party offering the reason seeks to establish the undisputed authority of the text being addressed. But in these amoraic generations reasons and justifications are most often accompanied by other reasons for the same ruling or opinion. Moreover, there is no evidence that the authors of these traditions thought this multiplicity of reasons to be in any way flawed. To the contrary, the evidence suggests that this condition is precisely what was intended, as can be seen from the great frequency with which such competing views were recorded. (If they were preserved, it was proper, in the estimation of those who did the preserving, that one reason or justification should be joined by others.) Furthermore, though in many instances the text records debates in which these sages defend their respective opinions, most often it records no conclusions. The deliberation itself was important, and in the end different views were deemed legitimate. Finally, these are precisely the generations during which we first find sages offering justification for their own opinions and for those of their opponents. Again, multiple views in law, reason, and justification are thought to be worthy of preservation. The need for reason and justification, therefore, must be more than mere defense of a specific opinion or ruling.

The meaning of the attention to reasons will be best understood, then, if we consider the meaning of the opposite stance held by the text that had earlier dominated modes of expression, the Mishnah. The Mishnah stated its authority through its silence to such concerns. It spoke for itself, on its own terms and by virtue of its own authority. The Mishnah's claim apparently was that it needed little else. Its connection to scripture was clear to educated readers, but it was unnecessary, in the Mishnah's estimation, either to justify its interpretation of earlier tradition or to give reasons for rulings that were unrelated to earlier tradition. The rejection of this stance by amoraim of the middle period indicates their assessment that the Mishnah's silent claim is not sufficient. Other sources of authority are necessary.

These other sources were to be found in multiple reasons and justifications, no one of them sufficient or necessarily correct. To put it otherwise, the source of authority now began to shift, modestly at first but then more confidently, to human reason as applied by the amoraic interpreters. Each of these shifts—seeking human reasons or human interpretations of earlier traditions, often noting the human processes by which decisions were made, and speaking more often in the language that the people in that time and place actually used—each was an assertion of human prerogative. There is, in this corpus of traditions, an increasing awareness of the human component of the system. The processes of the system were therefore beginning to become as important as its outcomes.

The same development *may be* present, in perhaps more explicit ways, in the significant body of argumentation that these generations produced. *If* the importance of this argumentation was recognized by the sages of that time, then this will confirm the trends delineated here. Being the purported record of the process by which rulings were produced or later justified, argumentation is perhaps the clearest evidence of the valuation of the human component of the tradition. It represents reason, justification, and process combined into one. Argumentation, if it was in fact valued, would be the most elegant expression of the sense that the authority of a given text (the Mishnah, baraita, or early amoraic traditions) does not speak for itself, but that it resides in the expression of those who, through their own assertion of authority, take the opinions of earlier authorities seriously, though not absolutely.

I am, however, cautious to say "if" in remarking upon the significance of the argumentation of these sages, because in the opinion of one of the major rabbinics scholars of this generation the importance of the argumentation was not recognized in this period, and it was not preserved by design. According to David Weiss Halivni the sages of these generations did not see fit to preserve argumentation. Rather, it was only the authors of the anonymous gemara (who, according to Halivni, flourished in the century following the death of R. Ashi in 427; Halivni calls these scholars stammaim) who first recognized the value of argumentation, and it is for this reason, in his opinion, that more argumentation survived from later generations of amoraim than from earlier generations. Of course, if Halivni is correct, then claims for the product of these sages will have to be far more modest than those offered thus far. Therefore, this question—Was the argumentation of these sages preserved by them or by their close contemporaries with intent?—will be the subject of the next chapter. The outcome of that deliberation will affect significantly the nature of the history presented in this book.

III.   But first, it is necessary to comment on the product of the later amoraic period (the fifth and sixth generations). As noted, the product of this period tends to assume the forms that were pioneered in the previous two generations, though in most respects it is less remarkable. Most of the traditions of Pappa and Ashi are interpretive, but in the case of Pappa, at least, brief traditions again are dominant. Although both sages prefer Aramaic over Hebrew by a significant margin, there is hardly an innovation in the overall corpus of traditions. Argumentation is most often very brief. There is attention to reason and justification, but always in modest ways. There are few cases of explicit preservation of argumentation, and none of the cases extends beyond a couple of steps. To describe the situation simply: the forms are here, but the energy is gone.

There is no question that the forms of the previous period, many of them then innovative, were accepted by this time. This may be the most significant contribution of these latter sages—the validation of forms that had been forged by earlier amoraim, but whose ultimate acceptance was nowhere guaranteed. In the traditions of these sages, in essence, lay the guarantee.

It must be recalled what was here being affirmed. The legitimacy of human reason in dialogue with tradition is the assumption that grounds these new forms. Process—human debate and deliberation—becomes a recognized value. Reasons and justifications, sometimes grounded in earlier traditions but often the product of human reason and always the product of human interpretation, are now essential elements of the enterprise. Making these things explicit—though they may always, in fact, have been present—self-consciously affirms their proper place in the emerging system. Tradition, in its most limited sense, is joined by the creative contributions whose source is human reason.

So, on the one hand, these later amoraim, by their admission of these forms, guaranteed that this innovation would not be lost. On the other hand, the broad absence of innovation in this period suggests that they did not allow for the full implications of these earlier contributions. Perhaps they did not understand what the outcome of these directions might be, or perhaps they did, and did not deem it proper to go any further. Whichever of these alternatives is correct, it is evident that there is no longer a will, in these later generations, to forge new forms and chart new territory. The implications of the innovations suggested in the middle amoraic period would only come to be explored by the authors of the gemara itself. It is only then that the impact of human reason would be recognized for its full power.

The only possible exception, the only glimmer of recognition of what reason might ultimately accomplish, is found in the scripture interpretations of R. Ashi. As we saw, Ashi participates in midrashic debate in a way unmatched by his predecessors. His methods are creative, and he is even willing to favor reason over scripture as a source for law. His activity in this realm represents an assertion of the ability of reason to transform scripture and draw new meanings from it. As we will see in a later chapter, the recognition of what this assertion of reason might accomplish would be fully realized only in the anonymous gemara.

But the full meaning of the traditions of these last generations also lies beyond us so long as we have not determined the precise nature of the relationship of amoraim to argumentation. For the presence of a large body of argumentation typifies the product of this period, as it had the previous. And as for the previous period, here too Halivni claims that the amoraim themselves did not value argumentation and did not see fit to attend to its preservation. This concern, it will be recalled, he believes to be the innovation of the authors of the anonymous text. It is to this thesis, and its implications for the present study, that we now turn.

3

The Preservation of
Amoraic Argumentation

THE EXTENT TO WHICH we understand the amoraim of the middle generations to have distanced themselves from earlier models depends heavily on our view of their involvement in the preservation of argumentation. There is of course no question that they participated in argumentation; there is ample evidence of the fact that they did. But there is also little question that their amoraic predecessors, or the tannaim before them, also participated in argumentation. The many differences of opinion that are recorded in their names must, at least in some degree, be the product of such argumentation.[1] We even preserve argumentational texts that are meant to represent such deliberations—more often in the case of early amoraim, but also, from time to time, in the Mishnah and baraitot. So what distinguishes the middle amoraim from those who came before them is not whether they argued but whether those debates were formulated and preserved. Preservation, or publication, thus was the crucial innovation. The question, then, must be: when and by whom was argumentation first preserved?

David Weiss Halivni's recent analysis of the gemara responds to these questions, though it raises certain problems. He suggests that the sages of the amoraic period, like their predecessors in the tannaitic period, thought that discursive, argumentational materials "were not worthy of being preserved, and were allowed to suffer neglect or disappearance."[2] The argumentational sequences "were not considered worthy enough to be transmitted to posterity—and did not survive."[3] Only the authors of the anonymous gemara finally recognized the value of the discursive material, and thanks to that recognition, the material we do preserve finally managed to survive.

In Halivni's view, the amoraic "indifference" toward argumentation is a consequence of more than mere practical considerations.[4] Although he admits that argumentation was more difficult to preserve than were brief traditions, it was not merely an awareness of this difficulty that lay at the root of the choice to "neglect" these materials. Rather, Halivni believes that the decision by the amoraim to disregard the discursive material in favor of the brief (which he terms argumentational and apodictic) was also ideological. In the ancient world, Halivni claims, it was only the apodictic resolution of the law that was considered important (or relevant) enough to preserve. Similarly in the rabbinic context, in the absence of any motivation to do the contrary, argumentation was normally overlooked by the official repeaters. In the end, it was only the authors of the unattributed text (the stammaim) who recognized the importance of the argumentation because "to the Stammaim, theoretical learning was a main mode of worship."[5] Torah and the examination of its intricacies (as embodied in the argumentation) were in their time viewed as central to Jewish religious expression. The stammaim, therefore, for the first time sought to preserve argumentation. What had survived from the amoraim they preserved and completed; what did not survive they invented anew.

This, according to Halivni, explains why, despite their exclusive commitment to preserving apodictic traditions, more argumentation did, nevertheless, survive from the later generations of amoraim than from the earlier generations. In his own language: "We attribute the preservation of the argumentational materials from Abaye and Rava more to the short [!] amount of time that elapsed between them and the Stammaim than to a special awareness by Abaye and Rava of the need to transmit the discursive as well. . . . It was the Stammaim who preserved for posterity the non-apodictic material of Abaye and Rava, and not Abaye and Rava themselves."[6] It was chronological proximity to the stammaim that determined survival, then. The argumentation that is left to us from these generations is not a matter of design, therefore, but a matter of accident.

The problems with this thesis should be stated immediately. First, nearly one hundred years passed between the so-called later generations, whose argumentation survived in some considerable numbers, and the stammaim, who were presumably the first to consider this material worthy of preservation. According to the dates preserved by Sherira Gaon, Abbaye died in 338 and Rava in 352. According to Halivni's theory, the activity

The Mind of the Talmud

of the stammaim began following the death of R. Ashi in 427. This means that in the case of Abbaye nearly ninety years at the very least would have passed between the time that the argumentation was articulated and the moment that it was first considered worthy of preservation. How are we to imagine, in a society whose publication (intended, formal preservation) was oral,[7] that these traditions nevertheless survived for such a significant period of time? Furthermore, since these fourth-generation sages are often represented as engaging in dialogues with their colleagues of the third amoraic generation, the dates of their deaths must be considered as well. Again according to Sherira, Yosef died in 323, Rabba in 320, and Hisda in 309. Granting that the latest date that a dialogue could have occurred is the date of the death of the first of its participants to die, this means that the many dialogues in which these sages are involved would somehow have had to survive for well over a century before they could have come to the attention of the stammaim. If the stammaim were the first to think that argumentation was important and therefore worthy of preservation, how then did this material come to their attention in the first place? This is a problem for which Halivni's thesis, at least in its starkest formulation, has no solution.

Second, though proportionally their number may be small, in terms of sheer numbers a *considerable body of sometimes lengthy deliberations survives from the first four amoraic generations.* In my enumeration, the total number of argumentational sequences of any length involving the most prominent sages of the first four generations is 2,449. If accurate, how could Halivni's reconstruction of the process possibly account for the presence of such a considerable body of argumentational amoraic texts? Unless virtually all of this argumentation is artificial, we must search for some other account of its preservation. Because evidence suggests that it is not a grand fiction, as I argued in both prior chapters, we must seek to explain its survival through a means that Halivni has not proposed. Whether the alternative I offer will be but a minor revision to his thesis or a complete displacement thereof will depend on the precise nature of the evidence at hand.

First, it is essential to note that Halivni is not unaware of these problems. It is the recognition of precisely these factors that causes him, at certain points, to compromise the absoluteness with which he at other times describes the division between the amoraim and the stammaim. For example, he writes that "the Amoraim did not deem it important enough to have the discursive material committed to the transmitters *with the same exactitude and polish with which they committed the apodictic ma-*

terial.'' [8] If the point was not whether they committed it to preservation at all, but only if they did so according to the same rigorous standards, then the problems discussed earlier will be far less troublesome. Later Halivni states it this way: "Once the law was arrived at, the argumentational that gave rise to it was neglected, *left to each succeeding academy to formulate as its members saw fit*. There was no *official version* of the argumentational."[9] Again, according to this formulation, "neglect" must be understood here in rather restricted terms. It could not mean that the argumentation was ignored completely, but only that it was preserved according to less demanding guidelines, and perhaps in a variety of versions. Nevertheless, this restricted definition still allows that such materials were preserved, and by design. It also eliminates the gaps that troubled Halivni's thesis when stated in its more extreme form.

In consideration of the problems already enunciated and the evidence presented in this chapter I will argue that Halivni's initial formulation of his proposals is not acceptable. His moderated view, however, will have to be considered seriously. Do the data support a picture by which amoraim preserved argumentation but recognized that it was distinctly less important than the brief traditions? Alternatively, did these sages preserve the argumentation with the same intent and recognition of value that directed their preservation of the brief traditions? This fine, although less severe difference will still affect our understanding of the amoraic contribution and thus will now be tested.

To determine which of these alternatives the evidence will support, I *method* have isolated all argumentational sequences attributed to major amoraim of the first four generations that persist for more than three steps.[10] My interest in sequences of greater than three steps is due to several considerations. First, though even shorter sequences might, in the end, represent a problem for Halivni's thesis, we could nevertheless admit the theoretical possibility that such cases survived without official attention to their formulation and preservation. It would be far more difficult to make such a claim for longer sequences. For such texts to have survived it would appear that concern for their formal preservation would have to have been necessary long before they came to the attention of the authors of the unattributed gemara. Second, in each generation there are far more cases of one- or two-step argumentation than there are of greater than two steps, and three-step argumentation represents a kind of middle ground, there being far fewer of these than of the briefer sequences but not quite as few as those which extend for more than three steps.[11] If these longer sequences are typified by unique, characteristic features, it might be argued that their preservation is influenced by such features and is therefore unusual. If, on the other hand, these sequences exhibit the same range of characteristics as shorter sequences, it will be difficult to argue that their preservation is unusual, making it necessary to account for the preservation of the whole body of amoraic argumentation on other than technical grounds. The precise characteristics of these texts should therefore tell us more about the nature of amoraic preservation of argumentation than any other evidence.

Of course, before employing these texts for such purposes it is necessary, to the extent possible, to confirm their basic textual reliability. Stated in other terms, is it accurate to consider each, individually, as a product of the period whose opinions it purports to record? For present purposes, such a determination must begin with a source-critical analysis of each. Since the anonymous author often combined sources that were originally unrelated to create deliberations, it is necessary to test each for evidence of such artificial formulation. Only if the text as a whole is supported by manuscripts, and if, at the same time, it is not apparently the product of later, artificial formulation, may it reasonably be considered as evidence in the present inquiry. It is only such argumentation that will be considered in the following analysis.

After such texts are isolated, it is of course necessary to consider those characteristics that might reflect upon the preservational intent (or absence thereof) inherent in their formulation. Is there something about these sequences that would suggest that their preservation is unique and therefore distinct from argumentation as a whole? Is there some feature, shared by many sequences, that could explain why they might have been preserved, whereas other lengthy sequences, now unavailable to us, were not? Is it possible, for example, that sequences survived only if they were subject to explicit attention by later generations of amoraim? If we could demonstrate that, for some reason, these sequences consistently drew the attention of successive generations of sages, then their survival would no longer be a mystery; we would be able to claim that preservation was assured only through ongoing amoraic attention. Alternatively, some formal characteristic shared by these texts might have facilitated their preservation, despite their length. For example, sequences introduced with the term *ba'i minei* ("he asked of him") more often exhibit traits of formal preservation than does other argumentation (pp. 312–18). In a similar way, stories describing argumentational exchanges or sequences preceded by narrative introductions often persist for more than a few steps (pp. 305–12). Do these lengthier sequences—unlike briefer argumentation, which assumes a variety of forms—tend to prefer these forms over others? If this is the case, this would suggest the possibility that these factors, rather than interest in argumentation as such, determined their survival. On the other hand, if these sequences are typical of argumentation in the Bavli, we might still find some hint as to the source of their preservation. For example, they might exhibit technical signs of formulation for preservation and transmission, such as mnemonic devices. Do any of these factors offer an explanation for the survival of this argumentation; if not, how else might their survival be explained?

The Evidence

The total number of argumentational sequences in the Bavli extending for more than three steps and involving the major amoraim of the first four generations was, by my initial, noncritical count, slightly more than 500. I based my analysis on approximately half that number (240), including all cases from the seders Mo'ed and Nashim and tractate Berakhot, because by that point I had concluded that there is no significant variation over the whole.

Of this initial number, 177 were found to represent genuine[12] argumentation of the sort described earlier. Of these, 18 include three steps of direct address plus a secondary response, 73 include four steps of direct address, 20 include five steps, 27 are six steps, and 39 are seven steps or more. These sequences include authorities from all of the first four amoraic generations, but the majority cluster in the third and fourth generations.

In terms of factors that characterize these sequences, the following was observed: 37 sequences begin with a *ba'i minei* question; 45 are introduced by brief narratives that set the context of the argument; 42 continue in a storylike form throughout. Only 25 show the explicit attention of later generations of amoraim. Other characteristics that might provide an explanation for preservation are far less common. In 9 cases preservation may have been a consequence of the transmittal of the tradition from Palestine to Babylonia. For a variety of reasons—connected primarily to the perception that Palestinian traditions, when repeated in Babylonia, might need to be buttressed by the explanatory context that argumentation can provide—such sequences were sometimes preserved with explicit amoraic intent (pp. 157–81). Finally, 12 of the cases include what I call provocative elements, an admittedly subjective category that includes such features as dramatic personal exchanges or self-conscious attention to the rabbinic process.

Such results do not permit us to conclude that these cases are in any way distinct from preserved argumentation as a whole. No single feature characterizes the majority of cases, and given the variety of features by which they might be described, it seems clear that they are, aside from their length, typical argumentation. This is particularly true in the thirty-nine instances that exhibit no noteworthy distinguishing characteristics. As the following examples will show, these sequences assume a wide variety of forms and deliberative stances. They are united, if at all, only by their awareness that the process itself is an important element of the rabbinic enterprise.

The texts described have been chosen for the variety that they represent, and for particular points that they help to illustrate. They are presented in the order in which they appear in the Bavli and are quoted only to the extent necessary for present purposes.

Eruvin 12a

(I have highlighted the steps of dialogue and other noteworthy features.)

a. *R. Yosef*[13] *said R. Judah said Samuel said:* A courtyard is permitted [for purposes of carrying therein on Shabbat] by one partition [to distinguish this area from areas outside the courtyard].

b. *Abbaye said to R. Yosef:* Did Samuel really say this? But *didn't Samuel say to R. Hanania b. Shila* "You should not do this deed except with . . . two partitions"?

c. *He [R. Yosef] said to him [Abbaye]:* And do I not know that there was [such] a case . . . ? It was [a case of] a small inlet of the sea that flowed into a courtyard, and [the owner] came before R. Judah and he required of him only one partition! [Therefore proving that I was correct when I said "one."]

d. *He said to him:* You spoke of an inlet of the sea; the sages were lenient with regard to water.

e. As [is evident from the following exchange in which] *R. Tavla asked of Rav . . . He said to him* [in response] . . . .

f. It is in any case [still] problematic [= the two contradictory opinions of Samuel, in (a) and (b)].

g. When R. Pappa and R. Huna the son of R. Joshua came from the School of Rav they explained it. . . .

h. R. Pappa said: *If it is difficult, then this is what is difficult to me.* . . .

The primary dialogue here (b–d), involving Yosef and Abbaye, is only three steps in length. But in at least one of these steps (b) Abbaye repeats to Yosef another single step of dialogue. This repetition is important because it reflects a willingness to repeat not only opinions, but also the process by which they came to be expressed. The same concern for process is evident in the following step (c), in which Yosef describes the context within which the ruling under consideration was delivered. The next step (d–e) may also record the quotation of earlier dialogue, though here it is less clear that the dialogue is being quoted by Abbaye; it is possible that it is the editor of the gemara who is filling in this supportive information (e). However, because this same two-step dialogue is quoted elsewhere on two occasions by R. Ashi (Shab. 101a and Eruv. 16b), demonstrating that this exchange was known to the amoraim, it seems reasonable to attribute its repetition here to Abbaye (who could then have been R. Ashi's source for the tradition). If this conclusion is correct, then the willingness to quote earlier argumentation is demonstrated here that much more strongly. In any case, the dialogue as a whole, at least in its essential elements, was already known to R. Pappa and R. Huna the son of R. Joshua. Its formulation as argumentation, therefore, must have been relatively early.

Pesaḥim 43b–44b/Nazir 35b–37a

(The following text is cited according to the version in Pesaḥim, with important variants from Nazir included in parentheses.)

a. R. Abbahu said R. Yoḥanan said: [With regard to] all prohibitions of the Torah, permitted matter does not combine with prohibited matter [to create a full measure of prohibited matter] except for those things prohibited to a Nazir. . . .

b. R. Dimi sat and repeated this statement.

c. *Abbaye said to R. Dimi* (Nazir: Abbaye objected to him): [Is this true?] . . . And has it not been taught [in a Mishnah]. . . . And we deliberated on it, asking . . . and Rabba the son of bar Hana said "What is the reason. . . ?" How is this to be understood? Is it not because. . . .

d. [Nazir, printed edition, though missing in MS Vatican: *He said to him:*] No. What is the meaning of "the equivalent of an olive"?

That there is the quantity of an olive in the time it takes to consume a piece [of bread].

e. And is "an olive in the time it takes . . ." [a law] from the Torah?

f. *He said to him:* Yes.

g. If this is so. . . .

h. Rather what? Is it because. . . ?

i. *He objected to him.* . . .

j. *He said to him* . . . [expressed anonymously in Nazir]

k. *He objected to him.* . . .

l. *He said to him.* . . .

(All of what follows is recorded anonymously in Pesaḥim. The version in Nazir is as follows:)

m. *Abbaye said to him:* For what reason [would one conclude] that this [proof text, used by R. Yoḥanan in (a)] comes to teach something about the combination of permitted with prohibited matter? Perhaps. . . .

n. *And Abbaye, originally he is troubled by what R. Dimi said, and he objects to him with all these objections, and now he says to him. . .?*

o.–p. [not necessary for present purposes]

q. *That sage said to him* [alt.: *He said to him*]: R. Abbahu [who originally repeated R. Yoḥanan's opinion] was following the [earlier] opinion of R. Aqiba.

(The gemara intervenes here with several steps.)

r. *R. Aḥa the son of R. Avia said to R. Ashi:* According to R. Aqiba. . . .

This is a very difficult text, and the relationship between the two versions in the gemara is very difficult to define. The number of steps of dialogue that derive from the generations that concern us, that is, the first four generations, depends, of course, on which of the versions is accepted, and on how precisely that version is analyzed. A few words of comparative analysis are in order, therefore, before a general statement can be made.

The first portion of the text (a–l) is paralleled relatively closely in Pesaḥim and Nazir. For a variety of reasons, it seems that the Pesaḥim version is more original, though the Nazir text may not be dependent on it, as I shall explain. The middle of this section (g–h) is in the Pesaḥim text quite clearly the product of the anonymous gemara. It refers to a lengthy deliberation in the gemara that precedes our text, depending heavily on that previous gemara for appreciation of its reference. Moreover, this deliberation as a whole is related only tangentially to the one that precedes it, and these few nonessential steps (g–h), therefore, can best be understood as the effort of the gemara's final author to weave the two larger deliberations together. This is true, I believe, despite the appearance in the Nazir version that these particular steps are a continuation of the direct dialogue. The text that gives this appearance, while supported by the Munich manuscript, is, however, denied by both the first printing (Venice) and the Vatican manuscript; in each of those versions these steps are also clearly the product of the gemara itself. The version of the present text (Vilna and MS Munich) can be explained on the basis of a scribal error,[14] one that is rooted in an original that is preserved either in Pesaḥim or in the Venice and Vatican versions. In either case, Pesaḥim presently records a more original version of these stages in the text, and they should not be counted as steps in the amoraic dialogue.

Hence the number of argumentational steps recorded in this text (Pesaḥim) in the name of amoraim is eight (c, d, e, f, i, j, k, l), and with one exception these are all relatively simple and wholly typical of argumentation preserved elsewhere in the Bavli. The exception (c) is worthy of comment. The first step of the exchange, in which Abbaye expresses his original challenge to R. Dimi, requires that he quote several pieces of information in order to make his point. These include (1) a Mishnah, (2) a question that was addressed to this Mishnah, and (3) the statement of an amora in response to this question. Abbaye articulates his challenge on the basis of the combination of these three pieces. What is of interest here is not merely the sophistication of the challenge, but the fact that Abbaye must repeat several steps (source text, question, solution) of an earlier deliberation. The willingness to do so is unprecedented in the earliest amoraic generations, and this is an excellent illustration of the creative attention to process that characterizes, for the first time, these middle generations.

The latter section of the text (m–r) is almost certainly preserved in a more original form in Nazir, which attributes several of the individual steps to amoraim. This is confirmed by the fact that several steps in the dialogue clearly depend on earlier attributed steps and therefore demonstrate that those steps were present before the author of the later dialogue.

In (n), for example, the anonymous author of the gemara remarks upon the apparent inconsistency in the approaches of Abbaye [(m) when compared to (c)], showing that those steps are clearly known to him as being attributed to Abbaye. Furthermore, the response to Abbaye [by either R. Dimi or "that sage," in (q)] is known later to R. Aḥa the son of R. Avia, a contemporary of R. Ashi, for his question already assumes that response (r). These several steps should thus also be attributed to Abbaye and his colleagues, and to our previous total we may now add two more steps. The fact that this whole deliberation is recorded anonymously in Pesaḥim, on the other hand, merely demonstrates that the author of the Pesaḥim gemara didn't know the attributions or, more probably, that he reworked originally attributed material for his own reasons, in order to create the final product.[15]

This sequence, whose full extent is evident only in Nazir, is most notable for its considerable length and complexity. The variety of differences that distinguish the two printed versions—and the larger number that are available in earlier printings and manuscripts—shows the overall difficulty of preserving lengthy argumentation. If the Pesaḥim text was borrowed from Nazir, then this borrowing took place at the time of the composition of that gemara; the weaving that we spoke of (with relation to g–h) was intended to create a coherent whole and, being essential to the overall form of the gemara, it could have occurred only when the text as a final product was being written. If this is an accurate picture of the textual history, then this sequence illustrates not only the difficulty of this sort of preservation, but also the general integrity of such a text. For despite the variations, what is also remarkable about this example is the numerous similarities that unite the two primary versions and the recognition that the gemara's final authors already knew the argumentation and used it in different contexts to serve their various agendas.

Pesaḥim 46b–48a

(Letters denoting steps in this deliberation do not correspond to steps in the gemara's overall argument but only to those that are part of the amoraic argument.)

a. It has been said: If one bakes from the festival for [use on] the weekday, R. Ḥisda said, "He is punished." And Rabba said, "He is not punished."

b. . . . *Rabba said to R. Ḥisda:* According to you . . . how do we bake from the festival for the sabbath?

c. *He said to him:* On account of *eruv tavshilin* [a legal fiction that causes such cooking to be permitted].

d. And on account of *eruv tavshilin* do we permit something that is prohibited by the Torah?

e. *He said to him:* According to the Torah needs of the sabbath may be prepared on the festival. . . .

f. *He objected to him.* . . .

g. *He said to him:* It is on account of the loss of his property.

h. And on account of loss of his property do we permit something that is prohibited by the Torah?

i. *He said to him:* Yes. . . .

j. He objected to him. . . .

k. He said to him. . . .

l. . . . *R. Meri objected:* . . . and if you say that needs of the sabbath may be prepared on the festival. . . .

m. There it is different, for scripture said. . . .

n. . . . *R. Ḥisda sent* [the following message] *to Rabba by the hand of R. Aḥa the son of R. Huna:* And do we say. . . .

o. R. Pappa the son of Samuel said [in response]. . . .

p. Mar the son of R. Ashi [or, according to MS Munich, R. Ashi] said. . . .

q. *Abbaye objected to him* (to Rabba). . . .

r. *He said to him.* . . .

s. . . . and is *muktzeh* [things not permitted for use on sabbath or festivals because they are not fit for or intended for use] from the Torah?

t. *He said to him:* Yes, for it is written. . . .

u. *He said to him*: But you are the one who said *"I asked R. Ḥisda"* (and there are those who say it "I asked R. Huna"): . . . *and you said to us* [that he said to you] . . . and if you say that the prohibition of *muktzeh* is from the Torah. . . .

v. *R. Aḥa the son of Rava said to Abbaye.* . . .

This deliberation, one of the longest of any kind in the Bavli, has for present purposes been reduced to its most basic structure. For the most part, steps that are the contribution of the gemara's later author have been eliminated. Only elements of the amoraic dialogue have been highlighted. By representing it this way, I have sought to allow the text to make its own impact. Only a few words of explanation are necessary for present purposes.

This is actually a collection of several dialogues, some lengthy, that take up issues inherent in the original difference of opinion between R.

Ḥisda and Rabba. The first two of these dialogues (b–l and n–p) involve the participation of the original disputants themselves; the latter (q–v) involves only Rabba, this time in an exchange with Abbaye. Halivni has demonstrated that, in the first dialogue, the second objection and response (j–k) is an artificial creation of the gemara's author,[16] and so the total number of steps in this sequence is nine. The second section (n–p) is introduced with only a single exchange, a challenge to which only later sages supply the response. The final sequence includes several possible later interpolations, which I have eliminated in this transcription, and so the total number of steps in its dialogue is at least six.

Of special interest in the final sequence is the challenge of Abbaye to Rabba at (u), which requires his reference to a dialogue that Rabba had earlier reported to him. This indicates, first, that Rabba had seen fit to repeat dialogue on a previous occasion and, second, that Abbaye recognizes the value of the earlier exchange in the pursuit of his inquiry here. On both accounts, the sensitivity to the potentially crucial nature of argumentation is undeniable. Also supporting this valuation of argumentation is the attention paid to these exchanges by several later sages. The challenge originated by R. Ḥisda at (n) is attended to not only by Pappa the son of Samuel (a contemporary of Abbaye), but also later by R. Ashi (or his son). The same is true in subsequent steps that I have not recorded. Attention not only to the subject at hand, but also to the variety of exchanges that the original subject generates, is evidence of the clear recognition in these generations that decisions and answers are not enough.

Sukkah 14b

a. It has been said: If one turned them [= overly wide boards] on their sides [in order to create the roofing for a Sukkah, thus exposing to the inside of the Sukkah only the narrow edge of the boards], R. Huna said "It is unfit," and R. Ḥisda and Rabba the son of R. Huna said "It is proper."

b. R. Naḥman went to Sura [Alfasi's version, according to manuscript: R. Ḥisda and Rabba the son of R. Huna went to Rav].

c. R. Ḥisda and Rabba the son of R. Huna went in to him.

d. *They said to him:* If he turned them [= overly wide boards] over on their sides, what is the law?

e. *He said to them:* It [= the Sukkah] is unfit; *[on account of their otherwise unfit status] they are as though made into spits of metal [which are always, by definition, unfit].*

f. *R. Huna said to them:* Did I not say this to you. . . ?
g. *They said to him:* And did the master tell us a reason, that we did not accept it from him [MSS: from you]?
h. *He said to them:* And did you ask of me a reason, that I did not tell [one] to you?

This exchange is relatively modest, involving only five steps of dialogue. Of great interest, however, is the content of the exchange. When R. Ḥisda and Rabba the son of R. Huna asked R. Naḥman (or Rav) for a clarification of the law, he gave them the same ruling as R. Huna. R. Huna then wanted to know why his ruling alone was not good enough. Their answer: you didn't give us a reason! Huna responds in turn that they did not ask for a reason; if they had asked, he surely would have offered one. At the center of this dialogue, then, is the quest for reasons. What is the meaning of this concern?

First, it should be noted that reasons are here assumed to empower the opinions that they accompany. If Huna had originally offered a reason, there would have been no reason to go further. At the same time, that opinions stated simply and not supported by reasons are considered inadequate is demonstration of the fact that the Mishnah's formal stylistic choice, at least, is here being questioned; something more than silent authority is necessary. Finally, reasons, being important justifications of opinions in law, must be sought. In the opinion of this text, at least, the search for reasons can now reasonably stand at the center of the interpretive enterprise.

For present purposes it is not essential to claim that the names recorded here accurately identify the authors of these traditions. On the contrary, as I argued earlier, what they reflect is opinions attributed to these authorities by near-contemporary disciples. We may speak here, therefore, of views held in these middle generations, and it is just views of this sort that the evidence noted in the previous chapter would have led us to expect. Reasons and justification have now achieved considerable value. For this reason, the traditions of sages of these generations so often supply justifications.

More Evidence and Conclusions

As these and other examples demonstrate, many argumentational sequences are recorded in the names of third- and fourth-generation authorities. These sequences are often long and elaborate, and they employ a variety of forms. Also, the deliberations are often built on discussion of the process itself; reasons, justification, and argumentation are represented as central concerns of the authors of these dialogues.

What does this corpus suggest concerning the history of the tradition? Is it possible, given the available evidence, to ascertain how this body of literature came to be preserved in the Bavli? In consideration of the interest expressed during these generations in argumentation and in other justificatory or interpretive forms, it seems less than reasonable to claim that the sages of this period did not esteem such forms. On the contrary, explicit evidence in both brief and argumentational traditions suggests that these forms were esteemed highly. Therefore, if we were forced to conclude that the argumentation was not preserved at this time, it would not be on account of a lack of interest. Other explanations would have to be found.

But there is, I believe, no reason for such a conclusion, for ample evidence of intention to preserve argumentation is available. Such evidence may be found in the following phenomena: (1) few cases of published commentary on earlier argumentation; (2) several dozen instances in which argumentation is explicitly preserved by amoraim; (3) cases in which it is possible to determine that argumentation had been formulated at a very early stage; and (4) building upon these factors, the presence of significant numbers of argumentational sequences whose preservation can otherwise not be explained.

The first body of evidence, involving only two examples, consists of those cases, discussed in the previous chapter, in which Abbaye comments at length on prior argumentation. One such case (the other is found at B.M. 55b–56a) follows.

Gittin 25a

a. R. Hoshaya asked R. Judah: If someone said to a scribe "write [a bill of divorce] to whichever [of my wives, both possessing the same name] comes out of the door first" what is the law?

b. He said to him: They have [already] taught it [in Mishnah Gittin 3:1] "More than this, if he said to a scribe 'write [a bill of divorce] to whichever I will want, that I might divorce her' it is improper to divorce with it [= the bill of divorce]."—therefore, there is no retroactive selection [= m. Pes. 8:3].

c. He objected to him: If someone says to his children "Behold, I slaughter this Pesach [sacrificial lamb] for whichever of you first enters Jerusa-

lem,'' as soon as the head and most of the body of the first enters, he
has acquired the right to his portion and he may grant the right to his
siblings [= m. Pes. 8:3].

d. He said to him: Hoshaya, my son, what do matters of the Pesach have
to do with bills of divorce? . . .

e. Abbaye said: He asks him regarding a matter in which the outcome
depends upon the will of others [in (a) the outcome depends upon
which of the wives chooses to come out first] and he answers him
from a case in which the outcome depends upon his own will [in the
Mishnah quoted in (b) he is the one who will make the final decision
of whom to divorce] and he objects to him from a matter in which
the outcome depends upon the will of others [in (c) the outcome depends on the efforts of his children, not on his own decision].

f. Rava said: What is the problem? Perhaps [it makes no differ-
ence]. . . .

g. R. Mesharshya said to Rava: But [I have evidence that it does make
a difference]. . . .

The nature of the comment attributed to Abbaye (e) has immense implications for our understanding of the assumed status of argumentation
at that time. This comment is in the form by which amoraic traditions
were officially published, that is, a concise, unadorned comment introduced by the formula "So-and-so said." Translated to replicate the form
and balance of the original, this comment would be rendered "He asks
him X and he answers him Y and he then objects to him X" (where X
and Y are three Hebrew words). Having employed this form, it is clear
that the authorities who promulgated this tradition assumed that it would
be preserved and transmitted to future generations.

But it makes sense to publish an interpretive comment in this way only
if one assumes that the object of its interpretation is similarly preserved.
Comments on a text are truly possible only when that text has an integrity
of its own. For this reason, comments on the Mishnah became widespread in the generations after its publication and reception. The same
could be noted in connection to many other texts as well. Furthermore,
to publish an interpretation an individual must assume not only that the
subject of his comment is likely to be preserved but also that the same
subject is worthy of comment, that is, he must value it. People do not
publish comments on texts that they deem unimportant.

These published comments of Abbaye are therefore eloquent statements of his valuation (or that of whoever attributed the comments to

him, again, representing his generation) of the argumentation he addresses. He assumes, first of all, that the argumentation is important; otherwise there is no reason to respond to it. Furthermore, he assumes that the argumentation itself has attained a certain integrity—that it will be preserved. On both of these accounts, but particularly the latter, we may conclude that the preservation of that argumentation was intended. It would not be unreasonable to believe that the opinions made explicit here might be extended to other argumentation.

Affirming this conclusion is the second body of evidence, that is, those cases in which amoraim are explicitly represented as repeating earlier argumentation.

There is ample testimony of the interest of amoraim in preserving and transmitting brief traditions. Such is the meaning of those thousands of cases in which a brief tradition is introduced with the formula "Rabbi X said Rabbi Y said." In these instances the first authority, "Rabbi X," is the primary repeater of the tradition of "Rabbi Y," and it is clear that he desires to preserve that tradition. Some of the most prominent amoraic authorities are active in this capacity, and there can be no doubt, therefore, that amoraim sought to assure the preservation of such traditions.

If there were equivalent examples in which amoraim repeated argumentational traditions, then we would have evidence of their similar interest in preserving that form. Though they are few, there are, in all, thirty-eight instances (according to my survey) of such preservation in the Bavli.[17]

None of these cases is associated with sages of the first two amoraic generations. The first examples occur during the third generation, and they are recorded in the names of Zeira (see Ber. 48a and Men. 7a), Yosef (Ber. 25b and Hul. 36b), and Rabba (Eruv. 17a, 40a–b, and Suk. 17a–b). The traditions quoted are generally brief questions and responses; the authorities who quote the earlier argumentation were themselves typically participants in that argumentation. There are exceptional examples of longer preservation (see Rabba at Eruv. 40b and Suk. 17a–b), but in these cases the sage who repeats the exchange had also been involved in it. The only exception to this rule is the latter portion of the preservation of Yosef at Ḥullin 36b.

Fourth-generation sages also quote earlier argumentation, although no more often than their predecessors in the third generation. Abbaye quotes argumentation in which he himself participated (Eruv. 45b) and that in which he had no direct part (Eruv. 12a and B.M. 10a). Rava quotes argumentation in narrative form (Pes. 103a and B.M. 48b) and also in straightforward report (e.g., see B.M. 10a). None of these cases is particularly elaborate, but neither is the bulk of argumentation preserved during these generations, and so it is precisely such cases the quotation of which we would hope to find.

Nearly half of the cases of explicit amoraic preservation of argumentation are cases that were transported from Palestine to Babylonia by scholars who acted as messengers. This is clear in many instances from the identification of the authorities who participated in the exchange. In six cases this factor is more pronounced, though, in that the repetition is introduced by the formula "When Rabbi X came [from Palestine] he said." Compared to traditions that involve only Babylonian sages, these cases are often far more elaborate, many being distinguished by careful literary crafting and formulation. The fact that they were transported from Palestine, I have suggested elsewhere (pp. 157–81), may have facilitated their preservation. Be that as it may, what is essential in the present context is that these argumentational texts were repeated this way at all.

These preservations are not many. Nevertheless, they do provide clear evidence of the desire of amoraim, at least at times, to record argumentation for transmission to later generations. By themselves, these cases would not be adequate to suggest convincing conclusions. In combination with the other proof, however, it becomes likely that this desire was not confined to these cases. (It should be recalled, in this connection, that the majority of brief traditions are also not recorded in a form in which the first repeater is identified. Yet in those cases most would not deny that there was intent to preserve the traditions. Why, then, in terms of argumentation should we assume such intent only if the repeater is identified? The presence of an identified repeater is clear evidence of interest in preservation, but the absence of such identification offers no evidence of its lack.)

One of the cases of explicit preservation of argumentation will introduce the third category that suggests the presence of intent to preserve argumentation at this time. At Yevamot 11b–12a Ḥiyya b. Abba repeats a four-step exchange involving R. Yoḥanan and R. Ammi. The deliberation is simple dialogue, and it is in itself not noteworthy. What is significant, though, is that R. Naḥman b. Isaac, a Babylonian sage, proposes an alternative version of the original Palestinian dialogue introduced with the formula "R. Naḥman b. Isaac teaches it this way (*mtni hkhi*)" This formula is indicative of a formally constructed tradition, and it shows that the original exchange, whose latest participant was a Palestinian sage of the third generation, had already assumed a formal literary character by the time of Naḥman b. Isaac, a fourth-generation Babylonian. This example proves not only that such exchanges were so formulated, but also that this was done within a relatively brief period of their initial articulation. Even if we were to imagine that these deliberations are wholly artificial, it is clear here that they were composed at least within a generation of the authorities to whom they are attributed.

The same phenomenon, also involving R. Naḥman b. Isaac, is found at Zevaḥim 85b (the structure there is virtually identical to this previous example) and Gittin 29b. In the latter instance, a group of sages directs Abimi the son of R. Abbahu to ask a question of his father. Abimi responds by saying that the answer to their question should be obvious, based on his reading of the Mishnah, and he suggests an alternative question. They, in turn, respond by saying that his question, too, has an obvious answer in the Mishnah. Following this report of their exchange, R. Naḥman b. Isaac reformulates the deliberation, including the same basic steps but suggesting that they developed in a different order. Clearly, then, this sequence has been preserved at least by the time of Naḥman b. Isaac, if not before. Other examples of early preservation, in this model and others, also occur.

Finally, and in some ways most crucially, there is the sheer quantity of argumentation that is recorded in the names of sages of these middle generations. To be sure, some proportion of these exchanges is artificial, as can be demonstrated through careful analysis. But even if 20 percent of the whole is artificial, and this is almost certainly an overestimation, there would still be nearly two thousand cases, of various lengths, involving these sages. If we are not willing to admit that these are all artificial formulations, then it appears that we must attribute their survival to the intent to preserve them.

As noted earlier, the evidence speaks against the conclusion that the argumentation is a vast fabrication. This is so, first of all, because the argumentation left from the first two amoraic periods, as I have defined them, is characteristically distinct one from the other. Early argumentation tends to be brief and direct. Objections depend on earlier authoritative sources. No argumentation is quoted by amoraim during these generations, and no comments on the process of argumentation are produced. In contrast, in the middle generations far more argumentation remains, and it is often far more lengthy and elaborate. Objections often depend on human logic alone. Dozens of argumentational sequences are explicitly quoted by amoraim, and a few comments on the process of argumentation are produced. These differences suggest that the formulation of these traditions precedes the hand of a final editor and most likely derives from the approximate periods to which they are attributed. That many of the features that typify argumentation are paralleled in the brief traditions (as discerned in the previous chapter) offers further support for this conclusion.

The presence in these sequences of dozens of names that are otherwise rarely represented in the gemara also supports this conclusion. Because many of these names do not appear often enough to create a characterization, we are left with no picture of the individual whom they purportedly represent. But if the argumentation were artificial, we would expect such names to be employed with a purpose—to represent a particular characterization or generalized point of view. Yet what purpose could be served by employing names that have no other context? We can make sense of these names if, and only if, the individuals whose names they record were actually active in the rabbinic community and these opinions were truly thought to originate with them. The very randomness of these names—one can never guess when they will appear—suggests that the argumentation in which they participated is the work not of a cunning final author but of an individual who genuinely means to represent the opinions of certain masters, and who, by virtue of his chronological proximity to those masters, actually knew who they were.

Yet if these argumentational texts did originate in these generations, how did they survive until the Talmud was finally composed? As I argued earlier, it would have been impossible for these traditions to have survived the century or more that would have been necessary if there was no intent to preserve them in the first place. On the contrary, their survival is ample testimony of the fact that there was intent. Since, as we have seen, the sages of these generations were interested in argumentation and recognized its worth, this conclusion should come as no surprise. Every piece of information we have examined supports it.

Even the variety of features that were found to characterize the lengthy argumentational sequences supports the conclusion that preservation was intended. For example, many of these cases began with *ba'i minei* questions. Elsewhere I have shown that such sequences often demonstrate characteristics of formal publication (pp. 312–18), thereby indicating intent to preserve. In addition, many of the deliberations were formulated with either narrative introductions or overall narrative forms. If the amoraim saw fit to conceive such formulations, this demonstrates that they were interested in assuring preservation. Literary forms of this nature facilitate memorization, and they are therefore evidence of the intent to preserve.

Nor should the fact that argumentation often survived in a flawed or truncated form be taken to contradict this conclusion. It is not unreasonable to suppose that argumentation was more difficult to preserve regardless of the intent to do so. If publication was oral, as we have assumed it to have been,[18] then even formal publication would not have been enough to ensure the integrity of long or sophisticated exchanges. Since such flaws are present in the argumentation of even the latest amoraic generations (pp. 255–57) clearly the argumentational form was in any case more difficult to preserve.

The solution that best accounts for the data, then, is the one suggested earlier: the amoraim, beginning in what we have called the middle amoraic generations, valued argumentation and sought on many occasions to assure its preservation. (This association between preservation and valuation is a necessary one. In oral cultures, or even in manuscript cultures, publication is by definition highly selective. Therefore, what was published, or preserved, was obviously greatly valued. This does not mean, however, that what was not preserved was necessarily not valued, as Halivni suggests in connection with the present discussion. Other analyses might be equally correct in explaining the absence of preservation of certain kinds of traditions.) In thus committing themselves to argumentation, they demonstrated their willingness to distance themselves significantly from formal conventions that had restricted earlier amoraim and the authors of tannaitic texts, laying the groundwork for the form that would ultimately come to characterize the gemara as a whole, that is, argumentation.

Their recognition of the value of argumentation is an affirmation of the many trends I detected in this same period. Argumentation is reason, justification, and process combined into a single form. Its representation of process—however artificial, in the historical sense, that representation might be—is inherent in the form itself. As noted earlier, argumentation claims to be either a record of the way a conclusion was produced or a deliberation on competing claims or interpretations. In either case, the function of recording such argumentation is justification. If argumentation represents the former, then it is meant to explain how a particular conclusion was reached. In such a case, its claim is that a ruling is well-founded. It shows that the outcome is reasonable. If, instead, argumentation records subsequent deliberation, then, similarly, it is meant to make sense of the subject being discussed. It may either defend both sides of a halakhic dispute, in which case it demonstrates that both parties have offered carefully considered opinions, or it may reflect different interpretations of an earlier view. If this is its purpose, then it shows that the substance of what is being discussed can be justified through a multiplicity of approaches. Whichever, finally, is the precise form of the justification, the claim of the justification is that whatever is being discussed is, in rabbinic terms, *reasonable*. The system here begins to make its logic explicit, and in so doing admits that the logic of the system is central. Precise rulings cease, at this stage, to be the only concern. Of equal import is the reason and structure of the system that produces those rulings.

The shift of these matters toward the center has another important implication. The system whose process is recorded in the argumentation is manifestly human. It may have been grounded in divine authority, and individual justifications may have made reference to the divine, but at the surface the system was profoundly human. The rabbis asserted the authority to define the law or to comment on it, and by allowing their deliberations to occupy a central position—together with scripture and earlier rabbinic canon (the Mishnah)—they advanced a claim for the hallowed status of their own efforts. The human endeavor, which had earlier been peripheral, came now, for the first time, to be a legitimate and explicit focus of rabbinic energies.

It would be a mistake, though, to overstate the extent of this shift. Even in the later amoraic generations brief traditions, and not argumentation, were more often recorded for transmission. In significant respects, the manner by which the later generations expressed themselves was not all that different from the way earlier generations did so. We are not speaking here of a revolutionary reform, much less a radical break. What we have uncovered, rather, is a significant evolutionary shift. It is a shift that has important ramifications, both actual and potential. In the amoraic period itself, the full potential of this shift never came to be expressed. The revolution, one which understood the full potential of the middle amoraic innovations, was left to the hands of the gemara's final, anonymous authors.

Appendix A: The Data at a Glance

Steps of Argumentation	Number of Cases
3+	18
4	73
5	20
6	27
7 or more	39
TOTAL CASES	177

Characterizing Features	Number of Cases
Ba'i minei	37
Story	42
Narrative introduction	45
Later attention	25
Provocative	12
Transport from Palestine	9

Appendix B: The Data in Detail

The following list includes only those argumentational segments deemed textually sound. Artificial sequences are not included. The list is restricted to sequences of greater than three steps that include sages of the first four amoraic generations. (For a more detailed explanation of the texts and the methodology applied to them, see pp. 53–55.)

In the "Text" column:

The name in parentheses following the citation identifies the individual with whom the dialogue or narrative begins. (Variants are not generally noted.)

In the "Number of Steps" column:

"3+" means that there are three steps of direct address plus a secondary response.

"3 + 2" means that there are two sequences, one of three steps and one of two steps, that are closely related but not obviously part of the same deliberation.

"3/2" means that the sequence might be either three or two steps in length, depending on a particular critical analysis; the first number is always the one I prefer.

"3–5" means that the sequence might be anywhere from three to five steps, depending on how the text is read but *not* depending on critical analysis questions.

In the "Notable Characteristics" column:

"b.m." means that the sequence involves, and usually begins with, a *ba'i minei* question.

"narrative" means that the connecting steps describe some action (so-and-so came before so-and-so and asked him . . .); often these narrative elements merely introduce the sequence, and in no case are they essential to the subject being discussed.

"story" means that various actions or events are described that are essential to the content of the discussion itself.

"formulaic" means that there are in the sequence elements that suggest formulation for memorization.

"transport" means that the sequence was transported from Palestine to Babylonia, which, as I explained previously, may be a factor that encouraged preservation.

"★" means that the sequence is what I call anomalous, meaning that, in my judgment, Halivni's theory could not account for its survival. This might be because it has no distinguishing characteristics or, in the presence of such characteristics, its length or sophistication makes its survival difficult to explain in the absence of interest in preserving argumentation.

"★★" means that there is clear evidence in the sequence of interest in the process of argumentation and/or its preservation. One way this interest might be expressed is through explicit amoraic quotation of earlier argumentation.

Text	Number of Steps	Primary Generation(s)	Notable Characteristics
akhot			
(Zeira)	6	3	story
(Avia)	7	3–4	narrative, ★
(Ḥisda)	4	3	★
(Resh Galuta)	11	3	story, ★
(Zeira)	4/7	3	story, ★
–b (Zeira)	2 + 2 + 1 + 4 + 5	2–3	narrative, quoted in later generation, ★

Text	Number of Steps	Primary Generation(s)	Notable Characteristic
Shabbat			
4a (Rava)	?	3–4	employs literary convention
29b (Resh Knishta)	4–6	3	narrative
37b (Shmuel bar Yehuda)	2 + 1 + 3	3–4	narrative, later attention
46a–b (Avia)	4	4	story
47a (Zeira)	4–6	3–4	★
48a (Rabba and Zeira)	6	3	narrative
53a (Asi bar Natan)	6 + 1 + 1	2–3	includes b.m., ★
66a (Rava)	2/4 + 1	3–4	b.m., later attention
71b–72a (Ulla)	3 + 4/2 + 1	3–4	★
95b (''that elder'')	3+	3–4	narrative, quotation of self
99b (Mordechai)	9	3	formulaic
101a (Huna)	6	3–4	quotation, later attention
108a (Huna)	3–4	3	early formulation★
108b (''they asked'')	3+	3	b.m.
112a (Judah the brother of . . .)	6/4	4	story, early formulation★
115b (Huna bar Ḥaluv)	6	3	b.m., complicated★
122b (Judah)	4+	3–4	★
123a (Rava the son of Rabba)	7	4	★★
124a (Rabba)	4+	4	★★
130b (Zeira)	8+	3	★★, b.m., narrative, pattern repeated elsewhere
134a (Abbaye)	2 + 2 + 4	3–4	★
138a (''they asked'')	3+	3	★
140a (Yoḥanan)	4	2	b.m., formulaic
140a (Aḥa bar Yosef)	5+	3	narrative
140a (Aḥa bar Yosef)	9+	3–5	★★, narrative
147a (Jeremiah)	4	3	narrative, later attention, provocative
148a (Avia)	7/5	3	narrative, formulaic
Eruvin			
10b (Dimi)	4/3	4	★★
11b (Naḥman)	5 + /2 + 2	3	story
12a (Yosef)	4 + 1 + 2	3–4	★★, later attention
20a (Abbaye)	4+4	3–4	b.m.
22b (Raḥaba)	6	3–4	b.m.
25b–26a (Huna bar Ḥinena)	4+	4–5	★, narrative
32b (Ḥiyya bar Abba)	5	3	★★, narrative
36a (Rava)	6	3–4	b.m., formulaic
38b (Ḥisda)	5+	3–4	★, slight narrative
39b–40a (Naḥman)	4+	3	narrative, later attention, provocative
40a (''those gardeners'')	4	3–4	narrative
40b (Rabba)	2+	3	★★, slight narrative

Text	Number of Steps	Primary Generation(s)	Notable Characteristics
–44a (Neḥemiah the son of . . .)	5+	3–4	narrative introduction, later attention
–45a (Rabba)	5	3–4	★★
(Rava/Rabba)	4–5+	4	★★, slight narrative
(Rava)	4	3	narrative, formulaic
(Rava)	4+6	4	★
(Zeira)	4	3–4	narrative
(Yosef)	4	3–4	★★, narrative, later attention
–64a ("Laḥman bar Ristak")	6–7	4–5	narrative
–68a ("that child")	12+	4	★★, narrative
–b ("that child")	6	4–6	★, narrative introduction, formulaic
(Judah)	6+	3–4	★
(Rav, Abbaye)	2+6+	3–4	★, narrative, provocative
–b (Yosef)	8+2	3	b.m., later attention
("they asked")	5+3	3–4	★★, b.m.
–b (Judah, Abbaye)	7+2	3–4	later attention, provocative
(Rabba bar R. Ḥanan)	4	4	repetitive
–93a (Rabba)	9	3–4	★★
a (Eleazar)	3+/5+	3–4	★★
a (Ulla)	4/3	4	

aḥim

Text	Number of Steps	Primary Generation(s)	Notable Characteristics
(Naḥman)	4(?)	3–4	
–b (Abbaye bar Avin)	8+2	4	★, narrative, transport
(Rabba)	4	3	★★
–44b (Abbahu, Abbaye)	9+	3–4	★, later attention
–48a (Ḥisda)	9+10+3	3–4	★★, later attention
(Yosef)	3+	3–4	
–51a (*bnei ḥozai*)	4	3–4	narrative, later attention
(Safra)	4	4	★★
("they asked")	1+1+2	4	partial quote
(Simlai)	10	2	story, later attention
a–104a (Ya'akov bar Abba)	12+3	4–later	story, later attention
b (Ulla)	4–7	4	story
a–b (Ravina)	8	4–5	b.m., later attention

sh Hashanah

Text	Number of Steps	Primary Generation(s)	Notable Characteristics
(Asi)	2+2+3	3	partial quote
(Yoḥanan)	4+2	2	b.m.
(Naḥman)	4	3	story

ma

Text	Number of Steps	Primary Generation(s)	Notable Characteristics
–4a (Rabin)	6–7	2	★, transport
–b (Rabba)	4+	4	★
(Abbaye)	3+	4	

Text	Number of Steps	Primary Generation(s)	Notable Characteristic
Yoma (*continued*)			
13b–14a (Rava)	3+	4	
20b (Rav)	4	1	story
72b–73a (Dimi)	4+	4	★, later attention (?)
80b (Zeira)	10	3–4	formulaic, ★, later attention
Sukkah			
14b (Ḥisda)	5	2–3	★★, narrative
17a–b (Rabba)	2+5	3–4	★★
19b (Abbaye)	4/2	3	narrative
43b (Yosef)	7/3+1	3–4	★
Bezah			
6a–b (Rav)	3+2	1–4	★★
16b ("that blind one")	6	1	story
21a (Avia the elder)	6	2–3	b.m., narrative, partial quote
21b (Abbaye)	6/4	3	★
22a (Abba bar Marta)	10+4+4	3–4–later	later attention, repetition
25b (Naḥman)	3+	3	b.m., narrative
27a (Ami)	7	4	story, transport
27b ("that man")	4–5	4	story
34b (Rava)	4	3–4	b.m.
38a–b (Abba)	6	3–4	narrative, transport
Megillah			
8b (Samuel bar Isaac)	3+	4	
28b (Resh Laqish)	6	2	story
Mo'ed Katan			
13a (Rava)	7+	3–4	b.m., later attention
17a (Judah)	long	2	story
19b–20a (Abbaye)	5/3	3–4	b.m.
28a (Rava)	5+6	3–4	story
Ḥagigah			
13a (Yoḥanan)	4	2	story
Yevamot			
11b–12a (Yoḥanan)	3/4+4	2–4	★★, b.m.
29b (Rabba)	4/2	3–4	b.m.
30b–31a (Rabba)	4(?)	3–4	
37a (Rava)	4	3–4	★
45a (Rav)	6	1	story, provocative
52a (Abbaye)	4	3–4	b.m.
57a (Yoḥanan)	3+2	2	★★, b.m., narrative
58b–59a (Ḥiyya bar Yosef)	4	1–2	b.m.
72b (Yoḥanan)	3+	2	narrative
78a (Rabba bar bar Ḥanna)	3+3+	3–4	★

Text	Number of Steps	Primary Generation(s)	Notable Characteristics
(Eleazar)	4 + 4	2	b.m.
–90a (Rabba)	3 + 1 + (2)	3	
b (Abbaye)	4	3–4	story
a (Abbaye)	10	4–5	story, provocative
a–b (Rabba)	6(?)	3–4	★★
tubot			
-b (Ḥisda)	5+	3–4	★
(Rabba)	4(?)	3–4	
(Naḥman bar Isaac)	4	4	
(Resh Laqish)	6+	2	story, provocative
(Meri bar Isak)	8 (in B.M. parallel: 16)	3–4	★
–37a (Pappa bar Shmuel)	5+	3	★
–b (Abbaye)	7+ /5+	3–4	★★
(Avina)	3+	3–4	★★
(Yoḥanan)	5	2–3	story
a–b (Anan)	7	2–3	story, provocative
–79a ("that woman")	6	3–4	story
("that man")	8	3–4	minor narrative
(Ulla)	6/4	3	b.m.
–95a (Yosef)	4	3	story
(Naḥman)	6(?)	3	★, narrative
a–b (Huna)	4	1–2	b.m.
larim			
(Huna bar Judah)	6	4	★
(Ulla)	5	2–3	story
(Rava)	4	4	story
–27a (Rava)	4	4–5	
–35b (Ḥiyya bar Avin)	4/5	4	b.m.
(Rava)	7	3–4	b.m., narrative, provocative
(Abba)	4	2	
–79a (Rava-?)	4(?)	3–4	later attention
zir			
–37a	parallel to Pes. 43b–44b		★
(Meri Ḥiyya)	4 + 4	1	b.m.
(Hamnuna)	5	4	★
ah			
(Abbahu)	4	2–3	transport
in			
Resh Galuta)	4	2–3	narrative, later attention
"they asked")	4+	4	★

Text	Number of Steps	Primary Generation(s)	Notable Characteristic
Gittin (*continued*)			
11b (Huna)	3	2–3	narrative, pattern
14a (Sheshet)	4	3	story
19a (Resh Laqish)	4	2	b.m.
25a–26a (Hoshaya)	4+3	2–4	★★
29b ("the rabbis")	3+4	3–4	★★
29b ("that man")	3–4	3–4	story, later attention
37a (Asi)	9	2	story, transport
37b (Abba bar Marta)	11	3–4	story
39b (Naḥman bar Isaac)	2+2+3	3–4	★★, story
52b (Naḥman)	6	3	story
60b (Shimi bar Ashi)	7+2+4		stories
72a (Rabba bar Abbuha)	6	2–3	★★, b.m., narrative
73a ("that man")	5+2	4–5	narrative, later attention
89a (Abbaye)	4	3–4	b.m.
Kiddushin			
9b (Abbahu)	3/4+	2–3	transport
21a (Huna bar Ḥinena)	4	3–4	b.m., later attention
25a ("the elder of . . .")	9	3	★★, b.m., story, provocative
29b (Ḥisda)	4	3	story
31b (Asi)	9		story
39a–b (Yosef)	3+	3–4	narrative
44a (Asi)	4	3–4	story, transport, early integrity
58a–b (Ulla)	2+5	2–3	★★, b.m.
59a (Giddle)	7+		story, provocative
62a–b (Asi)	4	2	b.m.
72a (Ika bar Avin)	3+	4	
81b (Aḥa bar Abba)	4	3	story

4

The Bavli Considered as a Whole

The Urgency for Argumentation

IF REASONS, JUSTIFICATION, and argumentation were already a focus of attention for the amoraim, as demonstrated in chapter 3, then what was the innovation of the authors of the anonymous gemara (the stam)? (By "the authors of the anonymous gemara" I mean those who compiled the earlier amoraic traditions and created for them an extensive, unattributed literary context as well as those who arranged these texts to form the final product. In my opinion, it is virtually impossible, at this stage of scholarship, to accurately distinguish between these levels; in any case, all involved shared the tendencies that I describe later.) What distinguished the text of the gemara itself from the traditions produced by the prior authorities?

The answer, stated simply, is this: for the amoraim there was both brief and discursive, conclusion and argumentation; *for the stam, there is only argumentation.* In the earlier period, a multiplicity of expressive forms coexisted; in the final period of the gemara's formation, virtually everything is impressed into an argumentational mold. The Bavli occasionally records brief interpretations of an antecedent Mishnaic text, but such brief interpretations are rare. In the vast majority of cases, brief comments are followed by questions or objections, which are themselves typically succeeded by responses, and then new questions, and then new responses, and so on. It is not only deliberation but the extent of deliberation that so characterizes the Bavli. At every step of the way, the urgent necessity to advance that process makes itself more and more felt.

This latter feature—the urgent necessity of argumentation in the ge-mara's later, compositional stages—must be illustrated in order to appreciate the full extent of the phenomenon with which we are dealing. What follows, then, is an exemplification of the gemara's imposition, through editorial, redactional, and compositional means, of an argumentational character on nearly all elements of the earlier tradition.

ⓘ *Building on Earlier Argumentation*

The first example, a sugya—a unit of sustained deliberation—whose argumentation is predominantly amoraic, nevertheless shows the intervention of the redactor to extend the range of the original argumentation. (To follow the flow of the argument and to appreciate the subsequent analysis, it has been necessary to record here a substantial portion of the argumentation. I emphasize those parts of the text that play a part in the discussion that follows.)

Baba Qamma 106a–b

a. *R. Huna said Rav said:* [If one party comes to another and claims] I have [a certain sum of money] in your hand, and the other says "you have nothing in my hand," and he swears [that his denial is true] but witnesses then come [and show him to have been lying, nevertheless] he is exempt [from payment], for it says (Exod. 22:10): "and its owners shall accept this [= the oath] and he shall not pay," [meaning] once the owners accepted the oath, money is no longer to be paid.

b–c. [not relevant for our purposes]

d. R. Naḥman sat and repeated this statement.

e. R. Aḥa b. Minyomi objected to R. Naḥman [quoting Mishnah B.Q. 9:7]: [If one party said to another:] Where is my deposit [that I left with you]? [and] he said to him: It is lost, [and the other said:] I call upon you to swear [that you are telling the truth], and he said: Amen [this being equivalent to taking the oath], and then witnesses testify that he ate it, he pays the principal. . . . [Thus the Mishnah indicates that payment might be made after an oath. How could Rav, presumably bound by the Mishnah, have made the claim he did in (a)?]

f. R. Naḥman[1] said to him: What are we dealing with here [in the Mishnah at (e)]? *Such as where he swore outside of the court* [and so the oath did not, therefore, have full legal force].

g. He said to him:[2] If this is the case, [then what about what] it says in the end [of the same Mishnah (9:8)]: "[If he said to him:] where is my deposit, [and] he said to him: it has been stolen, [and he said to him:] I call upon you to swear, and he said 'Amen,' and witnesses [then] testify that he stole it, he pays double payment [as in normal cases of stealing] . . . ," and if you should think [that the Mishnah is describing a case in which the oath took place] outside of the court, [outside of the court] is there double payment!?

h. He [R. Naḥman] said to him: I could have responded to you [by saying that] the first part [of the Mishnah is describing a situation that took place] outside of the court, and the latter part [a situation that took place] inside the court, however, we do not respond with forced responses, [rather] both took place in the court, and there is [still] no difficulty; *here [where the Mishnah requires payment] it is where he rushed* [to make his opponent take an oath before the court had a chance to do so, such an oath not having full legal power and permitting subsequent payment] and here [in Rav's case] it is where he did not rush [but instead let the court administer the oath].

i. *Rami b. Hama said to R. Naḥman: Being that you do not agree with Rav, why do you put yourself out for him?*

j. He said to him: *[My intent is] to explain Rav's opinion,* for this is the way Rav would resolve [the contradiction between his opinion and] the Mishnah.

k–l. [not relevant for our purposes]

m. *R. Hamnuna objects* [quoting m. Shev. 5:2]: "If he caused him to swear five times, whether before the court or not before the court, and he denied it, [if found to be lying,] he is liable for each and every one [false oath]. And R. Shimeon said: What is the reason? Since [after each false oath] he could go back and admit [the truth]," and *here you cannot say that he rushed* [and caused him to swear before the court had a chance to do so, because] it teaches "he caused him to swear [implying by the agency of the court]," *and you can't say [that he swore] outside of the court* [because] it teaches "before the court."

n. He brings the objection and he resolves it: [The Mishnah] is teaching two things—"he caused him to swear" outside of the court, or in the court he rushed [to make him swear before the court could do so].

o. Rava objects. . . .

p. Rather, Rava said. . . .

q. R. Gamda went and repeated the statement [of Rava, which contradicts the assumptions of the objection and solution of R. Hamnuna,] before R. Ashi.

r. He said to him: Now, *R. Hamnuna, the student of Rav,* knew that Rav said. . . .

First, it is essential to point out that R. Naḥman (at j) is here represented as explaining Rav's view despite the fact [noted at (i)] that he does not agree with it. This is typical of an interest in reasons that first flourishes in this generation. Furthermore, we see here that the proposal of reasons is not dependent on agreement with the opinion being clarified. As reasons become important in and of themselves, such agreement is irrelevant; it is not the conclusion in the law that is essential, but the examination thereof. This, of course, anticipates the methods of the gemara later on, when all opinions are the legitimate subject of attention, even those (such as those from the School of Shammai) that are explicitly rejected for purposes of law.

Most of the argumentation recorded in this text is amoraic in origin. Brief later interjections may be identified, but the substance of the deliberation precedes the anonymous authors. However, when we examine the exchange more closely, the contribution of the stam becomes readily apparent. The problem with the deliberation, as currently presented, is this: R. Hamnuna's objection and response (m and n) appear to assume the responses of R. Naḥman to earlier objections that were addressed to him. Hamnuna makes specific reference to both "he rushed" [Naḥman's solution at (h)] and "he swore outside the court" [Naḥman's solution at (f)]. However, this Hamnuna is clearly identified by R. Ashi (r) as being the sage of that name who was the student of Rav. This Hamnuna flourished, therefore, in the second generation. But R. Naḥman was active in the third generation, and the sage whose objections he here responds to was active in the fourth generation. It would have been impossible, therefore, for Hamnuna to object to Naḥman's responses; since they were suggested a generation after his own activity, he could not have known them. But if what we have before us now is obviously artificial, how can its present form be explained?

R. Hamnuna, and other students of Rav or of his traditions, knew that the ruling of his master was contradicted by several clauses in the Mishnah, one of which he quotes in this text. Hamnuna's purpose in quoting this Mishnah was to discover a solution to the dilemma—to explain the Mishnah in light of the opinion of Rav. The problem in the Mishnah from Shevuot was that it said "before the court," and it was obviously impossible, therefore, to argue that the oath did not have full legal force because it was administered outside the court. In light of this, Hamnuna proposed that, though it took place in the court, nevertheless the oath was not administered by the court. In essence, his original solution must have been: "in the court he rushed." The rest of what is recorded in his name, particularly the elaboration of the objection, following the quotation of the Mishnah at (m), is the addition of the stam in order to tie R. Hamnuna's comment to what came before it. The question, then, is this: Why did the author/redactor see fit to record this text in an achronological order? What did he hope to accomplish by creating this fiction?

The redactor of this text initially had before him two disconnected but substantively related argumentational sequences that sought to resolve the contradiction between the opinion of Rav and the rulings of the Mishnah. The first of these (chronologically) began with the effort of R. Hamnuna (m) and extended to include the attentions of R. Ashi and his contemporaries. The second began with the effort of R. Naḥman and his colleagues [beginning at (d)] but continued only to the fourth generation. Independently, these sequences each served their own limited purpose, but not more. The redactor, however, understood that they could be made to relate to one another and, moreover, that Hamnuna had (perhaps inadvertently) chosen to object from a Mishnaic text that logically was more difficult than the text that had served as the source of the objections of Aḥa b. Minyomi to Naḥman. Seizing this opportunity, the redactor ordered the sequence that began with Hamnuna after the other sequence and embellished what was now the latter part of a single, lengthy deliberation with an interjection [in the latter part of (m)] that guaranteed that the reader would understand the logical progression. Again, this combining of originally separate deliberations created a final product that was both lengthier and more sophisticated.

What is most noteworthy in this example is that we are dealing with a case in which the amoraic first level was already argumentational. One might think, therefore, that the stam would have had no need to embellish his sources; they already bore the form that the stam preferred. But argumentation, by itself, was not enough. Where the stam sensed the opportunity to embellish the argumentation—to make it longer and more elaborate—he could not refrain from doing so. Argumentation can be embellished; it can be made more argumentational.[3]

 Building on Brief Traditions

The authors of the gemara also saw fit to create argumentation out of amoraic sources that were originally not argumentational, as the following two examples illustrate.

Gittin 75a

a. Our rabbis taught: [If a man said to his wife] "behold, this is your bill of divorce, but the paper [upon which it is written] is mine," she is not divorced; [if he instead said] "on the condition that you return the paper to me," she is divorced.

b. What is the difference between the first part and the latter part [of this text]?

c. R. Ḥisda said: Who[se opinion] is this? It is R. Shimon b. Gamliel, who said "give her its worth"; here too it is possible that she could satisfy him with payment [and therefore the paper does not really remain his].

d. Abbaye objected to this: I will say that R. Shimon b. Gamliel said [this where] it is not available [for actual return], [but] where it is available did he also say [this]?

e. Rather, Abbaye said: Who[se opinion] is this? R. Meir, who said [that] we require a doubled condition [that expresses both the positive and the negative outcome], and here he did not double his condition.

f. Rava objected to this: Is the reason [then] that he did not double his condition, [meaning that] if he doubled his condition [and the condition were not met,] it would not be a [valid] bill of divorce? But from where do we learn [the requirements for] all conditions? From the condition of the children of [the tribe of] Gad and the children of [the tribe of] Reuven [see Kid. 61a–b and Num. 32:29–30]. Just as there [the expression of] the condition comes before the [description of the] consequence, so too for all [conditions the statement of] the condition must come before the [description of the consequence].

g. Rather, Rava said: [The reason the condition in the baraita (a) is invalid, and does not limit the effectiveness of the divorce bill, as was the husband's intent, is] because the [description of the] consequence comes before [the expression of] the condition.

h. Ada b. Ahava objected to this: Is the reason [then] that the consequence comes before the condition . . . [structurally this is exactly the same as (f)].

i. Rather, R. Ada b. Ahava said; Because the condition and the consequence are [inextricably bound] in the same thing.

This text, too, appears to be a straightforward amoraic argumentational progression. Each step responds to the previous one, and there is little elaboration that is not essential to the deliberation.

But when we consider it more closely it becomes clear that each step does not adequately respond to the previous one. Abbaye's solution to the initial problem (e) makes specific reference to the opinion of R. Meir (m. Kid. 3:4), who requires, for a condition to be valid, that it assume the form of the condition expressed in the Torah by Moses to the tribes of Gad and Reuven when they asked to inherit land in Transjordan. Abbaye points out that, as recorded in the baraita, the condition of the husband does not properly replicate that form, and hence is powerless to limit the possible validity of the divorce bill. But the objection and alternative solution of Rava (f–g) merely identify another way in which the condition described in the baraita does not assume the requisite form, and the same is true of the suggestion of R. Ada b. Ahava (h–i). In fact, as much as is Rava's or Ada b. Ahava's statement an "objection" to Abbaye, in precisely the same degree is Abbaye's statement an "objection" to them. To be more precise, on a basic level there is no difference of opinion between them at all. All three agree that what invalidates the condition in the baraita is the fact that it doesn't assume the form required by R. Meir in the Mishnah. They merely choose to emphasize different ways in which the requirement is not satisfied, and in this manner they supplement and strengthen one another, rather than object to one another.

It is only reasonable to conclude that the "argumentation" in this text was originally three complementary interpretations of the baraita. The compiler of this gemara, however, was not satisfied with merely presenting them as alternatives. He preferred, instead, to formulate them as an argumentational sequence, suggesting, perhaps, that their relationship is more complex than first might appear or that their difference of opinion is more than the choice of what to emphasize. Because these three parties really agreed in all but emphasis, the final formulation of the stam had to be highly artificial. For him, the benefit of creating argumentation apparently outweighed the logical inconsistencies that such a formulation might create.

A similar analysis and conclusion befit the following text.

Shabbat 74a

a. Our rabbis taught [in a baraita]: If a person had before him [on Shabbat] different kinds of food, he may sort and eat [or] sort and leave [them], but he should not sort, and if he sorted he is liable.
b. What is being said?
c. Ulla said: This is what is being said—He may sort and eat on the same day [or] he may sort and leave it for the same day, but for tomorrow he should not sort, and if he sorted he is liable.
d. R. Ḥisda objected to this: [But "sorting" is an act of work prohibited on Shabbat. Should it make a difference that he is doing it to be used on this same day?] Is it permitted to bake for the same day? Is it permitted to cook for the same day?
e. Rather, R. Ḥisda said: [This is what is being said:] He may sort and eat less than a measure [for which he would incur liability], he may sort and leave aside less than a measure [for which he would incur liability], but a full measure he should not sort, and if he sorted he is liable.
f. R. Yosef objected to this: And is one permitted to bake less than a measure?
g. Rather, R. Yosef said. . . .
h. R. Hamnuna objected to this: But is anything about . . . taught [in the text of the baraita]?
i. Rather, R. Hamnuna said. . . .
j. Abbaye objected to this: Is anything about . . . taught [in the text of the baraita]? . . .
k. Rather, Abbaye said . . .
l. The rabbis repeated this [suggestion of Abbaye] before Rava.
m. He said to them: Naḥmani [= Abbaye] said well. . . .

Here, again, steps of argumentation that appear to respond directly to the previous steps do not in fact respond at all. For example, Ḥisda (d) "objects" to Ulla by pointing out that what he proposes for sorting (a category of work prohibited on Shabbat) would not work for baking or cooking (another category of prohibited work). And yet his "solution" (e) has the very same problem. Similarly, though R. Hamnuna "objects" (h) to Yosef by pointing out that his solution finds no textual support in the baraita, Hamnuna's own "solution" is troubled by exactly the same shortcoming. These parties are not, in reality, talking to one another at all.

We must suppose, instead, that what is recorded here is a series of interpretations of a difficult baraita which were composed at approximately the same time but which do not originally relate to one another—only to a common antecedent. With one possible exception, each of these solutions was flawed, as is clear from the declaration of Rava preferring Abbaye's solution. But the problems with the other solutions were nowhere specified, and so it became the task of the redactor to explain their flaws. Rather than merely describing the problems, he chose to have them emerge in the course of a debate, a debate that he composed and many steps of which he provided. Some steps of this artificial debate made good sense, but others merely repeated mistakes that had only just been identified a step or two before. Again, the stam was not bothered that his insistence that *everything* be formulated as argumentation might create such logical inconsistencies—at least not enough to decide against the formulation. Virtually everything must be made to relate in argumentational progression, and this value is sufficiently weighty to sometimes put other considerations aside.

Fictional Argumentation

We have seen that, for the stam, argumentation yields lengthier argumentation, and independent statements, too, can be made to yield argumentation. But the urgency of creating argumentation does not stop with these relatively minor fictions (minor because in both cases the gemara's author builds on actual amoraic traditions; he merely enhances them by positing a particular kind of relationship). Even when there is no argumentation to begin with, or even amoraic traditions to use as building blocks, the stam will create argumentation. This is true not only in the many instances in which the gemara carries on a deliberation in its own voice. More remarkable are those occasions when the gemara puts the deliberation into the mouths of amoraic authorities, claiming that they exchanged words for which there is no actual source. These dialogues are theoretical fictions, for their only real source is the mind of the author of the final (not so) anonymous text.

Such fictional cases are particularly attributed to the Palestinian sages R. Yohanan and Resh Laqish (though they are by no means limited to these two). The presence of such cases was recognized by medieval rabbinic commentators, and the case for the artificial nature of these texts can easily be made. Just one example follows.

Nazir 16b–17a

a. It has been said: One who took a nazirite vow, and he was [at the time] in a cemetery [thereby creating a problem; nazirites are prohibited from impurifying themselves through contact with the dead (Num. 6:6–7). Does his presence in the cemetery therefore cause the vow to be void?]

b. R. Yoḥanan said: The nazirite vow takes effect.

c. And Resh Laqish said: The nazirite vow doesn't take effect.

d–e. [the gemara explains the reasoning behind these two positions]

f. R. Yoḥanan objected to Resh Laqish [quoting m. Nazir 3:5]: If someone took a nazirite vow and he was in a cemetery, even if he remained there thirty days they do count in the number [of days, usually thirty, that the nazirite state lasts] and he doesn't [have to] bring a sacrifice of impurity.

g. [This implies only that] he doesn't bring a sacrifice of impurity, but [the vow] does take effect!

h. He said to him: [The meaning of the Mishnah is this:] He is not bound by the law of impurity and he is not bound by the law of the sacrifice [i.e., he is not a nazirite at all].

i. He objected to him [quoting Tos. Nazir 2:14]: If someone was impure [as someone in a cemetery would be], and took a nazirite vow, he is [nevertheless] prohibited from shaving or drinking wine or becoming impure by virtue of contact with the dead [as any normal nazirite], and if he did [one of these things] . . . he must be lashed forty times.

j. It's fine if you say that [under such conditions] it takes effect, for this reason he must be lashed, but if you say that it doesn't take effect, for what reason must he be lashed?

k. [He replied:] What are we dealing with here? With [a case of someone] who went out [and purified himself, giving the vow a chance to take effect,] and [then] came back in [to the cemetery].

l. He objected to him [quoting a baraita]: There is no difference between someone who was impure and took a nazirite vow [= someone who took the vow in a cemetery] and [someone who was already] a pure nazirite who became impure, except that [in the first case] . . . his seventh day [of his purification period] counts, and [in the latter case] his seventh day doesn't count.

m. And if you should think that it [the vow] doesn't take effect, why does it count?

n. Mar b. R. Ashi said: *Nobody disputes that it does [in fact] take effect;* what they dispute is whether he is lashed. . . .

The comment of Mar b. R. Ashi at the end of this dialogue is astounding. How could he possibly have said that R. Yoḥanan and Resh Laqish did not dispute the question of whether the nazirite vow took effect if the entire exchange that lay before him—which chronologically would have preceded him by two hundred years—was based on this premise? The answer, of course, is that he would not have been able to do so; he could not have rejected that interpretation of their opinions if the interpretation was necessary from their own debate of the issue. Rather, we must conclude that the debate recorded here in the Talmud was not before Mar b. R. Ashi. Where, then, did it come from?

The medieval rabbinic scholar R. Asher b. Yeḥiel (thirteenth to fourteenth century, Germany and Spain) suggests in his commentary printed in the margin of the Vilna edition of the Bavli: "As to the objections of R. Yoḥanan to Resh Laqish . . . , it is the Talmud that is objecting, according to what we might have thought they were disputing, and there are many [examples] of this sort in the Talmud." I quote R. Asher not because of his recognized status in rabbinic Judaism but because I think that his solution is the only one possible. R. Asher's proposal is that the debate between R. Yoḥanan and Resh Laqish is not theirs at all. Instead, the later anonymous author of this gemara composed the debate, suggesting in effect what they might have argued if this were the correct interpretation of their difference of opinion. Because the anonymous author lived after Mar b. R. Ashi, there was no way that the latter could have known his debate or the interpretation that it assumed, and there was therefore no reason that Mar b. R. Ashi had to interpret the original dispute as would the stam. He was free to interpret as he saw fit.

But neither was the stam bound by Mar b. R. Ashi's earlier interpretation. To be more precise, the stam wasn't concerned that the interpretation for which he was composing a theoretical debate might not have been the correct one. He saw fit to create this fiction despite the fact that, in the end, its assumptions would be rejected. The argument itself— and the theoretical issues that it explored—was so important that it didn't matter whether it related to the outcome. Nor did it matter that it set up a glaring logical impossibility (Mar b. R. Ashi's reinterpretation in light of the prior debate). The fiction was justified by the need to explore the law and its justifications. As R. Asher remarks, there are many such instances in the Talmud.

In fact, scholarly analysis will show that virtually all debates of this sort (using the Aramaic term *eitivei,* "he objected to him") that involve R. Yoḥanan and Resh Laqish, as well as many that involve other sages, are the fictional creations of the authors of the gemara. The case for this conclusion can be stated briefly. Many of these sequences are built around obvious literary conventions, such as groupings of three objections and responses or other patterns involving triplets. Furthermore, many are plagued by the same sort of logical inconsistencies that we witnessed in this example. For this reason, as I have said, even medieval rabbinic authorities were willing to admit that some such sequences were fictional. Finally, though traditions of R. Yoḥanan and Resh Laqish that are recorded in the Bavli are often paralleled in the Yerushalmi, in the more than thirty cases of this specific type of argumentational exchange that is never the case.[4] Since it is reasonable to believe that debates that originated in Palestine would at least occasionally have been preserved in the Talmud of that community, and not only in the Talmud of the Babylonian community, it would seem that they were produced in Babylonia in the first place. Given that, as this example demonstrates, these dialogues were composed *after* Mar b. R. Ashi (mid fifth century), it is clear that they must have been produced by the postamoraic stam.

The stam's insistence on creating argumentation thus is not dependent on the nature of the sources that lay before him. If he began with argumentation, he may have enhanced it. If he began with simple, brief statements, he wove them together to create argumentation. And even where he had no traditions to weave together, even in such cases did he create argumentation. The argumentation was essential on its own terms and would not be limited on account of its absence in sources.

Argumentation for Its Own Sake

When I say that argumentation was "essential on its own terms" I mean, as this last example has shown, that the argumentation has a value independent of a given conclusion. In fact, argumentation that led to no conclusion at all was often composed. The following text is an illustration of this phenomenon. (This is an extremely long and complicated deliberation. Only what is necessary for illustration is reproduced here.)

Baba Batra 17b–18b

a. It has been said: If someone comes [to dig a pit] close to the edge of the boundary [of his property, perhaps restricting thereby where his neighbor might be able to dig a pit on his adjacent property] . . .

b. Abbaye said: He may do so.

c. And Rava said: He may not do so.

d–e. [two lengthy, alternative interpretations of the conditions to which this dispute pertains follow; they are offered as equally viable alternatives, and the gemara makes no attempt to decide between them]

f. We learned [in m. B.B. 2:1]: "A person should not dig a pit close by to the ditch of his neighbor." The reason [that this is prohibited] is that there is [another] pit, but if there were no [other] pit he could do so.

g. This is a fine according to the interpretation that says . . . but according to the interpretation that says . . . it would be difficult to Rava.

h. Rava would say to you. . . .

i. There are those who teach [this sequence] this way. . . .

j. Come and hear [an attempted resolution to the dispute, quoting from Tos. B.B. 1:1]: "[If there is] a clod [of dirt] that crumbles in one's hand [between the two properties] this one may dig his pit here and this one may dig his pit here, [but] this one must distance [his pit from the boundary line] three handsbreadths and plaster [his pit] with plaster and this one must distance three handsbreadths and plaster with plaster." [This suggests, contrary to Abbaye, that one may not dig right up against the edge of his property.]

k. [Abbaye's opinion could be defended by suggesting that] a clod that crumbles in one's hand is different [because, under such conditions, the ground could obviously not tolerate two nearby pits. This teaches us nothing about the law for normal ground, however.]

l–m. [the gemara here comments that this answer (k) was so obvious, that the attempt to learn anything from this baraita in the first place (j) must be defended]

n. Come and hear [another attempted resolution, quoting from m. B.B. 2:1]: "We distance olive-peel waste and manure and salt and plas-

ter and [heated] rocks three handsbreadths from his neighbor's wall
and [alt.: or] plaster [them] with plaster.''

o. The reason [that the distancing is required] is that there is [already]
a wall [there], but if there were no wall, he could place [them]
close [thereby supporting Abbaye's opinion].

p. No. If there is no wall he may also not place them close, but
rather, what does this [Mishnah] come to teach us? It comes to
teach us that these things [that it lists] are hard on a wall [and
therefore this Mishnah could also be explained according to the
opinion of Rava].

q. Come and hear [another attempted resolution]. . . .

The gemara continues for many steps in a variety of attempts to resolve
the dispute between Abbaye and Rava. It does so by making reference to
Mishnayot and other relevant texts, repeating in each instance, usually
almost exactly, the same pattern that we have seen here in these last
several steps. In the end both opinions emerge as equally valid, and for
that reason medieval rabbinic authorities who want to use this text as the
basis of law are forced to argue at length on behalf of one opinion or the
other. Of course, there is no unanimity in their decisions, because this
text intentionally provides no direction. It is this latter observation that
requires elaboration.

The most outstanding feature of this deliberation is its uncompromising
support of alternatives. This is evident, first, in its initial presentation of
the amoraic opinions, where it offers two comprehensive interpretations
of those opinions and allows both to stand as possibilities (d–e). It is
evident, again, in the first attempted resolution of the dispute (f–g) where,
after quoting from the first part of the Mishnah in this chapter, the gemara
considers the implications of this text according to both prior interpretations. The same support of alternatives is repeated when this very same
section is described in another order (i). Neither of the two versions of
the exchange is preferred in the gemara. Finally, the overall sequence
refuses to admit a decision. Virtually every time a text is quoted that
might seem to support one of the amoraic opinions (usually Rava), it is
responded to with an interpretation that makes the support of that opinion
unnecessary, and the single instance where a preference seems to be certain is excused as an exception. The cumulative impact is unfailing: alternatives are valid and decisions are to be avoided. Argumentation serves
to demonstrate the validity of alternatives; its primary purpose is not the
rendering of decisions.

This case, while longer and more elaborate than most, is nevertheless typical of the Bavli. Successful argumentation supports different opinions, it does not decide between them. This is not to say that the gemara does not render decisions. It often does (though less often than is commonly assumed).[5] But where it begins with a difference of opinions of amoraim, as it does here, its general preference is to support the alternatives as being equally defensible.

The reasons that alternatives are preferred are important and require elaboration in the context of our overall discussion of the meaning of the gemara's deliberative/argumentational form. But a few observations on this phenomenon are here in order. The desire to defend alternative opinions must begin with the assumption that at some level the alternatives are equally valid. This might be because the gemara wants to claim that the authorities whose opinions it discusses are intelligent, thoughtful individuals. If they said something, they must have had a good reason for doing so. It is the job of the student, therefore, to try to discover what that good reason was. The value of an opinion might be found, for example, in what it assumes about the interpretation of earlier texts, or in what it teaches about the law and its application. The defense of alternatives, I will show in the next chapter, might also reflect the assessment that, generally speaking, no one opinion embodies the whole truth. If one opinion *did* embody the whole truth, then it would be irresponsible to defend alternatives. Support of alternatives, therefore, speaks in behalf of a recognition that many views, even when contradictory, may share the truth, at least in part. This assumption, we will see, emerges from other elements of the gemara's form. Finally, the pursuit of alternatives may be an expression of the value of the examination of alternatives as such, even when they are not relevant for decisions in the law. We have seen this value expressed in earlier examples, and again we will come to understand this as an essential part of the Bavli's overall ideology.

The Bavli and the Yerushalmi Distinguished

As these examples illustrate, the Babylonian gemara is, at the level of its anonymous composition, an uncompromisingly deliberative/argumentational text. Virtually all of it assumes this form, there being relatively few exceptions. Typically, what emerges from the pens of the gemara's anonymous authors was sophisticated, sometimes tantalizing deliberation. These unidentified individuals created the unit of sustained deliberation, the sugya, that defines the gemara's discourse. When we go on here, as we did earlier, to ask "what is the meaning of this (in this case, the gemara's) form?" it will be the sugya, in its deliberative/argumentational glory, whose meaning we will be exploring.

But to do justice to this exploration, we must first distinguish the text that forms the subject of our inquiry, the Bavli, from its closest counterpart, the Yerushalmi, for the latter document is also, on some level, typified by deliberation and argumentation. Once again, then, what are the differences between these two works?

The Bavli and Yerushalmi, in some ways very similar, are nevertheless easily distinguished in details and in overall composition. Differences in details often can be attributed to the different forms of Aramaic that were employed in each, but certain details represent significant differences of method in the two documents. For example, the Bavli will resolve an apparent problem in a Mishnah by suggesting that the Mishnah is defective and that something needs to be added. This proposed solution, restricted to later amoraim and to the stam, demonstrates an extraordinary independence of will that typifies interpretations in the Bavli. The Yerushalmi is unwilling to utilize this same approach. Similarly, the Bavli—in its own voice or, on rare occasions, in the name of an amora—is frequently (i.e., hundreds of times) willing to propose that scripture should have expressed itself in a manner other than that actually recorded.[6] Some of these proposals even do violence to basic rules of biblical grammar. The Yerushalmi, on the other hand, admits this sort of proposal fewer than a dozen times.[7] The upshot of such proposed alternatives is that, since scripture did not express itself the way it might have, the way that it did choose to express itself may (because it is an intentional alternative) be used as the source of derivative interpretation (midrash). This phenomenon, again, is indicative of the independence of interpretation that the Bavli insists on and contrasts with the Yerushalmi's hesitating use of such a method. Furthermore, because the alternative way that scripture could have expressed itself can be proposed only by human reason, this phenomenon also shows the degree to which the power of reason extends itself in the Bavli, and here even with relation to scripture. Because of the theoretical implications of this method, it will be discussed at length and in detail in a later chapter.

The Bavli is also distinguished from the Yerushalmi in its willingness to question opinions derived by logical deduction. Both the talmudim observe, from time to time, that a certain tradition was known not to have been spoken explicitly by a given sage but to have been derived by another authority based either on his logical extension of another related tradition or on the logic of the sage's actions in a given event. The Yerushalmi apparently recognizes that such logical extensions were made to form new traditions but doesn't take such extensions to be meaningful. The Bavli, on the other hand, does think that it makes a difference. If a tradition began in logical deduction and was knowingly not enunciated by the authority to whom it is attributed, then, in the opinion of the Bavli, it is reasonable to ask whether the logic that produced the tradition is correct. When the Bavli sees fit to ask this question, almost without exception it concludes that the derivation was faulty. In doing so, of course, it again demonstrates the power of its own reasoning. The question (or perhaps more correctly, challenge) begins with the assumption that, if a ruling began in logical deduction, other logical analyses must be available. And where alternative analyses are available, as the Bavli has demonstrated before, there is often no reason to conclude that a particular analysis is the correct one.

The degree of its insistence on alternatives also distinguishes the Bavli from the Yerushalmi. "The sages of the Talmud of the Land of Israel," Neusner writes, "seek certain knowledge about some few, practical things. They therefore reject—from end to beginning—the chaos of speculation, the plurality of possibilities even as to word choice; above all, the daring and confidence to address the world in the name, merely, of sagacity. True, the Talmud preserves the open-ended discourse of sages, not reduced to cut-and-dried positions. *But the Talmud makes decisions.*"[8] Contrast the Bavli, where many options frequently are offered apparently for their own sake, and where decisions are frequently avoided, preference being given instead to the support of contradictory opinions. In the Bavli speculation is paramount and, we will conclude in the next chapter, sagacity (called "talmud torah") is a central value. This contrast in overall compositional preferences may be the most important difference between the Bavli and the Yerushalmi.

A specific phenomenon that best illustrates what I have described is the difference in frequency in the two documents of related formulas— "if you wish, I will say . . . [and if you wish, I will say]" in the Bavli and "there is he who wishes to say . . . [and there is he who wishes to say . . .]" in the Yerushalmi—that indicate the presence of alternative explanations or opinions.[9] This statement is found in the Yerushalmi a total of only 81 times. By contrast, it is found in the Bavli over 400 times. The Yerushalmi generally admits only one alternative, whereas the Bavli often allows several. Though this formula is only one way that alternatives are indicated, it may be the most explicit. It claims, very simply, that different rulings, answers, or interpretations stand side by side as equally valid alternatives. Its common presence in the Bavli is an expression of the Bavli's overall affection for that stance. That the Bavli employs it so much more often than the Yerushalmi again illustrates the difference discussed previously.[10]

It should come as no surprise that the factors enumerated here are limited in the Bavli either exclusively or predominantly to the anonymous layer of the text.[11] It is, after all, only in the later amoraic generations that these tendencies (in their more basic amoraic form) could be considered well established, and these are the generations during which communications between Palestine and Babylonia deteriorated.[12] At the time of their full expression in the anonymous gemara, we have no evidence of any significant contact between the two communities and there was therefore no opportunity for these developments to infiltrate from Babylonia into Palestinian rabbinic circles.

As suggested in the earlier discussion of alternatives in the Bavli and Yerushalmi, the most important differences between these two documents lie in matters of overall composition. To expand upon what I have already outlined, I will repeat here the observations of Zechariah Frankel:

1. The Bavli is far more verbose than the Yerushalmi. This tendency is expressed in a number of specific ways, including the likeliness of the Bavli to pursue matters in far greater length than the Yerushalmi.
2. The Yerushalmi will frequently raise questions or objections and never supply an answer to them. This phenomenon is extremely rare in the Bavli.
3. The Yerushalmi generally limits the number of objections and solutions that it will permit in a given sequence to a mere few steps. The Bavli, on the other hand, will commonly go on for several pages.[13]

The first and third of these observations are indisputably confirmed, the reader will recall, by comparing the respective commentaries of the two documents to the same Mishnaic tractates, as set out in the new English translations of Jacob Neusner and others.[14] When comparing the total number of sustained discussions of a single issue in the two talmudim, we find that, in a representative sample of tractates, the Bavli always records significantly more such discussions than the Yerushalmi (see p. 18). Since these discussions represent the variety of different ways that the Bavli is willing to examine the issues generated by the Mishnah, the authors of the Bavli were willing to explore a broader spectrum of issues, with less inhibition, than their Palestinian counterparts. In addition, the same sort of comparison shows that even discussions of single limited issues tend to be longer in the Bavli than in the Yerushalmi, and sometimes significantly so (see pp. 18–19). This too shows the great freedom of inquiry that characterizes the Babylonian text. The same freedom is also inherent in the Bavli's willingness to leave the Mishnah behind completely and, from time to time, to include lengthy and elaborate commentaries on blocks of scripture or on other independent issues.[15] In virtually all such matters the Bavli is willing to explore areas that the Yerushalmi does not touch upon. Far more than the details, this is what distinguishes the former from the latter.

Furthermore, the differences are not only differences in quantity but also, in the view of many, differences in quality. Such an evaluation is suggested, for example, in Frankel's comment equating the methods of the completed Yerushalmi to those of Abbaye and Rava. In other words, the Yerushalmi is less refined and incomplete when compared to the Bavli. Jacob Neusner is moved to make similar observations. In his detailed comparison of the Yerushalmi and Bavli commentaries to Mishnah Sukkah, chapter 1,[16] Neusner's descriptions of the Yerushalmi's commentary are brief and matter of fact. Where he sees fit to evaluate the Yerushalmi's contribution, he uses terms such as "routine" and "perfunctory." In contrast, Neusner frequently speaks of the Bavli's deliberations as "thorough," "elaborate," or "complex." One Bavli sequence is described as being "worked out with exceptional sophistication"; another is "beautifully articulated." In his summation, he writes that "the Bavli's authors went in a direction not imagined by the Yerushalmi's. The power and intellectual force of the Bavli's authors in that context vastly overshadowed the capacities of the Yerushalmi's."

Admittedly, such evaluations are a matter of taste. Where one reader sees lack of refinement and incompleteness, another sees intelligent conciseness of expression and sophisticated subtlety. But the differences reviewed earlier all support the same conclusion: the Bavli's independence of inquiry and broad creativity are not equaled by the Yerushalmi. The Bavli, like the Yerushalmi, is a deliberative commentary on the Mishnah. But it is far more than that.

In choosing to express themselves almost exclusively in the argumentational/deliberative form, the authors of the Bavli selected one of two major amoraic forms—the more innovative of those forms—and gave it virtually exclusive reign. This formal compositional choice represented an almost complete denial of the Mishnaic precedent. One could hardly imagine a text, related in subject and overall concerns, that is nevertheless more unlike the Mishnah than the Bavli. This dissimilarity utilizes, of course, models that had gained currency during the amoraic period. But during that earlier period the Mishnaic model had not been denied, just supplemented. The step taken by the Bavli at the end, therefore, was a deliberate rejection of an ancient precedent, or perhaps more correctly, the knowing affirmation of a particular alternative. The meaning of that alternative, and the reason behind its affirmation, is the subject of the next chapter.

5

The Meaning
of Argumentation

> The very nature of deliberation and argumentation is opposed to ne-
> cessity and self-evidence, since no one deliberates where the solu-
> tion is necessary or argues against what is self-evident. The domain
> of argumentation is that of the credible, the plausible, the probable,
> to the degree that the latter eludes the certainty of calculations.
>
> Chaim Perelman and L. Olbrechts-Tyteca
> *The New Rhetoric: A Treatise on Argumentation*, p. 1

A Philosophical Analysis:
The Indeterminability of Truth

IN THIS CHAPTER we seek to understand the meaning of the Bavli's argumentational form. We consider, as we did for the amoraic tradition in
an earlier chapter, what the literary form reveals about the ideologies of
the Bavli's authors. What was their relationship to earlier tradition? What
are the assumptions of the new tradition that they created? Before we
begin, it is essential that the subject of this analysis and the nature of the
likely explanations be delineated precisely.

First, the form that is our subject here, as spelled out in chapter 4, is
argumentation and deliberation. By argumentation I mean extended deliberation on a given topic, either narrow or broad, that involves questions,
objections, responses, and various forms of dialogue. Argumentation is
not to be confused with what has been called, in the work of Neusner
and others, the dispute-form. The dispute-form juxtaposes two disparate
opinions: "Rabbi X says A, Rabbi Y says −A." It includes no reactive
element and it suggests no necessary active engagement of the two parties. Argumentation, in contrast, always suggests active involvement (even

99

if fictional). It is to be found, in its simplest form, in what Neusner calls debates.[1] But debates, though present in tannaitic documents, typify none of these documents. Only the dispute-form is common in early rabbinic texts; debates or argumentation is rare in such texts and is found commonly only in the Yerushalmi and, to an even greater extent, the Bavli.

This does not mean that what we find about argumentation in the Bavli will not be relevant also to the dispute-form. From time to time it will. For example, the presence in argumentation of several concurrent opinions is a central characteristic of this form. My explanation of that feature might also pertain to the parallel phenomenon in the dispute-form. Obviously, much of what I say regarding argumentation in the Bavli will also be relevant to the less elaborate argumentation of the Yerushalmi. Still, as we have seen, the form of the Bavli is in some ways unique, and so my analysis will on the whole be specific to the Bavli.

The Talmud's argumentational form is also to be distinguished from the dialectical form of Plato's dialogues. To be sure, both forms employ directed questions and answers to arrive (or not to arrive) at a particular end. But the nature of the deliberation found in each is obviously distinct from the other. To begin with, Platonic dialogue is comparatively verbose; Talmudic argumentation, in contrast, is relatively concise, even elliptical. If Platonic dialogue is highly discursive, the Talmudic argument can almost be described as terse (again, comparatively). In addition, the Talmud makes frequent use of sources, often distinguished by the fact that they appear in a language different from that of the gemara itself. Plato employs no such sources, at least not formally or with any frequency, and his exposition is all, of course, in the same tongue. Finally, the argumentation of the Talmud is everywhere imprinted with formal conventions. Plato's dialogues, in contrast, are creatively diverse, exhibiting great "poetic" flexibility.[2] Nevertheless, here too what is common to the two forms would permit us to extend some of what is suggested in this chapter in connection with Talmudic argumentation to the dialectical form; in particular, my proposal that argumentational dialogue is posited on the ultimate indeterminability of a single, definable truth has its adherents among modern interpreters of Plato.[3]

Second, as already suggested, we are seeking here the meaning of a literary form, now in the strict sense of that term. For reasons that I will spell out later, it is reasonable to assume that, at the stage of its composition, the Bavli was a *written* work. In contrast, amoraic traditions, like the Mishnah before them, were oral. Undoubtedly this transition from an oral to a written medium facilitated the analytic approach of the gemara.

But this factor, by itself, does not explain the meaning of the Bavli's precise choice. Having assumed a written form, the Bavli could still have gone in many different directions. The question here is the meaning of its particular form of expression.

Finally, in explaining the Bavli's argumentational–deliberative approach, it will not be sufficient to claim that its methods are "mere" conventions. It is true that the frequency with which many of the Bavli's specific forms are repeated derives from their conventional status. But we have no evidence that these conventions were borrowed from elsewhere. Rather, such conventions in the Bavli are the creations of the Bavli and it is precisely the meaning of these conventions that we wish to explain. We therefore return to the original question: What is the meaning of the Bavli's form?

Argumentational discourse has been studied at length and in detail in the work of Chaim Perelman and L. Olbrechts-Tyteca. Their study entitled *The New Rhetoric: A Treatise on Argumentation* examines the theoretical underpinnings of deliberative or argumentational expression and elaborates the variety of ways that such texts relate to truth and authority. They do not actually examine the argumentational "form" as defined here. Rather, in their study argumentation is defined as "discursive techniques allowing us *to induce or to increase the mind's adherence to the theses presented for its assent,*"[4] regardless of the precise form of such techniques. Nevertheless, their analysis is relevant to our study of the Bavli's argumentation on two levels. First, as I have discussed elsewhere,[5] the Bavli is a rhetorical text in the sense that it wishes to convince. It attempts throughout to increase *our* minds' adherence to *its* theses. Second, in part the way the Bavli seeks to achieve this goal is by creating argumentational dialogues that ask us to take the position of each respective advocate in turn. In such dialogues there are at least two sides of the argumentational exchange, each of which seeks to persuade us of its correctness. On both these levels, the form and function of the Bavli is within the realm of concern of Perelman and Olbrechts-Tyteca's study. Furthermore, many of the forms of argumentational discourse that they address are found in the Bavli and, though much of their work is irrelevant in a study of the Bavli, few of the forms that characterize the Bavli are ignored wholly in their analysis. For this reason, and because of the general comprehensiveness of their presentation, no purpose is to be served by analyzing afresh material that they have already covered without reference to their work. Rather, it is for us to review the proposals that they have made, to assess their claims, and to consider how their observations might be applied to the Talmudic form in particular.[6] On the basis of this inquiry, we will be able to evaluate the meaning of the Talmudic form.

Let us begin with the introductory remarks quoted at the beginning of this chapter. Perelman and Olbrechts-Tyteca claim that deliberation/argumentation is, as a form, opposed to self-evidence and confident assertion of a single truth (where truth means "the way things really are").[7] If truth were readily evident, then no reasonable person would argue against that truth. Assuming that the deliberations we are discussing involve reasonable and not irrational parties, we must conclude that their willingness to engage in argumentation is evidence of their recognition that the answer to a given question or problem is not necessary or self-evident. To the contrary, if they are willing to debate the issue, they must agree that there are at least two possible answers or solutions.

We will reach the same conclusion if we examine argumentation from a second perspective, trying to understand its emergence. As Perelman and Olbrechts-Tyteca observe, "Recourse to argumentation is unavoidable whenever . . . proofs are questioned by one of the parties, when there is no agreement on their scope or interpretation, on their value or on their relation to the problems debated" (TNR, p. 8). If a proof is clear or certain, if there is a total agreement on the interpretation of the text or source being quoted in proof, then there is no reason, again, to engage in argumentation. Where, on the other hand, there is no agreement on the relevance of a given proof or on its interpretation, then argumentation will inevitably follow. The presence of argumentation therefore implies the absence of agreement. Again, it is evidence of the fact that we do not begin with self-evident proofs or interpretations.

Any student of the Bavli will recognize the correctness of this analysis with relation to argumentation in that document. The following selection will serve as an illustration.

Berakhot 13a

a. Our rabbis have taught: The Shema should be recited as it is written [in Hebrew; these are] the words of Rabbi [Judah Hanasi]; and the sages say: In any language.
b. What is Rabbi's reason?
c. Scripture said: "And they shall be (Deut. 6:6)," [meaning] as they are they should be [= in Hebrew].
d. And the sages, what is their reason?
e. Scripture said: "Hear (Deut. 6:4)," [meaning] in any language that you hear [= understand].

f. And for Rabbi, is it not also written "Hear"?

g. He requires that [scriptural term to teach the law:] make heard to your ears what you bring out from your mouth.

h. And the sages hold [the same opinion] as the one who says "if he did not make it heard to his ears, he has [nevertheless] fulfilled his obligation."

i. And for the sages, is it not also written "And they shall be"?

j. They require that [scriptural term to teach] that he should not read it out of order.

k. And Rabbi, [the ruling] that he should not read it out of order, where does he derive it from?

l. From [the difference between the word] "words (vs. 6)" [which scripture might have used, and] "the words" [which scripture did choose to use. The additional designation can be the source for derivation].

m. And the sages do not interpret . . . [this phenomenon].

Note the many differences that this gemara points out. Rabbi and the sages differ with respect to the law. This difference, the gemara suggests (this is all the suggestion of the anonymous gemara concerning the source of their differences), is the consequence of their disagreement over which proof text is relevant to the given question and how that proof text is to be interpreted. The sages associate "Hear" with the law of the language of recitation; Rabbi thinks that the term relevant to this particular law is "And they shall be." Rabbi thinks "Hear" teaches something about the volume of recitation; the sages think "And they shall be" teaches something about the order of recitation. Rabbi agrees with the sages with respect to the law of the order of recitation but derives that law from another proof; the sages think the same proof is in fact proof of nothing at all.

Here, we can see, there is no agreement on the relevance of different proofs or on the interpretation of any given proof. The argumentation is explicit in stating this absence of agreement. But we should not think that this recognition needs to be explicit. Obviously argumentation begins with differences of interpretation or other such differences; this must always be so. It is because a single, identifiable truth is not immediately available that it is worthwhile to engage in argumentation in the first place.

But argumentation—certainly as a comprehensive, unyielding form of expression—also implies that clear, undisputed truth is (at least often) unavailable at the end. If a given argumentation yielded "truth," that is, necessary and self-evident interpretations or conclusions, then this truth would effectively wipe out the argumentation that produced it. This is because truth, once identified, should speak with perfect clarity; it should be, if only retroactively, completely obvious. Once it has emerged, therefore, the process that produced it should be less important. Unless we are speaking of mathematical demonstrations (and even there axioms, once demonstrated, are usually employed unencumbered by their proofs), where the process may be of interest for its own sake, truths should speak for themselves, without accompanying support. The obvious valuation of argumentation in the gemara thus reveals that, in its view, "truth" is not at all self-evident. If proofs as such continue to be central, conclusions must be relatively less secure.

This relation of argumentation and truth is also inherent in another of the gemara's methods, that is, in its ever-present use of authority claims. Perelman and Olbrechts-Tyteca write:

> The argument from authority has been attacked in the name of truth. And indeed, insofar as any proposition is considered to be true or false, the argument from authority no longer holds a legitimate place in our intellectual arsenal. But is this always the case, and can all the legal problems, for instance, be reduced to scientific problems where only truth is involved? . . . [T]he quest for justice and the maintenance of an equitable order, of social trust, cannot neglect considerations based on the existence of a legal tradition. . . . Recourse to argument from authority is inescapable if the existence of such a tradition is to be attested. (TNR, p. 306)

This latter observation obviously pertains to the Bavli: the Bavli seeks to root itself in a tradition, and so it must argue on the basis of that tradition. But it is the former observations that are of particular interest here. The claim—which the authors do not wish to deny but only to gain some perspective on—is that questions of authority should be irrelevant in the presence of truth. If an opinion or interpretation is true, then, to state it bluntly, who cares who said it? What matters is only that it is true. On the other hand, where references to various authorities become important, truth as such becomes less so. What legitimates claims in a system that considers references to authority to be crucial is the tradition that that authority speaks for. If the system were concerned with philosophical purity, however, reference to authority would be far less crucial.

Theoretically, this analysis seems attractive. But it would appear that caution is warranted before applying it to arguments in the Bavli. "Truth" and authority stand in opposition in a system that posits a rational truth, for if the human mind is the source of illumination or clarification, then the authority of the individual within whom the mind resides should be irrelevant. All that should matter is the value of his or her claim, judged on its own terms. But in a system that posits other sources of truth—scripture, for example, or the authority inherited by rabbinic masters—this opposition is not at all necessary.

Obviously, the Bavli is a system that recognizes scripture as a source of truth, scripture presumably being an expression of the divine will. For the authors of the Bavli, therefore, "one must not look to nature for the ultimate reality, but to the divine creative word."[8] On a different level, Mishnaic canon might also represent an alternative source of truth. In analyzing the Talmudic argument, it would appear necessary, therefore, to consider the nature of the specific authority. With respect to arguments from amoraic authority, we must admit the validity of Perelman and Olbrechts-Tyteca's analysis. In such instances, the reference to authority indeed reveals that it is not the essence of an opinion that matters most but the support of an authoritative tradition. But in the case of Mishnaic and biblical proofs, the analysis they suggest might have no place, because in cases of this sort authority and truth might reside in the same entity.

However, although this caution is well taken, a more considered analysis of the place of authoritative sources in the Bavli will reveal that, even in such cases, the analysis of Perelman and Olbrechts-Tyteca is largely correct, for whatever the nature of its sources in a given argument, the Bavli often does not support single opinions or interpretations by reference to single sources or even by reference to several mutually supportive sources. On the contrary, as the previously quoted text from Berakhot illustrates, the Bavli's approach is typified by the support of multiple opinions and interpretations through reference to many, often contradictory sources. And, again speaking generally, where such a multiplicity of opinions exists, the Bavli will more often content itself with a successful defense of all competing opinions than it will decide in favor of one or the other. In such a context, reference to authoritative sources speaks not to a single divine truth but to the fundamental elusiveness of truth. It says, in effect, that the truth of scripture cannot be determined because its possible interpretations are many, and an authoritative source for this opinion or that can almost always be found.

In some sense, the validity of these observations can be demonstrated by comparing the Bavli to the Mishnah. The Mishnah, with rare exception, at most calls upon the authority of those few rabbinic sages to whom it attributes opinions. On those occasions when it quotes scripture, it generally quotes a single text to support a single view. But more often it simply states its opinion in its own voice and on its own terms, requiring for authority only the "truth" of its own opinions, that is, self-validating truths enunciated within the rabbinic system.⁹ The Bavli, on the other hand, explicitly constructs arguments within the context of a tradition, where the claims of earlier authorities become crucial and where the interpretations of given authoritative traditions are generally multiple and are rarely self-evident. Again, what this reflects is the gemara's compromised relationship to "truth." Its very form declares that truth is subject to question and that, in the end, truth is impossible to determine.

An ironic testimony to the correctness of these characterizations of the Talmudic form may be found in the lyrical polemic of the Karaite author Salmon ben Jeroḥam, against Saadiah. Ben Jeroḥam writes:

> . . . [I]f the Talmud originated with our master Moses,
>   What profit is there for us in "another view,"
> And what can a third and fourth view teach us,
>   When they tell us first that the interpretation of this
>   problem in law is thus-and-so, and then proceed to
>   explain it with "another view"?
> *The truth stands upon one view only,*
>   For this is so in the wisdom of all mankind,
> And *right counsel cannot be based upon two contradictory*
>   *things* . . .¹⁰

To be sure, ben Jeroḥam was an enemy of the rabbis and their Talmud. Nevertheless, his words are to the point: *the* truth can be embodied in one view only. Complete truth cannot be present in two different or even contradictory views. And yet it is these different views that stand at the foundation of Talmudic argumentation and that the argumentation, as noted, frequently does not resolve. It is not unreasonable to conclude, therefore, that the rabbis of the Talmud cannot rightfully claim to possess *"the* truth." The very form by which they chose to express themselves constitutes recognition of that same fact.

Returning to the matter of authority claims and authoritative traditions, I should add that, just as reference to such traditions attenuates the position of "truth" in argumentational dialogues, so too does the deliberation on such traditions compromise the very authority from which they speak. To use the words of Perelman and Olbrechts-Tyteca, "Mere questioning of a statement is . . . sufficient to destroy its privileged status" (TNR,

p. 68). If the statement were truly privileged, if its authority alone were sufficient, then there would be no room to question it. The fact that one can address it with a question is evidence enough that its authority is not absolutely respected.

Reference to authoritative traditions, therefore, has a dual, even contradictory effect. On the one hand, the use of authority claims in deliberation shows that "truth" must compete with tradition; in this manner such claims erode the position of the "truths" that they accompany. But as authoritative sources are used in such contexts, their authority is itself eroded by the application of reason. Neither authority nor reason stands unaffected by the other.

This is particularly so in a text like the gemara, where authoritative traditions almost never stand on their own; they always are quoted in a particular context, generally shaped by the gemara itself. What is the effect of such quotation in context? Perelman and Olbrechts-Tyteca remark: "The words of other people, when repeated by a speaker, have changed their meaning, for in the process of repetition he always adopts toward them a position that is in some way new, even if only in the degree of importance he attaches to them. *This applies to statements made in arguments from authority*" (TNR, p. 317; emphasis added). Quotation of an authoritative tradition by a later individual always affects the tradition being quoted, if even in imperceptible ways. Either the context into which he sets it or the comments that he makes upon it will cause the earlier remarks to be viewed through the lens of his understanding. Thus, although the fact that he quotes an earlier statement demonstrates that he deems it to be important—if he thought the statement to have no authority or importance, there would be no good reason for him to quote it—the mere act of his quoting it diminishes its independent authority and makes its impact dependent on his own interpretation. Using authority to support his own opinion, he compromises that authority by making it accord with his opinion.

Clearly, this process of quoting authoritative traditions characterizes nearly all of the Bavli. How such quotation in context affects the gemara's traditions has been widely demonstrated in recent scholarship, and there is little difficulty confirming the proper application of the preceding insights to the Bavli as a whole. The work of Shamma Friedman on the tenth chapter of tractate Yevamot, for instance, provides one illustration of how the meaning of sources is shifted when quoted in the later Talmudic context.

Yevamot 87b–88b

MISHNAH:

A woman whose husband went abroad, and [witnesses] came and said to her "Your husband has died," and she [went ahead and] married [another], and afterward her [first] husband returned, she should go out [by divorce] from this [first husband] and from this [latter husband]. . . .

GEMARA:

a. . . . Rav said: They taught this [law] only when she [re]married by the testimony of one witness, but if she [re]married by the testimony of two witnesses, she does not [need to] go out.

b. They mocked him in the West [= Palestine]: The man has come and stands [before us] and you say she should not go out?!

c. This [teaching] is required only for [a case where] we do not recognize him.

d. But if we do not recognize him, why must she go out [even] if there was [only] one witness [originally]?

e. This [teaching] is required only for [a case where] two witnesses came and said "we were with him from the time that he left until now, and it is [only] you who do not recognize him. . . ."

f. But in any case, there is a [dubious] case of two [witnesses testifying one thing] and two [testifying another], and [in such a dubious case] the one who has sex with her should [only] be obligated to bring [an appropriate sacrifice].

g. R. Sheshet said: [No sacrifice is mentioned] because she married one of her [original] witnesses [and that witness, presumably, was confident of his testimony. The sacrifice is to be brought only when there is doubt].

h. But she herself should bring the sacrifice [since she shouldn't be as certain as the witness].

i. [We are talking of a case] where she said "it is clear to me."

j. . . . Rava objects [quoting a baraita]: How do we know that if [a priest] didn't want [to hallow himself by separating himself from impurities and from prohibited marriages] then we force him? Scripture says "and you shall hallow him (Lev. 21:8)," [meaning, even] against his will.

k. How is this to be understood?

l. If you say that she did not marry one of her witnesses and did not say "it is clear to me," would it be necessary to say [under such dubious conditions] that you force him?

m. Rather, no, [we are talking, in the baraita, about a case] where she married one of her witnesses [= the priest with whom the baraita is concerned] and said "it is clear to me. . . ."

Friedman clarifies several source traditions that are read into this text, their meaning being changed thereby. To begin with, the statement of Rav (a), with which this whole deliberation begins, must be understood in a way that defies its simple meaning because of the gemara's initial, independent interpretation of the Mishnah, not quoted here. The gemara earlier claimed that this part of the Mishnah is, by definition, talking about the testimony of only one witness. If that were so clear, as the gemara wants to claim, then Rav's clarification (more correctly, limitation) would be unnecessary. Second, according to Friedman's analysis, the interpretation of R. Sheshet (g) is borrowed for this text from another, more original context. The details of Sheshet's comments are appropriate here, and their meaning is not effectively changed. But having inserted his words into a longer deliberation, the gemara has made it appear as though Sheshet actually participated in this exchange. In that way, it has contributed a new shading to Sheshet's activity.

Finally, most striking is the effect that the quotation of Rava's objection from the baraita (j) has had on the meaning of his objection. This is perhaps best understood by asking oneself, as one begins to read the gemara's amplification of his objection (k–m), "What does this have to do with the content of the text that Rava quotes?" Originally, Friedman suggests, Rava's objection was addressed directly to the opinion of Rav, without any intervening steps. But quoted in the context of the gemara, the baraita is made to assume a meaning that is in no way suggested by its words. The baraita says nothing about a priest who is confronted by the difficult case, the supposed concern of this larger deliberation; it merely discusses the need for a priest to separate himself from impurity and prohibited marriages. But the gemara's "clarification" of the baraita (k–m) assumes that the baraita addresses our specific case, that is, the case as defined by the gemara itself in the previous several steps (e–i). Placed into this context, the earlier tradition assumes a meaning for which there is no internal support at all. Again, its quotation demands that we read it through the lens that the gemara has provided, and while it is clearly meant to be a source of authority (in this case, an authoritative objection), in fact it has more profoundly been molded by the interpretive authority that the gemara has asserted. (See the appendix to this chapter.)

Moderation of authority claims, and of claims for truth in general, is also a consequence of several other elements of the gemara's precise deliberative approach. For example, the need to propose justifications demonstrates that authority claims are not by themselves sufficient. Dupréel is certainly correct in declaring that "every justification is essentially a moderating act" (quoted in TNR, p. 55). People who are unreasonable might demand that they be heeded for no reason at all; moderate, reasonable people understand the need to justify themselves. In fact, the gemara's incessant searching for justifications and reasons suggests that it consciously invites the "challenge" of authority (i.e., at least of rabbinic authority; because Talmudic justifications are so often found in scripture it would be unfair to suggest that this commonly extends to its authority as well). The Bavli was not unaware of the difference between letting traditions speak from their own authority and offering reasons for the same rulings; note the tradition at Avodah Zarah 35a: "When they issue a decree in the West [Palestine] they do not reveal its reason for twelve months lest there be a person who doesn't agree [with the reason] and come to deal lightly with it." In this document of the East (Babylonia), of course, it is reasons that are most often sought. The very act of seeking reasons, we see, invites someone to disagree. Authority may have some claim, therefore, but its power is consciously compromised by the recognition that other justifications—be they other sources of authority (such as scripture) or logical analysis—are also required.

The play of alternatives in the gemara—alternative interpretations, alternative rulings, alternative sources—is also a sign of moderation. The reader is constantly being asked to consider new perspectives. The very availability of alternatives often highlights the ambiguity of a situation (see TNR, p. 122). Even when the play of alternative interpretations gives preference to some over others, those that are denied will not be forgotten. The reader is always left with the impression that alternatives *were* available and that someone thought those alternatives to be reasoned and intelligent. Their echoes will always be a reminder that the conclusions, even when accepted, are not self-evident.

But with all of the ambiguity that argumentation might suggest, it would be improper to conclude that alternatives are endless, for argumentation, by its very nature, *must* take place in community. As Perelman and Olbrechts-Tyteca remark, "For argumentaion to exist, an effective community of minds must be realized at a given moment. There must first of all be agreement, in principle, on the formation of this intellectual community" (TNR, p. 14). We have all had, at one time or another, the experience of "arguing past" someone, realizing at the end that even the most basic assumptions were not shared. Without those shared assumptions, real deliberation cannot take place. Consider, as an illustration, the difficulty of those who try to study Talmud for the first time; not only is the vocabulary unfamiliar, but so too are the rules of procedure and other basic assumptions. The argumentation of the gemara assumes a rabbinic community. The theoretical multitude of its alternatives, as noted previously, is in practical terms constrained by the conventions of the community in which it operates.

Argumentation therefore may be taken to represent the ambiguity of truth and of authority claims within a defined community. But if argumentation begins with essential ambiguity, then what function does it serve in its particular community? To put it simply, when considered as a social act (for this is the perspective of community), what is the purpose of argumentation? The answer of Perelman and Olbrechts-Tyteca is: *"All argumentation aims at gaining the adherence of minds"* (TNR, p. 14; their emphasis). One argues with another in order, obviously, to persuade him or her. If authority is not absolute, if truth is not self-evident, and if force is not an option, then it will be necessary to persuade the other. Such persuasion is the aim of argumentation.

In other words, argumentation is an inherently rhetorical form, for only by means of rhetoric can it gain the adherence of which Perelman and Olbrechts-Tyteca speak. The frequent presence in the Bavli of common rhetorical devices is evidence of the close connection between argumentation and rhetoric and is testimony to the correctness of the proposed characterization with relation to the Bavli.

Consider what may be called "rhetorical objections." "Everything that furnishes an argument against the thesis being defended by the speaker, including objections to his own hypotheses, becomes an indication of sincerity and straightforwardness and increases the hearers' confidence" (TNR, p. 457). The gemara, as "speaker," often proceeds in this manner, suggesting an interpretation or opinion and then straightaway providing an objection. This might be an anticipated objection, in which case what it suggests will not bear great weight, or a genuine objection. It should be recalled that it is the anonymous gemara itself (as opposed to individual amoraim) which most frequently brings the objection; its doing so should be understood not only as an objection to the opinion being considered, but as a defense. The more objections against which the gemara successfully defends the opinion of rabbi so-and-so, the more secure his view will appear. There will be no doubt, moreover, that, following these objections, the opinion that has survived will not be considered capricious or baseless. If the gemara has "sincerely" tested the opinion, the reader will be convinced of its viability.

Persuasion, through "guided discussion," is also evident in the gemara's frequent proposal of theoretical answers that will obviously be quickly put aside. This is an expression of the rhetorical figure known as "suspension," which is described by Perelman and Olbrechts-Tyteca in this way: "The speaker asks a question, to which he gives an immediate answer, but this answer is simply a hypothesis which, more often than not, he will himself reject" (TNR, p. 493). In the gemara, this approach often begins with the question "What is X?" and is followed by an answer introduced with the words "If you say" or "If it be said" (*'i tema* or *'i lema*). As any student of the Bavli knows, any answer proposed in this manner will ultimately be rejected. The proposed answer must, at first glance, be a reasonable alternative; otherwise there would be no reason to consider it in the first place. However, the gemara at such times is really asking the reader to reject the given alternative. It is seeking to guide his thinking in other directions and to win his consent for other views.

More examples could also be presented, but the point has already been made. The Bavli, as an argumentational text, is rhetorical, that is, it seeks to persuade.[11] It does so within the context of community (the rabbinic community), and by doing so it seeks to strengthen that community. This is the nature of its approach because it begins with certain assumptions: (1) that it may not, finally, coerce the minds that it addresses; (2) that authority, by itself, is insufficient; and (3) that truth, finally, is ambiguous, and alternatives are always available.

The questions, then, are these: Why is this the form in which the rabbinic authors of the Bavli chose to express themselves? What, in their universe of experience—historical or intellectual—led them to prefer this approach?

Historical Underpinnings

To seek answers for these questions, we will begin where Perelman and Olbrechts-Tyteca end, that is, with their concluding remarks on the argumentational form, its meaning, and its purpose. Their words are meant as a defense of argumentation in a world that values, to an almost mystical extent, scientific and mathematical proofs and their conclusions:

The increased confidence . . . brought about in the procedures and results of the mathematical and natural sciences went hand in hand with the
casting aside of all the other means of proof, which were considered devoid
of scientific value. Now this attitude was quite justifiable as long as there
was hope of finding a scientifically defensible solution to all actual human
problems. . . . But if *essential problems involving questions of a moral,
social, political, philosophical, or religious order by their very nature elude
the methods of the mathematical and natural sciences,* it does not seem
reasonable to scorn and reject all the techniques of reasoning characteristic
of deliberation and discussion—in a word, of argumentation. . . . The assertion that whatever is not objectively and indisputably valid belongs to the
realm of the arbitary and subjective creates an unbridgeable gulf between
*theoretical knowledge, which alone is rational, and action, for which mo-
tivations would be wholly irrational. . . .*

*Only the existence of an argumentation that is neither compelling nor
arbitrary can give meaning to human freedom, a state in which a reasonable choice can be exercised.* . . . If the exercise of freedom were not
based on reasons, every choice would be irrational and would be reduced to
an arbitrary decision operating in an intellectual void. It is because of the
possibility of argumentation which provides reasons, but not compelling
reasons, that it is possible to escape this dilemma: adherence to an objectively and universally valid truth, or recourse to suggestion and violence to
secure acceptance for our opinions and decisions. The theory of argumentation will help to develop . . . the justification of *the possibility of a human community in the sphere of action when this justification cannot be
based on a reality or objective truth.* (TNR, pp. 512 and 514; emphasis
added)

The reasons for argumentation, as proposed in this masterful conclusion, are both theoretical and practical. To begin with, moral, social,
political, philosophical, and religious problems cannot be resolved by
scientific or mathematical demonstrations (though some philosophers might
take issue with the inclusion of their discipline in this company).[12] Such
problems are most effectively addressed through reasoned deliberation
and argumentational persuasion. Since these categories describe precisely
the nature of the problem the gemara is concerned with, *if there is concern with justification of opinions at all* (as in the gemara there clearly
is), it is natural that this is the form those justifications will (and did)
assume.

Moreover, these categories are not only theoretical. Moral, political,
social, and religious problems are also matters of practice. Being thus
concerned with practice, the gemara's argumentational form is appro-

priate to one of its fundamental purposes. Why so? As the authors explain, only theoretical knowledge can be purely rational. Only such a realm, untainted by the necessary human element (again, only in theory), can remain thoroughly rational. But action does not share this luxury, for human actions are motivated by numerous factors, and as a consequence such actions are assuredly not purely rational. Argumentation, in its persuasive character, seeks to create motivations and to affect actions, and so again, if the concern of the gemara is, on one level, human practice and action, then argumentation is the mode by which it can most effectively address that concern.

Argumentation also provides a means of assuring human freedom. It makes no claims to pure, final truth, and it always recalls the presence of alternatives. In so doing, it presents the listener (reader) with options, and it bids the listener to make a choice. It seeks to persuade the reader, but it leaves open the option of refusal or denial. In this regard, argumentation is a manifestation of a basic principle of the rabbinic system which at its foundation is a system of free choice. This is R. Aqiba's claim in Avot: despite God's omniscience, "free will is granted" (Avot 3:15). This principle is so important that it may be understood to be, in part, the reason for Maimonides's rejection of Aristotle's prime cause: the world had to be created in a purposeful way by a purposeful God. Only if things are not the way they are by necessity does it make sense to command, and to reward and punish. Reward and punishment may be deemed just only if the commanded being is not the way he or she is by necessity and retains freedom of choice. By making the choices evident even within the system, the Bavli's approach enunciates this commitment clearly and eloquently.

Although all of these reasons can explain the gemara's choice of form (at least in part), none explains why it was the Bavli that for the first time employed argumentation to this profound extent. After all, the concerns and assumptions discussed earlier were all presumably shared by the authors of the Mishnah, Tosefta, and Yerushalmi. These documents, too, presumably sought to shape and strengthen the rabbinic community and they also were essentially concerned with religious practice. Furthermore, the commitment to freedom of will was expressed already in Avot, and it too was shared by the communities of these other documents. Why, then, did the Yerushalmi not go to the same lengths as the Bavli, and why did the Mishnah or Tosefta not use this form at all? Why the Bavli's uniqueness?

First, it must be stated that conventional historical factors will not be able to answer these questions. Part of the problem is that we do not know precisely when the Bavli was composed. Present scholarship puts its writing (as a complete literary document) between the late fifth and early seventh centuries.[13] Furthermore, even if we could pinpoint its composition, we in any case can say very little about historical factors that might have precipitated such an undertaking. There is evidence of persecution of Jews in Babylonia in the mid fifth century, but its degree is not known and a precise reconstruction is impossible.[14] Legend speaks of a Jewish insurrection under the leadership of the exilarch in the early sixth century, but the evidence is mostly incredible and, if there is truth behind the legend, it is probably modest and insignificant.[15] Alternatively, the possible influence of some event like the literary composition of the Avesta is difficult to ascertain, because there too there is considerable scholarly debate concerning dating.[16] Given the nature of the evidence, therefore, we must look in other directions for the explanations we seek.

One development that was very likely a factor in giving birth to the Bavli's form was a shift in rabbinic circles from oral to written composition. Tannaitic and amoraic traditions had been composed and preserved (in their authoritative form, at least) orally, as noted in an earlier chapter. But internal evidence suggests that the Bavli was a written composition. This conclusion is supported, first, by the sequential, analytic quality of the Talmudic deliberation. Analysis of this sort is facilitated by written exposition and is not to be found in strictly oral cultures.[17] Second, the fact that the gemara leaves so much unexplained, requiring that the reader retrieve essential pieces of earlier information, strongly suggests that it was written. The oral experience requires, if anything, that too much be articulated, often in the form of repetition, for only in that way can the effectiveness of a message be ensured. In oral presentation, only the speaker—but *not* the listener—has the capability to review what he did not catch the first time. In contrast, the reader can always return to an earlier point in a text, and so a written composition alone has the luxury of expecting the reader to fill in the gaps.[18]

Nor should the obvious mnemonic features present in the gemara—repetition, three-step progressions, and so on—be thought to contradict this conclusion. As Walter Ong remarks:

> Manuscript cultures remained largely oral–aural even in retrieval of material preserved in texts. Manuscripts were not easy to read . . . and what readers found in manuscripts they tended to commit at least somewhat to

memory. Relocating material in a manuscript was not always easy. Memorization was encouraged and facilitated also by the fact that *in highly oral manuscript cultures, the verbalization one encountered even in written texts often continued the oral mnemonic patterning that made for ready recall.*[19]

This description obviously pertains to Babylonian rabbinic culture. Written documents within such a culture—as, I have suggested, the Bavli was—nevertheless retained powerful "oral residues." For this reason, written texts, in many of their features, *looked* oral.

Ong's analysis also explains why the claim that "people today even know the gemara by heart" proves nothing. Manuscripts were rare and precious and so manuscript compositions, though written, sought to facilitate subsequent memorization. The question, however, is not whether the gemara can be memorized but whether it was *composed* in that form. As I have said, the nature of its analysis and deliberation suggests emphatically that its origins, instead, were written. That condition is the first factor that explains why the Bavli, unlike the Mishnah and Tosefta (which were oral compositions), took the form that it did.

Second, the Bavli, unlike the tannaitic texts, already had an extensive documentary foundation on which to build. The Mishnah had a first-order task, that is, to articulate essential basic definitions for the early rabbinic community. The Tosefta supplemented these definitions, and the halakhic midrashim tied them to scripture.

The Bavli, in contrast, already had this extensive foundation, and its presence facilitated (perhaps even encouraged) the directed analysis that, in the pages of the Bavli, would extend from it. Because, for the Babylonian sages, the foundation was already secure, they could afford, with ever-increasing creativity, to speculate on both the practical and theoretical consequences of the law which they discussed.

The presence of the Mishnah, in particular, as a foundation document for the Bavli also explains its development in other ways. To begin with, the Mishnah was a document in which the land played a central role. Many of its agricultural regulations had no force in Babylonia, and its regulations as a whole placed heavy emphasis on land-based institutions (including the temple). The rabbis in Babylonia thus could not simply absorb the Mishnah and incorporate its strategies unchanged. Rather, they would have to decide the precise shape of rabbinic Jewish practice in that particular community, and since their decisions could not merely replicate earlier models—adaptation, at the very least, was necessary—they would have to justify their decisions. This, in part, may explain why so much of the gemara is justificatory. It takes interpretations and rulings that adapt

Mishnah regulations to a Babylonian context and justifies those traditions. The mere fact of changed conditions is one explanation of the Bavli's expository direction.[20]

Even more important than this, I think, is the Bavli's response to what Neusner terms "the crisis precipitated by the Mishnah."[21] The Mishnah, though it did respond to change, did not explicitly justify its response. For this reason, Neusner is correct in claiming, the Mishnah is inherently lacking. As eloquent as it may be, the Mishnah did not perform its full task, which, given the novelty of much of what it prescribed, would have required justification. It is to remedy this that so many of the interpretive statements of the amoraim are intended. The very silence of the Mishnah on these matters generated large parts of the subsequent tradition, and the task that it left undone was so vast that it took the Babylonian sages three centuries or more to finish the job to their satisfaction.[22] The amoraim responded to this challenge on one level; the gemara, in its lengthy justificatory deliberations, did so on another.

In sum, one of the main reasons that the Bavli does not look like the Mishnah is because the Bavli already *had* the *Mishnah*. The Mishnah, not only because of what it provided but also because of what it did not, supplied much of the generative energy for the later tradition, and the agenda of the Bavli can in part be understood, as described here, by appreciating this reactive aspect of its development.

Unlike the earlier documents, the Bavli also had the amoraic tradition on which to build. In the presence of the rulings and interpretations of the amoraim, the gemara was free to speculate on the meanings and relationships of these various elements of the tradition. Thus amoraic interpretation gave way to the even more liberal interpretive enterprise of the Bavli itself.

Also offering a foundation for the subsequent development of the Bavli was the birth during the amoraic era of the notion of Oral Torah. As has been documented by Neusner and others,[23] the oral tradition of the rabbis was not yet known as "Torah"[24] in the Mishnah or Tosefta or even, unambiguously, in Avot. The first such designations appear, rather, in the Midrashei Halakha and in the Yerushalmi.

The reference to the two Torahs in the Sifra (Behuqotai, 8:12) and Sifrei (Deut., par. 351) places the notion in what is purportedly a tannaitic context. The attribution to tannaim, however, is difficult to accept. Neusner's comment in connection to a similar attribution to Hillel in the Bavli (Shab. 31a) is relevant here: "The lack of evidence in the Mishnaic sector of the canon that people knew about the myth of two Torahs hardly enhances the credibility of [these attributions]."[25] Rather, it seems likely that the opinions expressed in these texts may be dated with confidence only to the time of their redactions (post-Mishnaic) and, in any case, there is certainly no evidence of the widespread acceptance of this notion during the earlier rabbinic period.

The record of the Yerushalmi, in combination with its Bavli parallel, is more conclusive. The Yerushalmi (at Peah 2:6, 17a; Hag. 1:7, 76d; and, in part, Meg. 4:1, 74d) attributes the view that there are two Torahs, written and oral, to, among others, R. Eleazar and R. Yoḥanan. Highly similar traditions—quoting the same verse, in the case of R. Eleazar, and emphasizing the dependence of the covenant on the Oral Torah, in the case of R. Yoḥanan—are recorded in the Bavli (Git. 60b). Because the Bavli, the later of the two documents, did not know the Yerushalmi (see pp. 22–23), the presence of what are essentially the same traditions in these two documents must be accounted for on the basis of a common third source. That source is the circle of disciples of these named authorities.[26] The notion that the oral tradition represented an Oral Torah was espoused by certain rabbinic groups, therefore, in the mid to late third century.

The view that rabbinic tradition constitutes a part of Torah in the opinion of late third-century amoraim is corroborated by the fact that it is during these same generations that study of this tradition begins to require the recitation of a formal blessing for Torah study (see pp. 159–61). Being part of "Torah," rabbinic study as such became the focus of inquiry and exposition, opening the option of properly "Talmudic" discourse. The *value* of rabbinic–Torah study, first articulated fully by these amoraim, came to be embodied in practice in the deliberative forms of the Talmud's authors.

Furthermore, specific amoraic models were also crucial in suggesting new directions to the later authors. This was particularly true with respect to the middle amoraic generations, whose concern for argumentation and theoretical interpretation opened the door for the gemara's vast theoretical argumentation and suggested to the later authors the possibility—which we will see exemplified in the next chapter—of Torah study as a pure and unconditional pursuit. In the absence of these models, the precise directions taken in the Bavli surely would have been more difficult to realize.

This latter factor—unlike those that precede it—begins to explain the differences between the Bavli and the Yerushalmi. Most of what we have seen to this point distinguishes not only the Bavli from earlier documents, but also the Yerushalmi from those same documents. We should find it assuring, therefore, that the Yerushalmi is distinguished stylistically from those documents in ways that are similar to the Bavli. But I have argued that there are also important differences between the Bavli and Yerushalmi, differences that similarly require explanation. If the middle amoraic model in Babylonia was crucial to suggesting specific directions to the authors of the Bavli, as I have proposed, this would in part explain why the Yerushalmi's choices were not precisely the same. The tradition of these amoraim, particularly as attributed to Abbaye and Rava, was generally unavailable to the authors of the Yerushalmi, or so the rarity of reference to their traditions as a whole would suggest.[27] Its influence, therefore may be found in the Bavli but not in the Yerushalmi.

A final factor that may explain the development of the Bavli in contrast to other rabbinic documents, including the Yerushalmi, is the nature of the Jewish community within which it developed. The Bavli, first, was composed centuries after the Mishnah and Tosefta (and perhaps as many as two centuries after the Yerushalmi) in a territory far removed from the world of those other documents. This factor, in particular, had a profound effect on the nature of the rabbinic movement in Babylonia, requiring (or permitting) numerous changes and adaptations from earlier rabbinic customs. Such changes showed up not only in specific matters of practice but also in approaches to the sacred and in overall attitudes.[28] These developments are reflected in the Bavli's unique personality.

Furthermore, the rabbinic movement in Palestine had been a relatively confined, relatively centralized community, reflecting the concentration of the Jewish community at large in the Galilee during the Talmudic period. Not so the rabbinic community in Babylonia, which was geographically far more diverse and which coexisted with a larger Jewish community that continued, as far as we can tell, to be incompletely assimilated into the rabbinic form of Judaism.[29] This condition is important for two reasons. First, the decentralized rabbinic community is an obvious influence in determining the plurality of practices and opinions that the Bavli records. Its variety is formed in the image of the community that was its home. Second, the rabbinic estate, which aspired to lead the Babylonian Jewish community as a whole, knew well how difficult an aspiration that was to realize. Though rabbinic power in Babylonia continued to increase after the third century, it is evident that the rabbis' power to coerce other Jews remained limited. To be sure, the rabbis claimed to have had a special relationship with the exilarch and claimed, as well, to have controlled the Jewish court system. But even if their claims are accurate (as they may be, at least in part), this power was one that the rabbis had to win, and once they succeeded, it is likely that the government placed significant restrictions on this power.[30] Whatever the precise extent of their power, it was certainly necessary for the rabbis to secure their position by gaining the voluntary support of the Jewish community at large.

For this reason, the rabbis must have understood the need for, and the power of, a persuasive presentation of their views. In connection with this factor, as well, the picture preserved in the Bavli reflects social conditions at large. The rabbinic station in Babylonian Jewish society preconditioned the rabbis to think in terms of justification and persuasion and caused them to recognize that such an approach was preferable to apodictic declaration.

Theological Underpinnings

It is more difficult, at least at first blush, to claim—as I did earlier in this chapter—that the rabbis thought "universally valid truths" to be inaccessible. After all, they possessed the written word of God, enhanced by an authoritative oral tradition. How then could they believe that truth was not fully available to them?

As difficult as this conclusion might seem, I suggest that it is precisely this recognition that is embodied in the Talmudic form, as I have argued from the beginning of this chapter. How, in light of the presence of "Torah," both written and oral, can this conclusion be justified?

We must begin with a rabbinic view that apparently gained ascendency long before the Bavli, namely, the opinion that prophecy, or direct communication from God in any biblically known form, was no longer present.[31] The Mishnah, first, records this view: "When the earlier prophets died, the Urim and Tumim were annulled" (Sot. 9:12). The Urim and Tumim were a means by which the High Priest could ascertain God's will; they would record God's response to specific inquiries (see Num. 27:21 and 1 Sam. 28:6). Their loss of power meant that communication with the Divine, originating on the human plane but expecting explicit divine response, was no longer available. The Tosefta adds: "When Ḥaggai, Zechariah and Malachi, the latter prophets, died, the Holy Spirit ceased in Israel, but even so they [= the Divine] would notify them [= Israel] by means of a Heavenly voice" (Tos. Sot. 13:2). Prophecy, being direct communication of the Divine with humanity, had therefore also ended. So-called heavenly voices (more literally, "echoes") remained, but these were not biblical. They were clearly inferior to prophecy itself, and, as we learn in later rabbinic literature, the rabbis considered it legitimate to ignore these voices (see b. B.M. 59b); the same course of action could never have been justified in the face of actual prophecy. Considered in combination, these texts make it clear that the divine will could no longer be known through its unambiguous emergence into this world. The rabbis, unlike their biblical predecessors, were largely cut off from active revelation of God's will.

However, the rabbis did, of course, preserve a record of divine will in scripture. The problem was this: if divine will was available only in a text, then that divine will could be known only through interpretation. God's part of the revelation was essentially complete; the human contribution to the divine record would now begin in earnest. But—and here is the difficulty—interpretation was (and remains) a profoundly *human* activity, human in all of its aspects. Hence interpretations would always be multiple because each human being reads a text in a different way, and each interpretation would always, in some degree, be incomplete. Humans are, by definition, imperfect; it is this that distinguishes them from God. Human interpretations must also, therefore, be imperfect, and even, on frequent occasions perhaps, wrong. Where the divine message ceases to be active and becomes dependent on human interpretation, it must always, in some sense, remain unavailable.

On a mythic level, the rabbis may have wanted to deny this conclusion (see Tos. Sot. 14:9: "When the students of Shammai and Hillel who did not serve [their masters] adequately increased, disputes multiplied in Israel and two Torahs were created"). But the very system that they constructed, in its broad willingness to include multiple opinions and interpretations, confirms that they recognized the meaning of the situation that they faced. This recognition was not complete, however, at the earliest stages of rabbinism. The Mishnah, though it does often record alternative opinions, also often does not. The overwhelming insistence on alternatives in interpretation would await the Bavli, and it was at the time of its composition that the full implications of the position described earlier would be recognized and affirmed. It should be no surprise, moreover, that the fullest extension of this recognition would wait so long. It is radical to deny that a single divine truth is available. This fact, at the earliest stages, had to be spoken softly. It could be fully realized only slowly and cautiously, and its comprehensive application had to wait until much later.

If divine truth could be approached (though never fully realized) only through human endeavor, then human reason, and the process by which it is applied, had to become central; the human effort, even when in error, had to be affirmed.[32] This latter point is extremely important. If one wants to claim, as the rabbis did, that the divine message could be reached only through human interpretation, then one has to legitimate the outcome of that interpretation. That outcome, being human, would also, from time to time, be wrong. Nevertheless, error must be legitimated. The alternative—to deny error—would mean the downfall of such a system, since any interpretation would by definition be more or less incomplete. Accordingly, the rabbinic system had to affirm the consequences of the human contribution, even if those consequences were "clearly" incorrect.

This affirmation is stated explicitly in the well-known story of "the oven of Akhnai" (y. M.K. 81c–d, 3:1 and b. B.M. 59b). Briefly, the story relates a dispute between R. Eliezer (ben Hyrcanus, a tannaitic sage of the early second century) and R. Joshua and other colleagues. R. Eliezer tries to prove that the halakha should follow his opinion by invoking miracles like the uprooting of a carob tree by his command. Finally, a heavenly voice declares that the halakha should follow Eliezer, but R. Joshua responds and says (quoting Deut. 30:12) "it is not in heaven!" The opinion of heaven is irrelevant in these matters; the decision is to be made by the sages.[33]

Of course, we must assume that if the heavenly voice supported R. Eliezer's view, his view must have been closer to the "truth." Nevertheless, his truth is rejected, and the view of the sages, though objectively in error, is affirmed. What justifies this position? Both the Yerushalmi and the Bavli agree that its source is scripture ["it is not in heaven" and "incline after the majority" (Exod. 23:2)], scripture that is read out of context and in patent disregard of its simple meaning. Yet such interpretations are clearly considered legitimate, and in this context they explicitly affirm the triumph of the view of the sages, however erroneous that view might be. Again, both documents agree: because God's will has been written (this point is noted explicitly in both texts) it is now available to interpretation by the human mind.

The agreement described thus far should have been expected, given the openness of both documents to multiple interpretations. The point that emerges from the "Talmudic" form common to the Yerushalmi and the Bavli is the same: the most important concern may not be truth, but the process by which that truth is approached. Yet despite their obvious similarities, there are also important differences, differences that also manifest themselves in their respective versions of this story.

The most obvious difference is their presentation of the ban of R. Eliezer. In the Yerushalmi, the dispute between R. Eliezer and his colleagues is provoked by their having previously banned him. We are not told the reason behind the ban. In the Bavli, on the other hand, the ban is a consequence of Eliezer's refusal to heed his colleagues' decision and his insistence on calling for miraculous intervention to buttress his position. For the Bavli, in other words, the stubborn insistence on "truth" is to be condemned, even to the extent of banning the individual who exhibits such stubbornness. The patently human aspect of the system is to be affirmed absolutely, and the person who doesn't appreciate that the system requires this affirmation must be restricted from participation therein.

The second important difference between the two versions is the response (or absence thereof) to the conclusion "it is not in Heaven." The Yerushalmi concludes its discussion of this matter with that quotation. The Bavli, in contrast, wants to know what God's response to his denial of divine intervention might be. Its suggestion, placed in the mouth of the prophet Elijah, is that God's response is to laugh.[34] God positively rejoices that divine truth had been disregarded in favor of human endeavor.

This particular view is appropriate for the Bavli, for it is the Bavli (and not the Yerushalmi) that pursues the human process, and the alternatives of interpretation, with such complete exuberance. If God would rejoice at God's own "defeat," then God would certainly rejoice at the deliberation of the Bavli, which pursues, to such joyful length, the human contribution to "revelation." The system unquestionably endorses the human endeavor, recognizing that, despite its shortcomings, it is the only option we now have.

This recognition, of course, is precisely what we saw take place in the Bavli. Concern for the process began, as far as the record shows, in the middle (third–fourth) generations of amoraim. By the time of the anonymous gemara, the process became virtually the sole concern. Since it was in this process that alternative approaches to truth were presented, it was the process, finally, which had to become the focus of inquiry.

The consequences of this recognition cannot be overestimated. Pursuit of God's truth is, of course, a pious act. But the rabbinic system claimed that the full truth, buried in the words of scripture, can never fully be uncovered. The best we can do is to seek the truth, to approach the truth. Since here, in the process, is where truth now resides, the process itself, *and the study of that process,* must become the ultimate act of piety. The process, known as *talmud torah,* is an independent value and therefore should be pursued for its own sake. The ultimate consequence of the admission that we no longer have prophecy is that talmud torah, the interface of divine word and human reason, becomes a meritorious act on its own terms, in service of nothing but itself.

It is for this reason that the Bavli insists on talmud torah. The Bavli does not merely record talmud torah but insists that the reader participate in it. That is the function of its "imaginary direct speech" (see TNR, p. 176). The text engages the reader personally in a dialogue, saying "and if you should say . . . ," "what might you say . . . ," "this comes to teach us . . . ," and so forth. By addressing you in this way, the Bavli demands that you speak to it. In addition, the Bavli is, despite its length, often extremely terse, requiring that you fill in the gaps. In this way, too, its voice is often only one side of a dialogue. You, the reader, must be its study partner.

It is also because of its sense of the independent value of talmud torah that the Bavli increases objections and responses at such length. Why, scholars have wanted to know, does the Bavli not go to the strongest objection or to the obvious answer first? Why does it repeat objections that are virtually identical? Why does it bring objections for which answers are already obviously available? The broad answer, again, is the same: all of these serve to increase talmud torah. Similarly, the variety of approaches that the Bavli records and the length to which individual inquiries sometimes go accomplish the same purpose. All embody the exuberant pursuit of talmud torah for its own sake.

Two examples will illustrate how central this "pursuit for its own sake" has become in the Bavli. The first is found at Beẓah 36a (Shab. 43a):

a. . . . R. Isaac said: A utensil may not be handled [on shabbat] except for purposes of a thing that [itself] may be handled on shabbat. . . .
b. Come and hear [a possible objection]: A mat may be spread over a beehive on shabbat, in the summer because of the sun and in the winter because of the rains, but on the condition that he not intend to capture [the bees. Now, a beehive may not be handled, so how, if R. Isaac is correct, could the mat be moved for this purpose?]
c. There too [we are speaking of a case where] there is honey [which, being food, may be handled].

d. R. Ukba from Meshan said to R. Ashi: This [answer] is fine in the summer, when there is honey [in the hive], but what can be said about the winter [when there is no honey]? . . .

David Halivni[35] suggests the following analysis of this text:

> It appears as though R. Ukba from Meshan [d] comes to refute the answer of the anonymous gemara [c]. . . .
>
> But why should someone imagine that the beehive in the baraita has no honey, and object from it to R. Isaac [a], and then force the respondent to say that it is not the case [that there is no honey], but rather "there too there is honey"?
>
> It therefore appears more likely that the initial supposition [b] (that the beehive has no honey) and the response "there too there is honey" are rhetorical, and do not represent bona fide opinions. Originally R. Ukba from Meshan himself objected from the baraita . . . and originally objected from the [condition that would pertain in the] winter, but the author of the anonymous gemara interrupted him in the middle . . . in order to explain why R. Ukba from Meshan objected only from [the condition that would pertain in] the winter.

In other words, the initial objection and response, as recorded in this gemara, are in their present form the artificial creations of the gemara's author. Obviously a beehive would have honey in the summer, and so again, obviously, the only part of this baraita that would present any problem to R. Isaac is that part which permits this action even in the winter. Unless all three steps of this exchange (b–d) were originally only one, the first objection and response make no logical sense.

Halivni suggests that the author created this artificial exchange (b–c) to explain, emphatically, why the objection was being brought only from the condition of the hive in the winter. But Halivni himself admits that such an explanation was not really necessary. Another factor must be at play here, therefore. That factor, I would suggest, is the mere love of increasing argumentation. The question and answer are "rhetorical" because it is the give and take of talmud torah for its own sake that the Bavli most highly values. The exchange, even if less than necessary, is meritorious on its own terms.

The same is true at Kiddushin 29b. There the gemara records the following tradition and brief deliberation:

a. R. Huna . . . said: If a man is twenty years old and has not taken a wife, all his days are [spent] in sin.

b. Would you think [actually] "in sin"?!

c. Rather, I will say "all his days are [spent] in thought of sin."

In evaluating this exchange, the question we must ask is whether it is reasonable to read R. Huna's tradition (a) as suggesting literally that such a man would spend all his days in sin (where "sin" means sexual impropriety). Would we, in the absence of (b–c), have understood it literally, or would we, in any case, have understood it to be an exaggeration? I see no way to avoid the latter conclusion and, if so, then (b–c) is telling us something, more specifically perhaps, that we already know. Again, it seems that there is no real problem with the meaning of the original tradition, and the brief exchange that accompanies it is suggested by this text's author only to increase the objection and response format that the Bavli prefers. Here the text speaks for us, voicing our natural interpretation, and defines precisely the steps for evaluating such a tradition that in our own minds might not have been apparent at all. The system flourishes, though, on making explicit the applications of reason that we would never, in the absence of such amplification, have seen fit to value so.

To recapitulate, the argumentational form of the Bavli represents a moderation of truth claims and an admission that divine truth is available only in the multifarious play of reasoning and interpretation, and even then, finally, only imperfectly. The words of scripture may embody truth, but because we can explore that record only through the application of our own reasoned judgment, in interpretive acts that are acutely human, in the end the full truth must elude us. Because any single interpretation (by definition) grasps only part of the truth, alternative interpretations are always called for. Because any interpretation may embody a kernel of the truth, even views that are for practical reasons rejected should be preserved and studied for their own unique wisdom.

All of this, as noted previously, is not without limits. The system of deliberation that the Bavli describes assumes a particular (rabbinic) community with particular norms and, presumably, with particular boundaries. It is clear, from the perspective of this community, that certain interpretations are to be rejected. For example, the destruction of the Temple cannot mean that God has rejected the Jews for failing to accept Jesus. Such a view, though not inherently less reasonable than rabbinic interpretations of the same event, are nevertheless outside the community. But, even given the boundaries assumed by the rabbinic community, the legitimate alternatives remain theoretically infinite and the room for dissent remains vast.[36]

For example, suffering may be the consequence of sin (see Ber. 5a), but then again it may not be (Shab. 55b). God may be responsible for the death of individuals, but others may die by sheer accident (Hag. 4b–5a). Something as basic (or so Jews have come to believe) as the recitation of the Shema, declaring the unity of God, may or may not be required by the Torah (Ber. 21a). And even the Torah itself, the source of the truth that the rabbis seek, may have been given in individual scrolls and combined at the end of the forty years in the desert or it may have been given in a "sealed" form and memorized by Moses, in whole or in part, until the last of it was revealed to Moses at the end of the forty-year sojourn in Sinai (see Git. 60a). It is true, on the one hand, that there are limits in the alternatives that talmud torah might admit; on the other hand, one ought to be extremely cautious with respect to what those limits might be.

I have argued, in this chapter, that the form of the Bavli itself carries with it the meanings and positions described here. If I am correct in these precise conclusions, there should be other, more "explicit" evidence of the views suggested here. The oven of Akhnai story, mentioned previously, is one example of such explicit evidence. Other examples, of a variety of sorts, are also available. In the next chapter we will examine such cases, expanding upon and refining the preceding analyses.

Appendix: The Erosion of Authority in the Bavli's Sources

I claim in this chapter that the Bavli's form, in its very nature, compromises or erodes the authority of the texts upon which it comments and of the sources that it employs. This claim will be difficult for some students of the Bavli and so, in addition to the theoretical analysis of this chapter, I will here justify the claim through detailed analysis of several illustrative texts.[37]

I begin with two brief, explicit examples.

I. Yevamot 46a–b

a. 1. Our sages taught: A [potential] convert who was circumcised but did not immerse, R. Eliezer says "Behold, he is a convert, for so we have found that our fathers [standing at Mt. Sinai] were circumcised but did not immerse."

2. [If he] immersed but was not circumcised, R. Joshua says "Behold, he is a convert, for so we have found that our mothers [at Mt. Sinai] immersed but were not circumcised.
3. And the sages say, "[if he] immersed but was not circumcised [or] was circumcised but did not immerse, he is not a convert until he [both] is circumcised and immerses.

b. [Several steps of deliberation follow, including case III below.]
c. R. Ḥiyya b. Abba said R. Yoḥanan said, "He is certainly not a convert until he [both] is circumcised and immerses."
d. Obviously! [If there is the opinion of] an individual and [of] a majority, the halakha is like the majority [and above, in (a.3), it was the sages—a majority—against R. Eliezer and R. Joshua, who expressed the opinion that R. Yoḥanan now confirms. Why is it necessary for Yoḥanan to do so, given that we could have arrived at the same conclusion ourselves?]
e. Who is "the sages" [of (a.3)]?
f. R. Yose, for it is taught [in a baraita]. . . . [Since what is called "the sages" in the original baraita (a) is now claimed to be, in fact, the opinion of an individual, it is necessary for R. Yoḥanan to confirm that opinion.]

The compromise of the authority of the source in this interpretive exercise is unambiguous. The opinion in the baraita that ought to be accepted, for reasons of halakhic procedure, is that of the sages (a.3). This turns out, in fact, to be the case; the gemara does not change the baraita's ruling. It does, however, change the baraita's authority. Because R. Yoḥanan (c) tells us something that we should already know ("Obviously!") the gemara concludes that the baraita does not speak for a majority at all, only for R. Yose. For this reason, what appeared to have unimpeachable tannaitic authority now requires the support of amoraic authority. The assent of the amoraic master, R. Yoḥanan, does not strengthen but instead weakens the authority of the source to which it is addressed. The amoraic tradition, in turn, is also weakened, for, though Yoḥanan's statement is no longer redundant, it is now aligned with an opinion that is not that of the majority but only of an individual.

A short sequence at 47a approaches its source in a manner similar to this first case. The precise nature by which it weakens the authority of that source is different, though, and in some ways more provocative.

II. Yevamot 46b–47a

a. 1. Our sages taught: If someone came and said "I am a convert," is it possible that we should accept him? Scripture says "with you" (Lev. 19:33), [meaning] someone who is confirmed to you.

2. If he comes and his witnesses are with him, from where [do I know that he is believed]? Scripture says "And if a convert dwells with you in your land" (ibid.).[38]

3. I know this only with regard to [the convert] in the land; for [the convert] outside the land, from where [do I know it]? Scripture says "with you" (ibid.), [meaning] in any place where he is with you.

4. If so, why does scripture say "in the land"? In the land he must bring proof, outside the land he needn't bring proof, [these are] the words of R. Judah.

5. And the sages say, "whether in the land or outside the land he must bring proof."

b. [several steps not relevant to our analysis follow]

c. R. Ḥiyya b. Abba said R. Yoḥanan said: The halakha is, whether in the land or outside the land he must bring proof.

d. Obviously! [If there is the opinion of] an individual and [of] a majority, the halakha is like the majority!

e. What might you have said? R. Judah's opinion makes sense, for scripture supports him.

f. [The tradition of Ḥiyya b. Abba in the name of R. Yoḥanan] comes to teach us [that Judah's opinion, nevertheless, is not the law].

Again, a tradition attributed to R. Yoḥanan (c) merely states that the halakha follows the majority opinion (a.5) expressed in a baraita. Since this should obviously be the law in any case, the gemara is troubled with R. Yoḥanan's ruling; it is unnecessary. To justify Yoḥanan's statement, then, the gemara argues that it *is* necessary because one might think that, despite a contrary majority opinion, the law should follow R. Judah since his opinion is supported by scripture. R. Yoḥanan must therefore teach us that, whatever the thrust of scripture, the halakha follows the sages.

As in the previous example, the support of R. Yoḥanan here weakens the opinion it comes to affirm, for to justify Yoḥanan's contribution we are forced to conclude that scripture supports a contrary opinion. We therefore see that, according to the gemara's thesis, scripture and halakha do not here align. Furthermore, the gemara's proposal for the function of

Yoḥanan's statement here (to declare halakha where scripture is not supportive) suggests that in other contexts, where rulings such as that of R. Yoḥanan are not present, it is legitimate to question the opinion of the majority on the basis of the sense of scripture. If such a suggestion were truly adhered to, the authority of the earlier system would be severely threatened, because rules of decision making (majority–minority) would now be secondary to fresh rereadings of scripture. It is difficult to imagine the rabbinic system actually sustaining such a compromise.

It would be easy enough to add many illustrations to these. But if, as I have claimed, this process is inherent in the very form and method of the Bavli, it would be of greater interest to inquire whether the Bavli's authors were sensitive to the effects of what they were doing. Did those who composed the Bavli understand that their deliberation on authoritative sources would inevitably erode the authority of those sources? The answer to this question is crucial because, if the answer is affirmative, then we will be forced to conclude that the authors of the Bavli were in a significant sense "untraditional."[39] If, on the other hand, the answer is negative, then we will view them as mere unwitting facilitators of a highly innovative, but not consciously untraditional, redefinition of Judaism.

One way to answer this question would be to accumulate cases of the sort examined earlier,[40] assuming that the greater the number of such instances the more likely it is that the authors of these texts understood their effect. But, in the end, this exercise would be of only limited value because one could still argue that it is only in cases that employ these and similar terms that the erosion of authority was recognized by the Bavli's authors. We will gain more by examining cases where the compromise of authority is embedded in larger deliberative structures. If we could show a trend toward the erosion of authority in extended, carefully wrought compositions, then we would be able, with greater confidence, to suggest that the consequences discussed previously were not unintended. If the author, in a variety of instances, orchestrates his sources to highlight the weakening of authority, then we should assume that such a consequence is a conscious outcome of the Bavli's overall approach.

Limitations of space restrict our examination to two texts that exhibit evidence of conscious weakening of authority.

The first text, taken from the same context as the preceding examples, follows the first baraita (I.a) with several comments on the opinions of R. Eliezer and R. Joshua. The immediate question is from where does

R. Joshua—who, in the opinion of the gemara, insists on immersion for all conversions—learn the law?

III. Yevamot 46b

a. From where does he learn it?
b. If you say, since it is written "Go to the people and hallow them today and tomorrow and launder their garments" (Exod. 19:10), and what if in a place where laundering is not required [such as when a man has had an emission of semen] immersion is required, in a place where laundering is required, doesn't it follow that immersion is required?!
c. But maybe [in that case the laundering was required] for cleanliness in general.
d. Rather, from here: "And Moses took the blood and cast it upon the people" (Exod. 24:8), and we learn [in oral tradition] that there is no sprinkling [of blood] without immersion.
e. Whence do we learn it for the mothers [meaning, for the women at Sinai]?
f. It is logic, for if not [for immersion], with what did they enter beneath the wings of the Divine Presence [= become partners to the covenant, or convert]?

This deliberation, seeking a source for the requirement that converts, both men and women, immerse in a ritual bath is remarkable for the way it attenuates the authority of its purported source. It begins by asking the source for the practice among men, and its first proposal, despite the gemara's explicit objection (c), is in many ways its strongest.[41] It points us to scripture—to the text that describes the preparations for the revelation at Sinai—and suggests that by means of a simple *qal vahomer* (a fortiori, reasoning from lesser to greater) we could derive the requirement for immersion (after the model of the people of Israel at Sinai, the first "converts"). It denies the viability of that source, though, and concludes that the correct source is, instead, a combination of scripture and authoritative oral tradition. For women, finally, the source is said to be logic.

To be noted here, first, is the sequence: scripture–tradition–logic. The first proposed source of the practice (b) is scripture "itself." Something derived from scripture by *qal vahomer* is thought, in the method of the rabbis, to be inherent in scripture, so much so that when a certain lesson can be derived from scripture in this manner, it is deemed unnecessary for scripture or for some later authority to state it explicitly (it would be "Obvious!"). The second derivation (d), though it employs scripture, is in fact dependent on oral tradition, for there is nothing in this scripture, in the absence of the tradition, to suggest this particular practice. With relation to the first proposal, therefore, this proposed source, though conclusive, is inherently less authoritative. Finally, the derivation for women (f) is unrelated to scripture, and logic alone is recognized in the Bavli to be the least authoritative possible source.[42]

It is not merely this progression that weakens the ultimate source of the immersion requirement. Rhetorically, the text fashions its arguments to create difficulties and inconsistencies that will support the same point. To begin with, it is curious that the first proposed derivation requires the assistance of the *qal vaḥomer* at all. The word that I translated (b) as "hallow" means, according to the *Hebrew and English Lexicon of the Old Testament*,[43] to hallow "by washing" (= immersion), and it is parallel in the same verse to "laundering." Moreover, this root still had the sense of "washing" in rabbinic usage (see, e.g., m. Yom. 3:6). To be sure, far more creative derivations than the one this would have required are known in rabbinic interpretation, and so, if the possibility of using this verse as a direct, unadorned source for the immersion requirement existed, the question of why this was not the case remains. The addition of the *qal vaḥomer* removes scripture one minute step from being the direct source of the practice in question, and this should be seen, therefore, as part of the gemara's overall attempt to remove scripture, the most authoritative source, as the possible direct source in this context.

This same impact is achieved by a second oddity in the gemara's argument. The source that the gemara deems conclusive for men should also have been sufficient for women (for this reason we read the two together, though they are seemingly two separate questions in the gemara).[44] The source for men [quoted in (d)] speaks of "the people," not of "the men" or "the children (presumably male) of Israel." Though there is room to argue that the biblical text did not include women in "the people"—at Exodus 19:13 "the people" are told not to approach women—this gemara, beginning with the baraita, obviously considers women to be included in the population that the term "people" describes in Exodus chapters 19 and 24. In any case, given the ambiguity of the term, it is at least noteworthy that women are explicitly relegated to another category at this point in the deliberation, and in a way that demands that the source for their immersion practice be further diminished in authority.

The direction of this progression is therefore from more to less authoritative. The way this diminution in authority is accomplished is twofold: first in the literal progression of suggested sources and second in the careful manipulations (the *qal vahomer,* the displacement of women from "people") that emphasize the distancing from scripture that is taking place. The thesis of this gemara is that the people of Israel at Sinai serve as the model for all future converts because they, for the first time, accepted Torah. What they did, therefore, future converts should also do. But when the text then seeks the sources for the conversion rituals that it obviously means to defend it winds up admitting that the sources are dubious indeed. As in the earlier brief examples, the halakha remains firm, but the sources for that halakha become ever less secure.

The second case that we will examine at greater length is in certain respects like the first, seeking a source in scripture for a particular practice (burial of the dead) and proceeding to weaken its case. The precise manner by which it compromises its source is more elaborate and demanding, and it requires detailed analysis.

IV. *Mishnah Sanhedrin 6:4–5, Bavli Sanhedrin 46b*

MISHNAH:

a. We remove him (the executed convict) [from his hanging position] immediately

b. and if he remains overnight, this is a transgression of a negative commandment, as it says "do not leave his body overnight on the tree, for you shall surely bury him . . ." (Deut. 21:23)

c. . . . and not only that, but anyone who leaves his dead [unburied] overnight transgresses a negative commandment. . . .

GEMARA:

a. R. Yohanan said in the name of R. Shimon b. Yohai: From where [do we learn] that if someone leaves his dead [unburied] overnight he transgresses a negative commandment?

b. Scripture says "for you shall surely bury him." From here [we learn] that if someone leaves his dead overnight that he transgresses a negative commandment.

c. There are those who say [that this is the correct version of the tra-
   dition]:[45]

d. R. Yoḥanan said in the name of R. Shimon b. Yoḥai: From where
   [do we learn] a hint for [the practice of] burial from the Torah?

e. Scripture says "for you shall surely bury him." From here [we learn]
   a hint for burial from the Torah.

f. Shapur the king said to R. Ḥama: Where [do we learn] burial from
   the Torah?

g. He was silent and said nothing to him.

h. R. Aḥa b. Jacob said: The world is given into the hand of fools, for
   he should have said "for you shall bury."

i. [But this can be taken to mean] that he should make him a coffin.

j. "Surely" [can instead be used as the source!]

k. He (Shapur) doesn't take this [repetition of the verbal root, translated
   here by the emphatic "surely"] to be meaningful.

l. And say [that it is required] since the righteous [biblical figures] are
   buried.

m. It is merely the custom of the world.

n. [Say that it is required] since the Holy One, blessed be He, buried
   Moses.

o. [God did so] in order not to change the custom.

p. Come and learn [an answer from this verse]: "And all of Israel shall
   mourn him and bury him" (1 Kings 14:13).

q. In order not to change from custom.

r. "They shall not be mourned nor buried, but they shall be as dung
   on the face of the earth" (Jer. 16:4).

s. In order to change from custom [as punishment for the evil].

t. They asked: Is burial because of shame or because of atonement?

u. What difference does it make?

v. [It makes a difference] if he said "I do not want them to bury that
   man (= himself).

w. If you say that it is because of shame [to the living who survive him,
   then] he hasn't the power [to do this],

x. but if you say that it is because of atonement [to himself], well, he
   said that he doesn't want atonement [and that he has the power to
   do].

y. Come and learn from [the fact] that the righteous [in the Bible] are
   buried, and if you should say that it is because of atonement, do the
   righteous require atonement?

z. Yes, for it is written "there is no just man on earth who does good and does not sin." (Eccles. 7:20)

aa. Come and learn: "And all of Israel shall mourn him and bury him" (1 Kings 14:13), and if you say that [burial] is in order that he have atonement the other [males of the house of Jeroboam, who are to be denied burial] should also be buried in order that they have atonement.

bb. This one who is righteous should have atonement, the others should not have atonement.

cc. Come and learn: "They shall not be mourned nor buried, but they shall be as dung on the face of the earth" (Jer. 16:4) [suggesting that burial is not for atonement, for the wicked too should be atoned].

dd. [Burial is denied here] that they not have atonement.[46]

This text first suggests a definitive source in scripture for burial of the dead (or for the prohibition of leaving unburied overnight) (a–b). An alternative version then suggests that there is no definitive source, but only a "hint" at the practice (c–e). Following, an exchange involving, among others, Shapur the king, reveals that the derivation is, for non-rabbis at least, dubious (f–k) and concludes that the most that scripture will indubitably yield is the fact that burial is required by custom (l–s). Finally, the gemara asks why burial is required (t–x) and, after several failed attempts at determining a solution, leaves the matter without conclusion (y–dd).

Again, a description of the potential sources considered in the several attempts to find a source or reason for this practice is revealing. The sequence traversed in the gemara is this: scripture–"hint"–custom–logic. As in the Yevamot text, the first attempt is strongest and each following attempt rests on reasons of lesser authority. Moreover, each successive step undermines the authority proposed in the steps that preceded.

The first attempt (a–b) suggests a simple midrash halakha, one that is in no way more difficult than other rabbinic "derivations from Torah." Nevertheless, the reformulation of the Yoḥanan tradition (c–e) reveals that the first attempt is, in the minds of some, flawed, and the best that can be said of this verse is that it hints at the practice of burial. The following exchange (f–k) points to the same fact—that the initial derivation is flawed—and in a way that is more precise. The gemara admits here that Shapur would remain unconvinced, leaving us with the distinct impression that the proposed scriptural source is, in fact, unconvincing.

Seeking, then, other sources from scripture (l–s), the gemara admits that none is definitive and that they may, at best, be reflecting accepted custom. Last, the gemara asks the reason for burial, and its very doing so reflects its assessment that no answer has yet been given—the answer is not, in other words, "because scripture says so." The initial thrust of each of the proposed answers is that burial is to avoid shame to the living (each seeks to show why the answer could not be "atonement"), but even this remains unresolved, and the very absence of resolution serves to comment on the status of the enterprise as a whole.

The exchange with Shapur is a puzzling one. Why would the gemara want to step outside the rabbinic system (though it persists in claiming that Shapur shares certain concerns with that system) to show the weakness of the proposed rabbinic derivation? To be sure, the gemara is not addressed to Persians but to rabbis, and it is here bidding the rabbinic student to put himself in Shapur's place and similarly challenge the proposed derivation. For this reason other attempts at discovering a source are necessary. The first possible source is unequal to the task of proving what requires proof.

The final sequence (t–dd) is the most corrosive to the authority of any proposed source. By asking for a reason, the gemara suggests that reasons are as yet not definitive and thereby weakens the institution as a whole. In connection with this point the gemara is explicit: if the reason for burial is atonement, then it is possible, in certain circumstances, that burial would not be required at all (even *despite* the Mishnah which claims that "anyone who leave his dead [unburied] overnight transgresses a negative commandment). Maimonides is sensitive to the effect of the gemara's question here when he writes "if a person commanded that he should not be buried we do not listen to him, for burial is a commandment, as it says 'for you shall surely bury him' " (Laws of Mourning, 12:1). If it is possible to refuse burial, in other words, then it must obviously not be a commandment from the Torah, and despite Maimonides's subsequent opposition, this is clearly a possibility that the gemara considers seriously.[47] Appearing, as it does, as the final step in the deliberation on burial, this question–answer sequence leaves the matter of burial and its source unresolved and denies definitively the availability of an undisputed supportive authority.

So, like the preceding Yevamot example, the gemara here is straightforward in its attempt to weaken the authority of the institution that it treats. Moreover, since the immediate source of this institution is the Mishnah itself, the gemara's deliberation also compromises the authority of that text. In truth, the gemara's purpose here is to question the source of the Mishnah's ruling (why does it say that "anyone who leaves their dead unburied is transgressing"?) and, carefully fashioning a stalemate, the gemara declares that the Mishnah is in fact without an authoritative source.

Why do these texts weaken the authority of the institutions for which they seek sources and of the texts upon which they comment? What do they accomplish by leading us further and further from scripture?

First, they self-consciously make evident the consequences of the gemara's method. They reveal an awareness of the fact that deliberation is a claim to one's own (the gemara's own) authority. By questioning an earlier authority, even if that question purportedly seeks a support or a defense, the result is an inevitable shift in authority to the questioner and a compromise of the power of the earlier authority. As the halakha itself states explicitly: "What is fear [of one's father]? . . . [One] should not support him [in a dispute]" (b. Kid. 31b). Commenting on the opinion of one's "father," even in support, extends him no honor; it implies that he needs such support, and all that does is weaken his authority. The texts examined illustrate the gemara's recognition that its method has this effect on its "father" texts and they apparently reflect its desire to affirm this consequence. Moreover, such examples show that the gemara is unapologetic in this regard; if its commentary compromises the authority of the earlier tradition, displacing the authority to its own masters, then so be it.

Second, if these examples are representative, it seems reasonable to conclude that the gemara here is saying something about its relationship to scripture. Despite the widespread effort in the gemara to seek scriptural sources, these texts seem to suggest that the consequence of that effort is not always a drawing-near to scripture. On the contrary, even when such sources are sought, the ultimate judgment concerning their viability is the gemara's alone. The gemara might admit a particular derivation or, as in these cases, it might deny a derivation and claim that the authority for a given practice resides elsewhere. In either case, there is in all instances a certain distance from scripture, because the gemara itself will dictate its relationship to scripture (as well as to all of the earlier tradition), not vice versa.

I have suggested in these final paragraphs that the gemara was aware of the consequences of its method. I have done so because the examples discussed, given their meticulous composition, reveal, in my reading, the

conscious intent of the gemara's author to treat his subjects with assertive, self-confident authority. The fact that the erosion which was mentioned takes place, in these texts, not in individual steps but in the deliberation as a whole suggests to me that the manipulation is not naive but
mindful.

Reading other Bavli texts with a sensitivity to these possibilities will
yield additional examples of this phenomenon. For example, in his analysis of the first gemara in the tenth chapter of Yevamot, Shamma Friedman notes that the gemara considers three possible sources for the law
that one witness might be believed in certain circumstances, those sources
being, in order, the Torah, logic, and an enactment of the sages (which
is not, however, necessarily "logical").[48] In light of our discussion, we
should now consider this to be evidence of the same trend.

Though I have not conducted the research to identify other similar
instances, I am confident that they can be found. Be that as it may, the
cases outlined here should be sufficient evidence of at least the more
modest claim regarding the gemara's form or method and its consequences: the gemara, in its reference to various sources and authorities,
compromises their authority and makes their voice essentially secondary
to its own.

6

The Bavli on "Truth"

The Separation of Truth and Practice

As NOTED IN chapter 5, the form of the Bavli has certain specific implications regarding the ideologies of its authors. These include a recognition that truth is indeterminable and that alternative views can encompass different aspects of the whole truth. Since, for this reason, final answers may be unavailable, the process by which answers are sought assumes far greater interest and acts of study and interpretation become, on their own terms, expressions of piety. Furthermore, in recognition of the elusiveness of a single, definitive truth, practice is effectively divorced from truth, and coercion, which may be justified in the presence of truth, yields to considered persuasion.

In this chapter, we examine specific texts that more explicitly support the analysis previously suggested. These cases are meant not only to confirm that analysis but to demonstrate that the authors of the Bavli were conscious of the consequences of their method.[1]

We saw that the oven of Akhnai story admits that halakha and truth are not synonymous. Because practice must therefore be determined independently from truth, this implies that "Torah" is constituted of two autonomous pursuits, each of which is meritorious on its own account. Whatever the merits of this conclusion, it is precisely this step (the separation of practice and truth) that the Bavli finally takes. The point is made explicit in a text, without parallel in the Yerushalmi or elsewhere, that discusses the "history" of the disputes of the Schools of Shammai

139

and Hillel. At Yevamot 14a the Bavli notes that there are some sages who believe that the disciples of Shammai never followed their expressed opinions in practice, and others who believe they did. The gemara asks, in its own anonymous voice, what period in the history of halakha this dispute pertains to:

a. When [does this dispute apply]?
b. If you say [that they are arguing about the period] before the heavenly voice [in Yavne (late first century) announced that the halakha follows the School of Hillel], then what is the reason of the one who says they did not act (why not, being that no heavenly decision had yet been made?)?
c. But if after the heavenly voice, then what is the reason of the one who says they did act (being that the heavenly voice had already decided against Shammai)?
d. If you wish I will say [that the dispute applies to the period] before the heavenly voice, and if you wish I will say [to the period] after the heavenly voice.
e. If you wish, I will say before the heavenly voice, and in a case where the School of Hillel is the majority. [Under those conditions] the one who says [the School of Shammai] did not act [on the basis of their opinions says so] because the School of Hillel were the majority [and the law generally follows the majority]. And the one who says that they did act [said this because] we go according to the majority where they (the competing parties) are equivalent, *but here the School of Shammai are sharper*.
f. And if you wish I will say after the heavenly voice. The one who says they did not act [says this] because the heavenly voice had come out [and announced a decision]. And the one who says that they did act, it is R. Joshua['s opinion that he follows], for he said that we pay no heed to a heavenly voice. [emphasis added]

This gemara was composed, of course, centuries after the decision in favor of the views of the School of Hillel had been made. Its argument thus is quite remarkable. It begins by suggesting that even before the heavenly voice, the School of Shammai should probably not, in principle, have acted on the basis of its decisions. Why not? Because the School of Hillel was even then in the majority. But if this was so, then even before the heavenly voice it would be difficult to justify the position that the School of Shammai acted on the basis of their opinions. Nevertheless, this position is justified, and in a truly startling way. The gemara supports the view that they followed their opinions by asserting (e) that the School of Shammai were "sharper" than the School of Hillel. Having been sharper, they could ignore the general principle that the law follows the majority and could act on the basis of their own sharper insights.

The second part of the gemara's argument (f) reinforces this assertion. Even after the heavenly voice, the gemara notes, the School of Shammai could have followed their opinions if they, like R. Joshua in the oven of Akhnai story, concluded that heavenly voices have no business meddling in halakhic decision making. But even if this position had been accepted, we must still recall that (certainly) after the heavenly voice the School of Hillel was in the majority. This being so, the heavenly voice should at most only have been confirming an already obvious conclusion: the law follows the School of Hillel, the majority. How could they have denied this conclusion, then? Again, they could obviously be justified only by the principle that the majority does not rule when one party is sharper. Whether before or after the heavenly voice, it is necessary to posit that the Shammaites were sharper; otherwise, the position that suggests that they followed their opinions in practice could not be justified.[2]

What is the meaning of this text? It was clear to everyone, the author(s) of this text included, that the halakha in general followed the opinions of the Hillelites.[3] Yet this text admits that the Shammaites might have been sharper than the Hillelites. Being sharper, it was more likely, on the average, that their views were "correct." Halakha therefore is not to be equated with truth. On the contrary, according to the scenario created in this text, truth is more likely to be on the side that is not the halakha. This being the case, we can understand why the authors of the Bavli's commentary were just as willing to explore the meanings, assumptions, and consequences of the opinions of the Shammaites as they were those of the Hillelites. Because the Shammaite views might just as readily (or perhaps even more readily) contain true insights into God's will, they too, certainly, are worthy of extended attention.[4] Again, practice and truth might be independent of one another, and although the Bavli is certainly interested in the former, its preference is to explore the latter.

Another demonstration of the separation of truth and practice and of the value of pursuing theoretical truths independently of practice is found at Eruvin 13b. I quote those parts that are relevant for this discussion:

a. R. Aḥa b. Ḥanina said: It is revealed and known before "The One Who spoke and the world came into being" that there is none in the

generation of R. Meir who is comparable to him, and for what reason
[then] did they not fix the law according to him? Because his colleagues could not comprehend the fullness of his opinion. For he would
say for [that which is actually] impure "pure," and give it reason,
and say for [that which is actually] pure "impure," and give it reason.

b. It is taught [in a baraita]: His name is not really R. Meir, but R.
N'horai.[5] And why is he called R. Meir? Because he enlightens
(*"me'ir"*) the eyes of sages with halakha.

c. . . . Rabbi[6] said: The fact that I am sharper than my colleagues is
because I saw R. Meir from the rear, and had I seen him from the
front I would have been [even] sharper. . . .

d. R. Abbahu said R. Yoḥanan said: R. Meir had a student by the name
of Symmachus who would, for each and every impure thing, give
forty-eight reasons for its impurity, and for each and every pure thing
[he would give] forty-eight reasons for its purity.

e. It is taught [in a baraita]: There was an experienced student in Yavne
who would purify the crawling creature [who is explicitly declared
impure in the Torah; see Lev. 11:29–38] with one hundred and fifty
reasons.

f. Ravina[7] said: I will do so. . . .

g. R. Abba b. Samuel[8] said: For three years the School of Shammai and
the School of Hillel disputed, these saying "the law is like us" and
these saying "the law is like us." A heavenly voice emerged and said
"[Both] these and these are the words of the living God, and the law
is according to the School of Hillel."

h. Now, being that "these and these are the words of the living God,"
why did the School of Hillel merit having the law fixed according to
them?

i. Because they were pleasing and humble, and they taught their own
words and the words of the School of Shammai, and not only that,
but they [even] gave priority to the words of the School of Shammai
before their own words.

j. Like that which we have taught [in m. Suk. 2:7]: He whose head and
most of whose body were in the Sukkah, but his [dinner] table was in
the house, the School of Shammai declare this unfit and the School
of Hillel declare it fit. The School of Hillel said to the School of
Shammai—"Wasn't the case thus, that the elders of the School of
Shammai and the elders of the School of Hillel went to visit R. Yo-

ḥanan b. Ha-ḥoranit and found him sitting with his head and most of his body in the Sukkah and his table in the house!'' The School of Shammai said to them—''Is that a proof?! Even did they say to him: If this is how you have practiced you have never in your days fulfilled the commandment of Sukkah!''

k. . . . Our sages taught [in a baraita]: For two-and-a-half years the School of Shammai and the School of Hillel disputed, these saying ''it would have been better if man had not been created than been created,'' and these saying ''it would have been better if man had been created than not been created.'' They voted and decided ''it would have been better if man had not been created . . . but now that he has been created he should examine his actions. . . .''

Several ideas in this text stand out. To begin with, R. Meir is spoken of as being without rival in his generation because he can skillfully demonstrate that what is impure is pure, and what is pure is impure. One might think that such a skill is to be condemned in a society where matters of purity and impurity are so important. That is clearly not the case here. Despite the fact that Meir's colleagues do not understand his subtleties, he is spoken of as ''enlightening the eyes of the sages with halakha'' (b). Furthermore, the very sight of R. Meir would make someone sharper (c), as confirmed by Meir's student Symmachus, who could give many reasons for the purity or impurity of given things (d). Of course, this latter testimony shows that, despite his ability to confuse matters of purity and impurity through reasoned argument, his students knew what was really pure or impure and could give ample explanations of their rulings. Still, because of this same capability, R. Meir's view in the law was not generally accepted.

As the text progresses, it becomes clear that the capability to reason against halakha, as R. Meir could, is highly valued. The baraita (e) teaches approvingly of a student who could, through careful and abundant reasoning, argue for the purity of something that the Torah itself explicitly declares to be impure. Ravina (or Rav or Rava) boasted that he could do the same, giving at least one reason; though the gemara, in a step not recorded here, rejects his precise reasoning, the fact that such a capability would be praiseworthy is unambiguous throughout. The gemara wants to argue, through its combination of these traditions, that there is something valuable in the sharpness of reason, even when playfully turned against the halakhic tradition. The play of alternatives (as seen in the ''forty-eight reasons'' and the ''one hundred and fifty reasons'') is a demonstration of excellence, and the more alternatives a sage is able to suggest, this text claims, the more excellent is the Torah that he teaches.

Moreover, this text does more than separate practice and study, halakha and truth. It declares that the determination of truth—meaning a single, decisive, clear truth—is not the point. There is no other way to explain its insistence that even arguing against explicit rulings of the Torah is valuable. Although it can be difficult to ascertain precisely what the Torah means, it should not be difficult to conclude that an opinion that obviously and directly contradicts a law of the Torah (''pig is kosher'') is not possibly a part of divine truth. But in an almost perverse way we are told here that even such opinions are worth offering and pursuing. Because truth is so difficult (read: impossible) to ascertain, kernels of truth might reside in strange places. Even views that appear to be patently untrue, therefore, should be explored.

Before continuing, I should explain why I speak of these opinions as the views of ''the text'' and not of the individuals who are named in the text. In an earlier chapter I argued at length that attributions in the gemara should not be dismissed; they are likely to accurately identify the period in which a particular opinion was actually expressed. Why, then, ignore the attributions here? Because what makes the meanings delineated previously so eloquent in the text is not the individual opinions alone, but the way they are combined. No individual tradition states clearly and unambiguously what their combination does. It is necessary, for this reason, to ask when these traditions were combined. The answer, according to my understanding of the evidence, is at the time of composition, when the Bavli was finally constructed. This conclusion seems necessary because of the achronological arrangement of this text, suggesting that it did not form through natural accretion. Its logical progression, despite its lack of chronological arrangement, is too powerful to attribute to anyone but a later composer—one who already possessed the constituent traditions. It must be at the time of final composition, therefore, that these views emerge in their fullness. This is not to say that the individual views did not exist earlier; as I have made clear elsewhere, the evidence suggests that they did. But the full power of the chorus is not evident in the individual voices.

Indeed, the next part of the text confirms the interpretations suggested earlier. The tradition of Abba b. Samuel [(g), perhaps quoting an earlier tradition; cf. y. Yev. 1:6, 3b and parallels] declares that, even in disputes where diametrically opposed opinions are offered, ''these and these are

the words of the living God.'' How can this be so? Again, if either of
the opinions held the whole truth, then this evaluation would be absurd.
Since, however, no opinion contains the truth fully, divine truth may
reside in multiple opinions.

But if both the opinions of Hillel and Shammai (or their disciples) were
"the words of the living God," then why did the opinions of Hillel become halakha? Because, the text suggests (in a tradition paralleled in the
Yerushalmi; see y. Suk. 2:8, 53b), the Hillelites taught the Shammaite
opinions along with their own, even giving priority to the Shammaite
views. Why was such an approach so praiseworthy? Because it embodied
the notion that no opinion or interpretation fully contains the truth, and
alternatives must therefore be offered.[9] The Shammaites, who presumably taught only their own views (otherwise their opinions too could have
become halakha), did not recognize this essential fact. The Hillelites,
admitting that truth could be found even in contradictory views, merited
the fixing of halakha in accordance with their admittedly less than true
opinions.

Despite this one important shortcoming in the School of Shammai—
their failure to look beyond their own opinions—the context provided by
this text suggests that it is not in other ways to be considered inferior.
We should recall that a question of "fixing the halakha in accordance
with . . ." is the way this lengthy deliberation began. We were told (a)
that the law was not fixed in accordance with the views of R. Meir "because his colleagues could not comprehend the fullness of his opinion."
Here (h–i) it is the Shammaites who stand in the position of Meir (not
having the halakha fixed in accordance with their opinion), and so, while
the Hillelites may be humble and understanding, by association we are
led to conclude that the Shammaites are brilliant and clever. Again, as in
the Yevamot text, the Shammaites are sharper and so again, as there,
truth and halakha are less than likely to coincide.

Furthermore, the very Mishnah that is quoted to demonstrate why Hillel is preferred in halakha (j) is one of the few cases where the law might
actually be the opposite. What is striking in the Mishnah from Sukkah is
that the Shammaites respond to the attempted proof of the Hillelites, and
the Hillelites appear to have no rejoinder. The Yerushalmi (referred to
previously) takes this to mean that in this case the law should follow the
School of Shammai, and for other reasons the Shammaite view is also
supported in the Bavli (Suk. 3a). In either case, it is almost absurd to
demonstrate the halakhic preference for the Hillelite view by using a text
that both talmudim agree demonstrates the opposite! What possible rea-

son could there be for doing so? The answer, I think, is again to moderate claims for definitive halakha and for the connection between halakha and truth. Exceptions are plentiful and alternatives are often available. Even our confidence in rules such as "the law follows the School of Hillel" should not be complete, and for various reasons, including their possible greater theoretical brilliance, the School of Shammai might still, from time to time, emerge on top.

The text here (k) concludes with the same point. Perhaps to emphasize the fact that halakha is only a part of its concern, the text quotes a dispute between the Schools of Hillel and Shammai that has nothing to do with halakha proper. The question is whether the creation of mankind was a good thing or not, the negative opinion apparently being associated with the Shammaites and the positive opinion associated with the Hillelites (this because the Shammaites and the negative opinion are both mentioned first and the Hillelites and the positive opinion are mentioned second. The general sense of the personalities of the two schools and their founders would also lead us to make this association). It turns out, though, that the negative view, associated with the Shammaites, is the accepted one, and so at the end, notwithstanding halakhic preference to the contrary, the Shammaites emerge victorious. We thus can predict neither what will be accepted nor what will be rejected. Moreover, as far as this text is concerned, we cannot predict which view will be convincing or which will be closer to the truth. As in earlier texts, truth and practice, or even systemic rules and practice, do not necessarily align, and for this reason it is important to pursue many opinions. Human reason is worthy of examination even if it contradicts Torah; even more so if it contains part of the Torah's truth.

The Centering of Human Reason: Reason and Revelation

The opposition of scripture and reason, and the willingness even to let human reason prevail over Torah (and to be conscious of that willingness, stating it explicitly), is found in the Bavli as in no rabbinic document that preceded it.[10] It is particularly obvious in texts that compare and contrast the proper place of scripture (*kra'*) and logic (or reason, *sevara'*) in the formation of the tradition, including cases that derive identical lessons using both means interchangeably and others that suggest the possibility that scripture is unnecessary in the presence of compelling logic.

The former phenomenon, occurring in fourteen cases in the Bavli, is
identified with the formula "if you wish I will say [the opinion is justified
by] reasoning and if you wish I will say [that the opinion is justified by
a certain interpretation of] scripture.[11] Typically, though not always, this
approach is used to explain an earlier difference of opinion, and it often
responds to the explicit question "In what do they differ?" Crucially,
this interpretive approach is found only in the later anonymous level of
the Bavli, and there for the first time.

An example of this phenomenon follows:

Baba Batra 9a

a. R. Huna said: We investigate [the truthfulness of a beggar who comes
   asking] for food, but we do not investigate for clothing.
b. If you wish I will say [that his view is a consequence of his interpretation of] scripture, and if you wish I will say [that it is a consequence
   of his] reason.
c. If you wish I will say it is reason: this one (the one asking for clothes)
   is shamed [because of his nakedness] and this one [asking for food]
   is not shamed.
d. And if you wish I will say scripture: (Isa. 58:7) "Is it not (or, in
   context, "should you not") *parosh* your bread with the hungry . . .";
   it is written with a *shin* (making the word *parosh* = examine, and
   not *paros* = share), [meaning] examine [him] and then give it to him,
e. And there it is written (ibid.) "when you see the naked, you shall
   clothe him," [meaning] when you see him [you should do so] immediately.
f. And R. Judah said: We examine for clothing, but we do not examine
   for food.
g. If you wish I will say it is reasoning, and if you wish I will say it is
   scripture.
h. If you wish I will say it is reasoning: this one [who is hungry] is
   suffering and this one [who is naked] is not suffering (meaning, there
   is no actual pain),
i. And if you wish I will say it is scripture; here it is written (ibid.) "Is
   it not *paros* your bread with the hungry," [meaning] share immediately, as we actually read [the verse],
j. And there it is written (ibid.) "when you *see* the naked you shall
   clothe him," [meaning] when he is [clearly] seen to you [that he is
   not a liar].

Here, though the question is not asked explicitly, it is clear that the concern of the gemara is "in what do they (i.e., the disputing parties) differ?" The answer the gemara gives is that their difference of opinion may derive either from different reasoning (independent of scripture) or from different interpretations of scripture. Neither opinion is at this point preferred and, as is typical of this genre of explanation, the intent is to show that both reason and scripture can support either opinion.

Most striking in this approach is the willingness of the gemara to place human reason side by side with scripture as an essentially equal partner. Both are equally viable sources for rulings, and there is nothing in this or similar texts to suggest that scripture is in any way superior for these purposes. Earlier, such an approach would not have been thought legitimate. We already noted in chapter 2 (pp. 36–37) that in the earliest amoraic generations human reason was suspect and sources of recognized authority were obviously preferred. Hence both justifications and objections in earlier generations tend to depend on scripture or tannaitic sources; consider the multitude of occasions when an opinion is supported with a simple "scripture says. . . ."

Reason is also equated with scripture in the sense that neither offers access to unambiguous truth. Both, after all, are merely interpretations, and both can yield either of two contradictory opinions. When the question is "in what do they differ?" and the answer takes this form, inevitably both sides of the dispute will be supported. Both (interpretation of) scripture and human reason, therefore, are equally imperfect sources of law. The willingness to admit this condition is present, as noted previously, for the first time in the anonymous layers of the Bavli.

In fact, in related examples, the Bavli is even willing to admit that human reason may precede scripture (!). The texts that make this claim are repeated here.

Pesaḥim 21b = Ḥullin 114b

a. It is taught [in a baraita]: "You shall not eat anything that dies by itself, you may give it to the stranger who is in your gates, that he may eat it, or sell it to the foreigner . . ." (Deut. 14:21) . . . therefore, either to the stranger or to the foreigner you may sell it or give it, [these are] the words of R. Meir. R. Judah says: Things are as they are written [literally, meaning] it may be given to the stranger or sold to the foreigner.

b. What is R. Judah's reason? If you should think [that the law is] as
R. Meir says, let the Merciful [God] write [in scripture]: "To the
stranger who is in your gates you may give it, that he may eat it, and
[you may] sell''; why do I need [the word] "or"? Learn from it that
things are [literally] as they are written.

c. And R. Meir['s reasoning is this:] "or" [is needed to teach that] giving to the stranger has priority over selling to the foreigner.

d. And R. Judah [would answer this by saying:] this does not require
scriptural proof; since you are commanded to sustain a stranger but
you are not commanded to sustain a foreigner, *this does not require
scripture, it is [knowable by] reason.*

The point requires little elaboration. The Talmud here, in considering
the reasons for the difference in interpretation of R. Meir and R. Judah
in the baraita, suggests that a certain conclusion that R. Meir derives
from a particular scriptural phenomenon should not require scriptural proof
at all. Why not? Because the same conclusion could be known from the
application of reason. If reason could have given us the same conclusion,
then scripture didn't have to do the same. In other words, in the opinion
of this text, we can know what scripture *may mean* only after we first
know the lessons of human reason. Apply reason first, then ask what we
do not yet know. It is the details that have not yet been defined that
scripture may relate to. But, again, the possible meanings of scripture are
known only after human reason has been applied.

Ketubot 22a

a. R. Asi said: From where in the Torah [do I derive the principle] "the
mouth that prohibited is the mouth that [by right also] permitted?"
For it says (Deut. 22:16) "I gave my daughter to this man as a wife
. . . ," [meaning that when he said] "to the man" he prohibited
her [to all men, not, at that instant, knowing whom he would desig-
nate, but then saying] "this" he permitted her [to that particular man].

b. *What do I need a scriptural proof for? It is logical* (= reasonable;
this is the same Aramaic word—*sevara'*—as above) [that if] he prohibited her he should [have the right to] permit her! . . .

The point here and in the last example is the same. Again, reason
renders scripture unnecessary. Again, as well, this is the belief of the
anonymous Bavli. This approach is typical at the final level of the Bavli's

inquiry, and there is little evidence for this view, in an explicit, self-conscious form, at an earlier stage.

If the gemara admits, as we have seen, that the meaning of scripture is dependent on an independent system, not found within the boundaries of scripture itself, then this independent system, human reason, is to a significant extent the very source of the meaning of scripture. Theoretically, at least, human reason becomes an even more powerful source of meaning than the words of scripture itself, for scripture can be judged only against the background of what it is not (human reason). If the implications of this position are recognized, and if the position extends beyond this couple of examples, then the authors of the anonymous Bavli who pioneer this approach are making a radical statement indeed.

In fact, the assertion of the power of reason over scripture, in the manner described, can be found in the hundreds of cases in which the Bavli suggests "scripture should have said. . . ." The theoretical implications of this interpretive approach are so profound that it merits a careful and somewhat detailed consideration.

There are in the Bavli over two hundred occasions in which the text proposes that scripture "should" have been written in a form other than the one it ultimately assumed.[12] Approximately a dozen of these are attributed to amoraim, and the rest (over two hundred) are recorded in the anonymous voice of the gemara itself. The precise nature of the proposed alternatives covers a relatively wide range of possibilities; nevertheless, most assume the following reasoning. If scripture could have expressed itself in other ways, the way it ultimately did choose to express its (= God's) opinion must be taken to be meaningful. If so, its precise form, in light of the alternative (or alternatives), may serve as the source of interpretation. In some sense this method suggests that all scripture may be said to be "superfluous," because more economically worded alternatives can almost always be proposed.

The cases that are presumably the earliest, that is, those that are attributed to amoraim, tend to be the least daring. Almost all either point out a simple allegedly superfluous element in scripture or ask the reader to read the scriptural text more closely, without genuinely considering an alternative.[13] A more daring example at Yoma 81a finds several amoraim suggesting how scripture might have communicated a particular concept. Their proposals are pure invention though, because they apparently believe that the given concept was not actually recorded in scripture. While they try their hands at composing scripture then—a radical concept indeed—they do not actually propose alternatives to specific scripture. As we will see, more specific alternatives of the anonymous author turn out, in fact, to be far more radical.

One case, attributed to R. Yosef (Zev. 99a), is not only purportedly the earliest of the recorded examples of this phenomenon, but in some ways it is among the most remarkable. Referring to Leviticus 6:19 ("The priest who offers the sin-offering should eat it . . .") Yosef remarks: "Being that what is [true meaning of] 'he should eat it'? 'He should divide it.' So let the Merciful write [in scripture] 'He should divide it.' What is [the meaning when God writes, instead,] 'He should eat it'? . . ." R. Yosef assumes here that the rabbinic understanding of the scriptural term (i.e., that "he should eat" really means "he should divide") is its correct meaning and that the "alternative" term actually employed by scripture may, therefore, be taken as the source of an additional teaching. This means that the "real meaning" of scripture can be proposed only by the rabbis themselves, and since they know the "real meaning," theoretically any time scripture expresses itself in a less than straightforward fashion (when, again, what is straightforward is defined by the rabbis) this may supply an additional source for midrash.

The assumption made here was certainly developing among the amoraim. It is implicit, sometimes, even in earlier texts. But, as the sheer numbers demonstrate, its full force was not appreciated until the period of the composition of the Bavli itself, and it is therefore in that period that the greatest number of these examples, and certainly the most radical such examples, are found.

To appreciate the impact of these interpretive approaches, it is essential that we understand the assumptions that they make. The Bavli proposes a particular scriptural economy that, in its literalness and comprehensiveness, is unparalleled in most earlier rabbinic texts. What it claims is that every scriptural feature teaches one specific matter of halakha, no more and no less. Several lessons may not be derived from a single such feature, and every single feature, theoretically, should yield one particular lesson. This economy is expressed in graphic terms at Menahot 94a:

MISHNAH:
The two loaves [to be offered on the Shavuot holiday (see Lev. 23:17)] are to be kneaded one by one and baked one by one. The show breads (Lev. 24:5–9) are to be kneaded one by one and baked two by two. . . .

GEMARA:
a. Where are these words [of law derived] from?
b. [From that] which our rabbis have taught: "two tenth measures shall

be in one cake (Lev. 24:5)," this teaches that they [= the show
breads] are to be kneaded one by one. How[14] do I know that this is
true also for the two loaves? Scripture says "shall be (ibid.)." And
from where [do I know] that they are baked two by two? Scripture
says "And you shall place them (ibid., vs. 6)." Is it possible that this
is true also with the two loaves? Scripture says "them" [meaning
them and not others].

c. *[But] this [word] "them," you have [already] interpreted it!*
d. If so [meaning, if it may not be used for anything else, then] let
   scripture say "placethem" [i.e., let it use the pronominal suffix to
   express this idea]; what is [its intent when it writes, instead,] "and
   you shall place them" [using a separate pronoun]? You may [there-
   fore] learn from it two things. [emphasis added]

Both the general method and its assumptions are explicitly articulated
in this example. In theory, a single phenomenon may yield only one
lesson (c). For this reason "them" could not have been used to teach
two different things. But since scripture might have been written in another fashion [as suggested at (d)], "them" turns out to be not one phenomenon, but two. *It is both what it is and what it is not.* Being actually
two phenomena, it can serve as the source of two lessons.

The nature of the alternatives, the "what it is not," tends, even in the
anonymous gemara, to be rather modest. Most cases simply point to possible superfluous phenomena in the text, just as had the amoraic examples. But some of the cases proposed in the Bavli are radical indeed,
suggesting even alternatives that are clearly intolerable according to normal rules of biblical grammar or syntax. The following example will
suffice to demonstrate the extent to which the Talmud is willing to go.

Baba Qamma 85b

a. R. Pappa said in the name of Rava: Scripture said "he shall surely be
   healed *(verapo' yerape')*" (Exod. 21:19), [meaning that a damaging
   party is] to give [payment for] healing [even] in a place [where payment for] damage [is given].
b. [But] this [phrase] is needed for the teaching of the school of R.
   Ishmael, who taught: "and he shall surely be healed," from here [we
   learn that] permission is given to the physician to heal.

c. If [this is all it is intended to teach] scripture should write "and the physician shall heal *(verofe' yirpa'),"* [the fact that it didn't write it this way means that from the alternative] you may learn [the ruling described in (a)]. . . .

d. Still, it is needed, as we said, to teach a scriptural source for healing [when damage has been done].

e. If [that is all it intends to teach,] scripture should say either "to heal to heal *(rapo' rapo')"* or "he should be healed he should be healed *(yerape' yerape')";* what is [the intended lesson of the alternative] "to heal he should be healed (or, he shall surely be healed; *verapo' yerape')"?* To teach [the lesson suggested at (a)]. . . .

The first proposed alternative (c) is not distant from the biblical original, nor does it offend biblical rules of expression. But the second alternatives (e) do violence to rules of grammar and are patently unacceptable to anyone (like the rabbis) even casually familiar with the biblical idiom. What this, and other examples like it,[15] means is that the alternatives the rabbis propose, which as we have seen are the source of additional derivations, may even extend beyond the limits that scripture would seem to suggest. At this level, the only true limitation is the imaginations of the Talmudic authors.

Let me spell out the implications of this Talmudic method. The Torah (and to a lesser extent the rest of scripture) is the source, by derivation, of much of Jewish law. By reading the Torah the rabbis believed that they could know something of the divine Will. But they did not allow for a simple reading of the divine text. Numerous rules were assumed that directed their reading and influenced their derivations. One of these rules, suggesting that each feature of scripture could yield only one lesson, would seem to have limited the breadth and variety of laws that could emerge from the text.

However, the rabbis of the Bavli worked around this apparent limitation. They granted that one scriptural feature could yield only one lesson (actually, they seem to be the ones who suggested this in the first place), but they defined "scriptural feature" in an extremely creative way.[16] Any expression of scripture had to be considered, they believed, not only for what it was, but also for what it wasn't. Scripture could in theory always have been written in a way different than it finally was, and so each positive choice represents a rejection of one or more alternatives. Each decision not to express something in a particular way is also a meaningful "scriptural feature," and so each such decision may itself act as the source for derivation.

Of course, all these alternatives could be proposed only by the rabbis. There was no other source for them. Because, in theory, the meaning of Torah can be fathomed only in relation to the rejected alternatives and because those alternatives could be invented only by the rabbis, in theory the meaning of any given scripture is in a profound way dependent on the contribution of the rabbinic imagination and on its sense of "the other Torah." By this scheme, the revealed scripture always echoes a suppressed alternative, an alternative that might be brought to the surface at any time by the rabbis, and so the fullness of revelation can emerge only after the rabbinic imagination is asserted and its alternatives proposed.

In theory, the number of such alternatives is endless. There is always another way that the Torah might have been written. Since the alternatives all yield new derivations, this means that the Torah may be, for the rabbis who propose the alternatives, an infinite source of derivation. As long as there is another alternative, scripture has another lesson to give. This is particularly the case because the rules by which the alternatives are regulated are, in effect, known to no one. As we saw, even alternatives that the Torah could never in fact have included, contradicting as they do basic rules of biblical expression, were nevertheless proposed by the Talmudic authors, and just as the alternatives are theoretically without limit, therefore, so too (in theory) are the new lessons that can be discovered in the biblical text.

To state matters simply, what we witness here is *the triumph of human (rabbinic) reason over scripture*. No scripture has any meaning in the absence of reason not merely because basic interpretation and explanation are necessary, but because no interpretation or explanation is theoretically complete without considering the alternative scriptures—those existing in the rabbinic imagination, which has now become an essential part of revelation itself. The human mind becomes here an ongoing source of revelation, and it renders written revelation absolutely dependent on its dictates. In this way, the claim attributed to R. Avdimi of Haifa at Baba Batra 12a, that "from the day the Temple was destroyed prophecy was taken from the prophets and given to the sages," is literally realized in the pages of the Bavli.

One might imagine that so radical an approach permits a nearly complete dissolution of boundaries or limits. This is not so, however, and it is for this reason that I have been careful to emphasize the *theoretical* nature of this approach. On most of the occasions in which this approach is used, the gemara seeks to explain either how two views can coexist simultaneously or why one sage did not interpret a particular scriptural passage like another sage. In the former instance, the problem is generated by the "scriptural economy" discussed earlier. The Bavli insists that one scripture can yield only one lesson, but earlier traditions often belie this insistence. It is thus relatively common to find several derivations that emerge from the same text. For the Bavli this cannot be tolerated, and so one of the ways that it solves this problem is by suggesting that what appears to be one scripture is actually several scriptural features (in consideration of the theoretical alternatives, as the method reviewed previously proposes) and the multiple derivations therefore do not contradict the rule of scriptural economy. The point, then, is to support earlier traditions, not to invent new ones. The same is true in the latter instance, when the Bavli uses this method to respond to the question "why does so-and-so not interpret this like so-and-so?" The answer, according to this method, is that one of the parties recognizes a meaningful alternative that the other party does not. Again the point is to explain earlier traditions, and so, in fact, the inventive creativity of this approach remains theoretical, not practical.

A method to explain or support earlier traditions, this interpretive approach remains strongly bound by the community of those traditions. The alternatives are never proposed in a vacuum; quite the contrary. The author who suggests such an interpretation always knows the answer before he begins, and so, as outrageous as a particular scriptural alternative might be, nothing new—indeed nothing not yet proposed within the rabbinic community—can emerge from this method.

Though it is bound by community, however, this in no way diminishes its radical theoretical implications. The claim made by the authors of this method is that the "torah" of human reason is an essential foundation of the written Torah of God. This is a resounding affirmation of that reasoned Torah, that *Torah sheb'al pe*. Symbolically, this places the rabbinic contribution to the broad tradition at a level similar to the written revelation itself. The process that dominates the Bavli's approach emerges here confident and triumphant. The argumentational/deliberative process, called talmud torah, is no less central to the enterprise than the recorded word of God.

The *idea* that alternative scriptures can be proposed is not unique to the anonymous Bavli. It is on a number of occasions, as we saw, attributed to amoraim. It also appears, though rarely, in the Yerushalmi.[17] What makes it so meaningful as a phenomenon in the Bavli is the frequency with which it appears in that document. Appearing, as noted, on over two hundred occasions, it ceases to be a mere idea and is transformed into a method of symbolic impact. It represents the Bavli's willingness to place the human imagination at the center of the enterprise and to privilege it to virtually the same extent as written Torah. This centrality of human reason is that much more remarkable in view of the theoretical origins of this precise method. It will be recalled that the notion of suppressed alternatives to Torah is necessitated with some frequency by the assumption, insisted upon by the Bavli itself, that one scriptural feature teaches only one lesson, what we have called the Bavli's "scriptural economy." The Bavli, in insisting upon this economy, is investing the Torah with an immense mythical power. It is imagined, according to this assumption, that the Torah is a kind of grand divine code, and it is up to the rabbis to figure out the precise meaning of each detail of the code. The Torah, in other words, does not "speak in the language of human beings."[18] To the contrary, it is so infused with the divine that no element of it should escape scrutiny or fail to yield a teaching. But at the same time that the Torah is thus mystified, it becomes largely dependent on the contribution of human reason and its alternative scriptures before it can mean anything at all. Those very same authors who transformed the status of the written Torah, therefore, were the ones who sought to equate with it the Torah of the sages. Doing so they enhanced, as never before, the status of both.

Human Reason on Its Own Terms: Learning Becomes Torah

The enhancement of the position of human reason, both on its own terms and in relation to Torah, is widely evidenced in the Bavli. In some ways, the most interesting illustration of this development is the well-known story, found at Shabbat 31a of the exchanges between potential converts and Shammai and Hillel. Its interest derives from the precise nature of its proposals, which we shall see, and its elaboration of the figure of Hillel, the great (legendary?) "founding father" of rabbinic Judaism. Still, this text must be considered with caution because it claims to be of tannaitic origin—at least in significant part; some elements are formulated in an Aramaic that is clearly not tannaitic—and it is partially paralleled in another treatise that claims tannaitic origin, Avot d'Rabbi Nathan.[19] Nevertheless, it is my claim that it may justifiably be used to illustrate a view elaborated fully in the Bavli, and not before. I reach this conclusion because the Bavli text is not paralleled fully in the Avot d'R. Nathan version (neither in version A nor B),[20] and the part that finds no parallel (II below) is in many ways the most important for the claim I will make later. The absence of this segment before the Bavli allows us to consider its version independently.[21]

The part of the narrative that concerns us follows.

I. a. Our Rabbis taught: It happened that a gentile came before Shammai and said to him "how many torahs do you have?"

   b. He said to him: "Two, a Written Torah and an Oral Torah."

   c. He said to him: "With respect to the written one, I believe you, but with respect to the oral I do not believe you. Convert me on the condition that you teach me [only] the Written Torah."

   d. [Shammai] rebuked him and sent him out in anger.

   e. He came before Hillel [and stated the same condition, and] he converted him.

   f. On the first day he said to him [in naming the letters of the Hebrew alphabet] "aleph, bet, gimel, dalet." The next day he reversed them.

   g. He said to him: "But yesterday you didn't say it to me this way!"

   h. He said to him: *"Have you not [inevitably] depended upon my [words]? With respect to the Oral [Torah] also depend on me."*

II. a. It happened at another time that a gentile came before Shammai and said to him "convert me on the condition that you teach me the whole Torah while I stand on one foot."

   b. He pushed him with the beam of the building that was in his hand.

   c. He came before Hillel [and said the same thing, and] he converted him.

   d. He said to him: "That which is hateful to you do not do to your fellow—*this is the whole Torah and the rest is interpretation.* Go and learn." [emphasis added]

This text has been quoted typically as a demonstration of the rabbinic value, exemplified by Hillel, of forbearance and humility, because this is the subject of the broader Talmudic context into which it is set. But to demonstrate such a value, many different specific subjects could have been chosen for the content of the exchanges. The question must be, therefore, why these specific exchanges? What value or attitude is expressed in these subjects in particular that makes them the focus of attention in these narratives?

The precise subject of both of these exchanges is the Oral Torah. In the first instance, this is explicit. The potential convert approaches Shammai and Hillel and asks them about the existence of a second, Oral Torah, and they both insist that it too is part of "Torah." The manner in which Hillel, in the end, persuades his interlocutor is particularly meaningful: he demonstrates that, on the most basic level, the Written Torah is dependent on oral tradition and that, in fact, we have no access whatever to the Written Torah without the aid of its oral explanation. Written Torah requires Oral Torah, therefore, and it is nonsensical to insist on the former without the latter. Of course, as this story had it, the convert is convinced.

In the second instance, the question does not address the matter of Oral Torah explicitly but, on a different level, Hillel's answer does. His claim in his answer is that, aside from one particular teaching ("that which is hateful . . ."), the rest of the (written) Torah is *interpretation*. The Oral Torah, too, of course, is largely interpretation—so this response turns out to be a fundamental equation of the Written and Oral Torahs. The Oral Torah is interpretation, but so too is the written. What, then, is the essential difference between them? Furthermore, even "the whole Torah" is not actually a verse from scripture but is itself an interpretation (i.e., of the intent of the Torah as a whole). Therefore, not only is "the rest" of the Torah interpretation, but so too is "the whole Torah." Everything in the Written Torah is, according to this claim, interpretation, and in this sense the Written and Oral Torahs are fundamentally (we might even say ontologically) the same.

In these stories, Hillel, the "founding father" of rabbinic Judaism, is represented as being a competent defender of the oral tradition. What he does, in more or less explicit terms, is to equate the Oral and the Written Torah and to claim that the two are totally interdependent. As Neusner properly notes, the fact that this combination of narratives appears for the first time in the Bavli demonstrates only that at the time of its composition Jews (or, more precisely, rabbis who composed texts such as this) "believed in the myth of the two Torahs . . . [and] ascribed that conviction to Hillel."[22] Since the ideology described explicitly here echoes directly the views that emerge from other phenomena that are restricted primarily to the compositional levels of the Bavli, as noted at length earlier, it seems reasonable to conclude that this strong an equation of the oral and written traditions is an innovation of the Bavli. It is the Bavli that enhances the status of the human contribution and transforms the process of "Oral Torah" into its central concern.

This equation is also evident in the Bavli's extension of its scriptural economy to earlier rabbinic texts. Just as the Bavli considers redundancies in the Written Torah to be problems requiring explanation, so too does it consider redundancies in earlier rabbinic traditions. Again, since this development parallels those suggested previously, it seems reasonable to conclude that it was in the Bavli, for the first time, that the equation of Written and Oral Torahs was assumed with such absolute confidence.

what does it effesy?

If the process that both yields Oral Torah and is itself Oral Torah, which is here called talmud torah, in fact underwent a transformation in status in the Bavli, we would expect to find evidence of this transformation in texts that address talmud torah (Torah study) explicitly. Such evidence may be found in two areas, in those texts that discuss the requirement of reciting a blessing before studying Torah and in those that discuss the value of *torah lishma,* that is, Torah study for its own sake.

The question of whether a blessing is required for Torah study, and for what forms of Torah study, is important, because it reveals to us whether a particular type of study was considered by the rabbis to be a *mitzvah,* that is, a fully compelling religious requirement. If a blessing was required, that means it was deemed reasonable to say, with respect to a specific act of study, "blessed are You Lord, our God, King of the universe, who has commanded us to perform this act." The issue, then, is one of divine imprimatur, and a blessing would be evidence that such divine sanction was thought to exist.

The Mishnah knows nothing of a blessing for Torah study. The Mekhilta speaks of a blessing for "Torah,"[23] but there is no reason to believe that "Torah" in that context is anything more than study or recitation of Written Torah. The first clear mention of a blessing for study of something more than Written Torah is found in the Yerushalmi.

Berakhot 1:5 (3c)

a. Samuel said: If someone awakes to study before reading the *Shema,* he must bless. . . .

b. R. Huna said: It appears [proper that] *midrash* [interpretation of scripture] requires a blessing, [but the study of] *halakhot* [laws] does not require a blessing.

c. R. Simon [said] in the name of R. Joshua b. Levi: Both *midrash* and *halakhot* require a blessing.

That the "mitzvah" of Torah study extended, in the Yerushalmi, beyond the study of scripture should be no surprise. Its own agenda of study clearly includes far more than Written Torah. Still, what is significant in these rulings is not only what does require a blessing, but also what does not. On the one hand, in all of these statements, something beyond the strict study of scripture is viewed as being a divinely sanctioned commandment. According to the final opinion (c) both rabbinic interpretation of scripture and the study of rabbinic rulings merit the recitation of a blessing. What is missing, on the other hand—as will become evident when comparing this text to a similar discussion in the Bavli—is reasoning and argumentation, that is, sophisticated rabbinic analysis of earlier traditions (the form of both talmuds, though far more elaborate in the Bavli). In the Bavli, for the first time, such study merits the recitation of a formula of divine confirmation.

The Bavli's discussion is highly problematic, there being a wide variety of versions recorded in manuscripts and elsewhere.[24] I translate according to the Vilna edition.

Berakhot 11b

a. R. Judah said in the name of Samuel: If someone awoke to study before reading the Shema he must bless. . . .

b. R. Huna said: For [study of] scripture one must bless, but for *midrash* one need not bless.

c. R. Eleazar said: For scripture and *midrash* one must bless, but for *mishnah* one need not bless.

d. And R. Yoḥanan said: Even for *mishnah* one must bless. . . .

e. And Rava said: Even for *talmud* [sophisticated reasoning and deliberation] one must bless.

As I said, it is difficult to depend on a particular version of this text, given the many alternatives. What is crucial, though, is that most versions—like the one recorded here—include reference to *talmud*.

Only in the Bavli is *talmud*—that is (in the present context), *the study of study*—thought to be a *mitzvah* of essentially divine status and therefore requiring a blessing. This development is reflected in the Bavli's overall affection for rich, open-ended deliberation, and this text represents an explicit admission of the implicit valuation of study that the Bavli's form suggests. Moreover, if the attribution of this view to Rava is correct, then this tradition will correspond to a broader phenomenon that we earlier associated with this generation. As noted, it was Rava and his generation who for the first time thought argumentation to be worthy of extensive preservation and who often addressed argumentation *(tal-mud)* on its own terms. In that generation its value was first recognized, and so it would make sense that it was then, for the first time, that *talmud* admitted definition and enhancement with the statement "You have commanded me to engage in this act."

The second phenomenon that reflects the enhanced status of Torah study (talmud torah) in the Bavli is a shift in the expressed purpose of Torah study. In rabbinic documents before the Bavli, Torah study is clearly valued; their very form is often an expression of this fact. But when those documents express a judgment concerning the purpose of such study, it becomes evident that it is valued primarily for its capability to lead those who engage in it to the practice of God's commandment (i.e., whenever it is possible to fathom the purpose ascribed to Torah study at all). It seems to be for this reason, too, that Torah study is understood to lead to reward (though one shouldn't study in order to gain reward).

The study of Torah is rarely discussed in the Mishnah (aside from Avot, to be considered later). In the single text[25] that is relevant to our present concern (Peah 1:1), where Torah study is evaluated with relation to other mitzvot, the act is simply a source of reward. This Mishnah's well-known statement, "These things have no measure . . . and Talmud Torah," makes no claim for the independent value of Torah study. "No measure" means merely that the time allotted to it is not precisely determined by the law, not (necessarily) that study is cherished on its own terms. Similarly, the claim, in the end of the same Mishnah, that "talmud torah is equal to them all" is only a declaration that its reward exceeds that for all of the other acts listed in the Mishnah—perhaps for the very reason that it leads to the performance of all of those other acts. In the absence of other evidence, there is no reason to assume that this text would claim study to be an act of independent merit even when not connected to performance of the mitzvot being studied.

Avot, which speaks at great length about the value of Torah study, is more explicit, but not qualitatively different. Regular study of Torah is mentioned several times in Avot (1:15, 2:12, 2:14). Its association with reward is also common (2:16, 3:2, 4:10). But when the purpose of study is explored, the emphasis is clear: "He who learns in order to teach, he will be granted sufficient [power] to learn and to teach. He who learns in order to perform [the commandments that he is learning], he will be granted sufficient [power] to learn, to teach, to observe, and to perform" (4:5). The hierarchy of values leads to performance. If this is the purpose of one's study, then he will gain all the benefits of study. Learning to

teach is inferior to this and, by derivation, there can be little doubt that
learning for its own sake would not be viewed kindly. The same emphasis is articulated elsewhere: "What is essential is not study, but practice"
(1:7). The one possibly noteworthy variation is the parallel drawn at 3:3
between speaking words of Torah (= Torah study) and the sacrificial
service. Sacrifice is, of course, a gift to God, of independent merit. If
words of Torah study are also such gifts, as this text suggests, then this
may be the first occasion that the value of Torah study for its own sake
is alluded to. The allusion is modest, however, and, its presence notwithstanding, it is clear that, when Avot considers the purpose of Torah study,
its opinion is that study is meant to serve practice. It has little essential
value independent of this end.

The same view persists in the tannaitic midrashim. Again, there is no
doubt that study is a meritorious act, but where its purpose is discussed,
study is—with one possible exception—meant to serve action. Consider,
for example, the following text from Sifrei Deuteronomy:

> "And you shall learn them and you shall observe to do them" (Deut. 5:1)—
> this teaches that performance is dependent on learning, but learning is not
> dependent on action. . . . And R. Tarfon and R. Akiba and R. Yose the
> Galilean had already taken a meal at the house of Aris in Lydda, and this
> question was asked before them: Which is greater, study or performance?
> R. Tarfon said: performance is greater. R. Akiba said: study is greater. They
> all responded and said: *study is greater for study leads to action.*[26]

Study is considered here to be "greater" than performance, but this is
only by virtue of its capability to lead to performance. Performance is
dependent on study because one cannot perform properly unless one first
studies, but study is meant to serve performance, and the highest value,
therefore, is the performance of the commandments.[27] "Greater" in this
context should be understood in mere utilitarian terms; performance is
impossible without prior study, but the priority of study is not a priority
of values. Performance is a greater value, and the "greatness" of study
is only in its service of performance.

The same point is equally as straightforward in the Sifra. There we
read: " 'If you walk in the ways of my precepts, and observe my commandments, and perform them' (Lev. 26:3)—[this teaches that] one should
learn in order to perform, and not learn in order not to perform, for the
one who learns in order not to perform, it would have been better had he
not been created" (Beḥuqotai, beginning). The translation "in order not
to perform," though literal, is not fully accurate. The opposition being

set up in the midrash is between the one whose study is meant to lead to performance and the one whose study is not meant to lead to performance. The opinion expressed here, therefore, is that study that is not meant to lead to performance is to be condemned. Study, once again, is intended primarily to serve performance, and to separate study and performance is, according to the rabbis who composed this text, an indefensible move.

The single case in the Midrashei Halakha that I have found that may contradict this opinion is a brief text in the Sifrei, immediately preceding the text quoted earlier, that discusses the mitzvah of Torah study and when that mitzvah came to be incumbent upon the people Israel. The midrash addresses its subject in this way:

> "And it shall be if you heed my commandments . . ." (Deut. 11:13)—
> why is this said? For it is said "and you shall learn them and take care to
> do them" (Deut. 5:1). Do I understand [from this verse] that they were not
> obligated to study until they were obligated to perform [a given command-
> ment]? Scripture says "And it shall be if you heed . . ."—this teaches that
> they were obligated to study immediately [even before the commandments
> that they were to study would become practically applicable].

Clearly, this midrash separates the study of a given commandment from its performance, making study an independent commandment, required in its own right. The context, however, must be considered. The specific problem that confronts the author of this text is the strange and unique situation of the Israelites in the desert, who already had the Torah but could not yet practice significant elements of it. Did they have to study mitzvot that could not be practiced, the midrash asks. Surely they did. But what is the intent of the author in drawing this lesson? Does he intend for this to be a lesson to later Jews, such as the community of the rabbis following the destruction of the Temple, who also were unable to perform some of the Torah's commandments? If so—and this seems reasonable— then this is a claim for the independent worth of Torah study, at least in circumstances where the Torah's content is no longer practicable. But we may also understand the midrash's lesson to pertain only to the special situation of the generation of Sinai, in which case its discussion is purely academic. In any case, even admitting the first interpretation, the most we can claim on the basis of this text is that commandments should continue to be studied even after, for historical reasons, they have fallen into disuse. There is no suggestion that study of relevant commandments might similarly be thought meritorious when independent of practice.

The Tosefta also expresses the possibility that, in limited circumstances, study as such might have independent value. This is true in the three instances—the first involving the rebellious son (San. 11:6), the second involving the condemned city (ibid. 14:1), and the third outbreaks on the walls of houses (Neg. 6:1)—when the Tosefta declares that the law at hand was never meant to be practiced and was included in the Torah only in order that the student might "study and receive reward." These traditions record unambiguously the opinion that study merits reward even independent of performance. But we should, at the same time, recognize how limited this claim is. It applies in the Tosefta (subsequent variations will be noted later) only to three mitzvot that were so problematic for the rabbis that they wanted to claim that they had never been and would never be in force. For this reason they had to justify their inclusion in the Torah. But there is no hint here or elsewhere in the Tosefta that the same principle could be extended to Torah study in general. This extension would not be made in rabbinic texts until considerably later.

The opinion of the Yerushalmi, as far as I have been able to find, is identical with the predominant view expressed in Avot and the Midrashei Halakha—though dissenting views are recorded in context. The Sifrei text quoted earlier, discussing the relative worth of study and performance, appears in the Yerushalmi (Pes. 3:7, 30b; Hag. 1:7, 76c) with a difference that is potentially crucial. Unlike the Sifrei, which qualifies its claim for the primacy of study by explaining that "study leads to practice," the Yerushalmi records the same claim without any qualification, suggesting that study truly is primary. However, while understanding this in fact to be the lesson of the tradition at hand, the Yerushalmi goes on in its own deliberation to limit the extent of this claim. Study is primary, we learn, only if there is someone else available to perform a given deed (in this context specifically the burial of the dead). But if there is no one else available and it really comes down to the decision "which do I do, study or performance?" then performance takes precedence over study. The same is true in certain circumstances, such as the burial of a stranger, even when someone else could perform the mitzvah. In any case, where there is an outright conflict—where the mitzvah will go unfulfilled unless you interrupt your study—then study is to be interrupted and performance is to be preferred.

In Berakhot [1:2 (5), 3b], too, the relative merits of study and performance are discussed at length, and the conclusion is again resoundingly in favor of the primacy of performance. The text quoted earlier from the Sifra ("one who studies without intention to perform, it would have been better had he not been created") is repeated and elaborated ("it would have been better if his placenta had been turned over on his face and he never emerged into the world") in that context, and study as an independent pursuit is questioned even for a zealot of study such as R. Shimon b. Yohai.

Finally, the same point is made in tractate Hagigah (1:7, 76c), but there with an important linguistic twist. In a tradition attributed to R. Huna, the gemara declares: "Learn Torah [even] not for its sake, for as a consequence of [doing so] not for its sake one will come to [do so] for its sake." From context it is clear that "for its sake" means "in order to perform"; the same story from the Sifrei which questions the relative value of study and performance is also quoted here. So, again, the emphasis of the Yerushalmi is on performance. But the linguistic shift from "in order to perform" to "for its sake" *(lishma)* may have important consequences. The term *lishma* is nowhere used in connection with Torah study before this Yerushalmi text.[28] Its meaning from context, as noted, is identical with the phrase "in order to perform," but it introduces an ambiguity that is crucial in this context. "For its sake" might mean, as it does here, "for the sake of the commandment that is described in the text" (or something to that effect).[29] But it might also mean "for its own sake," meaning for the sake of Torah [= study], as such, independent of the commandments that might be performed. It is this ambiguity of meaning that will allow this second interpretation to develop, and it is in association with this ambiguous but pregnant phrase that the independent value of Torah study will finally be fully realized (though not yet in the Yerushalmi).

This phrase "for its [own] sake" is used commonly in the Bavli in connection with Torah study. At Taanit 7a the phrase appears in a purportedly tannaitic text; at Sukkah 49b its use is amoraic. On both of these occasions its meaning is ambiguous, and if one approaches them with no preconceived notion of the meaning of this term, there is no reason to claim that it suggests the independent value of Torah study "for its own sake."

On the other hand, the statement attributed to R. Huna in the Yerushalmi is repeated in the Bavli with a crucial variation. In a tradition attributed to R. Judah in the name of Rav (Pes. 50b and parallels, a total of seven times) we find the following recommendation: "One should cer-

tainly engage in Torah and mitzvot even not for its sake, for as a consequence of [doing them] not for its sake one comes [to do them] for its
sake." The parallel between "Torah" and "mitzvot" (commandments)
necessitates that we understand Torah to be independent of performance.
Just as commandments may be done for their own sake—that is, with no
ulterior motive—so too may Torah study be done for its own sake. This
means that Torah study is considered here to be an independent mitzvah,
meritorious in its own regard and worthy even separate from immediate
application in practice. Just how far this independent merit extends, however, is not yet clear. We will return to this consideration.

The fact that the term "for its own sake" *(lishma)* does take this meaning in the foregoing tradition should not lead us to conclude that this is
its meaning in the earlier texts or that this opinion is the predominant one
in the Bavli. The alternative opinion, that study is important primarily
because it leads to action, is also common in the Bavli. The Sifrei story
that gives priority to performance is repeated in the Bavli (Kid. 40b)
essentially without comment (and cf. B.Q. 17a). The statement of the
Sifra and the Yerushalmi that a person who studies without intention to
perform should not have been created is also repeated in the Bavli (Ber.
17a), though there with the term "for its [own] sake" replacing the phrase
"in order to perform." As in the earlier documents, there is no ambiguity
in the Bavli's rendition of this tradition that performance is the primary
concern. In this context the meaning of *lishma* is clearly the same as that
in the Yerushalmi, and the potential ambiguity yields nothing new.

But, as noted, there is at least one tradition in the Bavli that, unlike
all precedents, suggests that Torah study, broadly conceived, is an act of
independent value and merit. Though that tradition does not define the
consequences of its opinion—what, practically, does it mean that Torah
study has such independent merit?—another Bavli text, at Sanhedrin 99b,
discusses "Torah study for its own sake" in a context that has the broadest implications.

The gemara there reports a tradition in the name of R. Alexandri:
"Anyone who engages in Torah [study] for its own sake creates peace in
the family above and in the family below." From the wording of the
tradition, it is impossible to know the meaning of the term "for its own
sake." But the deliberation earlier on the same page, which creates the
context within which this statement must be understood, suggests that its
meaning here expands significantly upon what we have seen before. The
text includes the following traditions.

Sanhedrin 99b

a. R. Eleazar said: Every person was created for toil, as it says "for man is born for toil" (Job 5:7).

b. I do not know if he was created for toil of the mouth or for the toil of work. When He [then] says "[The soul of a laborer toils for him,] for his mouth presses upon him" (Prov. 16:26), say [therefore] that he was created for labor of the mouth.

c. And still I do not know if he was created for the toil of Torah [study = with the mouth] or the toil of [ordinary] speech. When He [then] says "this book of the Torah should not depart from your mouth" (Josh. 1:8), *say [therefore] he was created for the toil of Torah.*

d. And this is [the same as] what Rava said: All bodies are mailbags; *it is well for the one who merits being a "mailbag" for Torah.*

e. "The one who commits adultery with a woman lacks understanding" (Prov. 6:32)—Resh Laqish said: *This refers to one who learns Torah [only] periodically,* as it says "For it is pleasant if you keep them in your belly, let them be set together upon your lips" (Prov. 22:18; emphasis added).

f. Our sages taught: "But the person that acts presumptuously . . ." (Num. 15:30)—this is Menashe, the son of Hezekiah, who would sit and teach slanderous teachings.

g. He said: Did Moses have nothing [better] to write other than [the following apparently purposeless scriptures]: "And Lothan's sister was Timna . . . and Timna was concubine to Eliphaz . . ." (Gen. 36:23 and 12)

The gemara goes on to discuss Menashe's offense and to explain why the verses in question were in fact crucial.

Because this deliberation begins the broader discussion of Torah study to follow, it must be accounted for in any attempt to understand the meaning of the tradition of R. Alexandri. It is these traditions that, by creating the context for Alexandri's statement, suggest a definition for the term "for its own sake" as the gemara understands it.

To begin with, we must recognize that the quoted text, in combination with Alexandri's tradition, creates a meaningful contrast that underlies the gemara's whole point. The introductory traditions contrast proper devotion to Torah study (a–e) to improper devotion, exemplified by the activity of Menashe (f–g). When Alexandri immediately thereafter speaks of "Torah study for its own sake," such study is obviously to be contrasted with what Menashe did and associated with the proper devotion described earlier. What, then, is the meaning of "Torah study for its own sake" as it is elaborated in the earlier text?

Torah study is described here as "toil," that is, something that should be engaged in constantly without any guarantee that the fruits of one's labor will be immediately realized (cf. Eccles. 1:2–7). Furthermore, one's relationship to Torah study should be like the relationship of a "mailbag" to its contents, meaning that one should fill oneself with words of Torah and carry them within oneself always. Finally, what is to be condemned, by comparison to adultery, is occasional, periodic study of Torah, suggesting that Torah should be studied at all times and presumably without limitation. To sum up, Torah study should be engaged in always, as a toil, and without promise of a pragmatic outcome. The act is recommended on its own terms.

In contrast, what is condemned in the following steps (= the *opposite* of Torah study for its own sake) is the act of engaging in "slanderous teachings," that is (as the text makes clear), in teachings that suggest that some words of Torah are unnecessary or have no purpose. The alternative, and what is therefore recommended by this text, is to involve oneself in interpretation in the belief that every element of the text will yield fruit. This too, therefore, bids that we engage in Torah study, with proper intent, virtually without limitation (to make sense of every detail of Torah is a potentially infinite task); consequently, the same interpretation of the term "for its own sake" emerges from this broader context. Torah study for its own sake now means for the sake of open-ended study—with the right attitude, to be sure, but not necessarily in direct relation to practice. Study is emphasized here as an independent value, and its purpose need only be the study of the divine (or divinely sanctioned rabbinic) message.

This meaning of *lishma* ("for its own sake") is suggested strongly here for the first time. Because, as we noted, there is nothing in the actual statement of Alexandri that requires this meaning, it must be the suggestion of the authors of the Bavli. The context, of course, is the creation of the Bavli's authors, and it is only the context that suggests this direction. This is an editorial meaning, not necessarily an original meaning, and it must therefore be considered an innovation at that level, and not before.

Also supporting the conclusion that the conception of the purpose of Torah study underwent a transformation in the Bavli is the significant extension, in its pages, of the application of the recommendation "study and receive reward," seen first in the Tosefta. The Bavli, with the Tosefta, believes that the institutions of "the rebellious son," "the condemned city," and "the afflicted house" are included in the Torah only for this purpose (San. 71a). It goes beyond this, though, and, in its modified version of an earlier Tosefta text, suggests that this advice may be taken to be a general recommendation of scripture (Sot. 44a and cf. Tos. Sot. 7:21). And, most notably, in a discussion recorded in two contexts (San. 51b and Zev. 45a), Abbaye is reported as suggesting that virtually any study, though disconnected from practice, is meritorious. The context for his comment is this: In both texts an amoraic tradition declares the halakha for a matter that is irrelevant in current practice, the first in a matter of death penalties imposed by the Sanhedrin and the second in a matter of sacrifices. To these, the gemara records an amoraic response: "[Do we need] halakha for [the time of] the Messiah?!" Responding to this objection, Abbaye declares "But if this is so, then [even any matter of the laws of] the slaughter of holy things (= sacrifices) should not be taught [and that would be unthinkable]! Rather, study and receive reward. . . ." Rabbinic study is often about impracticable things. Large parts of the Mishnah speak of institutions destroyed. Yet clearly they are to be studied. The Mishnah's inclusion of these matters may be understood, in fact, to support such study that is independent of practice. But, at most, this value is merely implied in the Mishnah or other earlier texts. It is made explicit only in the Bavli and that, I claim, is significant.

Again, I do not claim that the notion of Torah study independent of its connection to practice or application did not exist at all before the Bavli. As we have seen, the Tosefta records this opinion modestly, and I have just suggested that the Mishnah itself may support this view in its inclusion of laws that are obviously irrelevant in practice. But practically speaking, there is no evidence in any of the earlier documents that this notion was transformed into an ideal (and much explicit evidence against it); in any case, there is immense significance to the labeling of such an ideal. If it exists without precise identification—without a *name*—then its full status cannot yet have been attained. Only the Bavli finally labels this value *(Torah lishma)*, and thus only in that document can we be confident that independent Torah study was thus valued.[30]

I have sought in this chapter to present more explicit evidence for the analysis proposed in the previous chapter. But whatever the merit of the specific demonstrations, the meaning of the Talmudic form claimed there stands, I believe, on its own foundation. What is finally the most articulate evidence for that analysis is the Bavli's form itself. Its ideology is not explicit in the sense with which we generally use that term, but it is explicit nonetheless.

Virtually every page of the Bavli records arguments that have no conclusion, or contrary opinions that are equally well defended. Nearly every deliberation includes manipulations of tradition and reason wherein the latter transforms the former. The indifference of these arguments to "truth" (where "truth" means a single, ideal truth) and their primary concern for human (rabbinic) community is evident at nearly every turn. The shape of the Bavli bespeaks this meaning and bids the rabbinic community to be persuaded that this is the road to be followed. The modesty and moderation of the document, with all of its sophistication and brilliance, is what contributed to the success of its reception into the Jewish community as a whole and what made it the foundation of Jewish theory and practice for so many centuries to follow.

7

The Bavli in Comparative Perspective

IN THE PREVIOUS CHAPTERS I suggested that the form of the Bavli reflects its authors' opinion that truth is ultimately indeterminable. The text juxtaposes interpretations or rulings, frequently without preferring one or the other, in order to declare that a single confident truth is beyond the reach of human understanding. Because revelation is no longer a means of divine communication and because the divine record (scripture) is dependent on human interpretation, human reason becomes the arbiter of the divine will—but only at a cost; human reason, as the Bavli admits explicitly from time to time, is fallible. The single truth is therefore inaccessible, and the variety of approaches to truth must be (and are) systematically affirmed.

In this chapter I will compare the Bavli's approach to "truth" with those of other religious and philosophical systems. The purpose in doing so is not to suggest influence or historical relations; it is unlikely that any of the systems discussed were known well, if at all, by the rabbis who formed the Bavli. Rather, what I intend is a kind of phenomenological survey, the question being, simply, how did others who were concerned with the question of truth, men of religion or philosophy, respond to the problems that any pursuit of truth presents? Did they believe that human beings could ascertain the truth? If so, how and by whom? What were the sources of truth and the means for its discovery? With these being the questions, it will be appropriate to consider approaches that were put forth also after the completion of the Bavli; to elucidate the range of possibilities and to clarify the Bavli's unique approach even later statements are relevant. By defining our task this way, our understanding of the Bavli's particular approach may be deepened and light may be shed on how its authors, compared to other deeply thoughtful men, understood their relationship to the world's universal categories (God, the Truth).

Obviously, this review will have to be highly selective; the question of truth in philosophy and religion is ample enough a topic for many books and can hardly be handled comprehensively in the space of a single chapter. The following criteria, therefore, will direct our examination.

First, in the philosophical tradition, consideration will be restricted primarily to major elements of premodern Western philosophy. Because the Bavli is a premodern system, little purpose would be served by reviewing more recent treatises. Furthermore, the philosophical tradition in later Sasanian Iran—the world from which the Bavli emerged—was dominated by Greek/Hellenistic philosophy.[1] Being in this way the most proximate tradition, this is the philosophy that can be expected, in contrast with the Bavli, to be most instructive.

Second, of religious traditions, those with a scripture will obviously be most relevant in a comparative study of this sort. Because, at a fundamental level, our concern here is the Bavli's relationship with a particular revelation, it will be instructive to consider how other scripture-based traditions translated and communicated their revelations.

Finally, because the Bavli mediates a particular approach to revelation and reason, making one dependent on the other and insisting on the essential position of both, it will be useful to consider others who sought to plot a path between revelation and reason. In particular, we will consider the approaches of those philosophers who defended the legitimacy of rational inquiry while at the same time remaining committed to the truth of a particular scripture. Of course, the meaning of "reason" in the Bavli and in rational philosophy are not synonymous. In the Bavli, reason need not be a formal, tested operation and often it seems to be identical with what we would call common sense. Furthermore, the philosophers who addressed the potential conflict between revelation and reason perceived an explicit, essentially philosophical problem, whereas the rabbis, in the Bavli and elsewhere, probably did not; for the latter the tension developed and was resolved organically. Nevertheless, in both cases human reason was perceived to be a source of truth independent of scripture (remember the Bavli's question: "It is reasonable, what do I need scripture for?") and this comparison is therefore both legitimate and essential.

It is necessary to add that we will not be considering the philosophy of law as a distinct field, though the Bavli is apparently predominantly a legal text. This focus is avoided for two reasons. First, it would be incorrect to equate the Bavli's concerns with law as generally conceived. Law can be conventional or natural. Law in the Bavli is certainly not the former and is only in a restricted sense the latter. The law of the Torah is an expression of divine will—there is nothing conventional about it. Furthermore, if by natural law we mean law that is derived by means of the analytical application of reason, again there is no essential equation between it and God's inspired, nonrational law. Only if natural law is, as for Aquinas, that part of divine law that revealed itself not in scripture but in human reason[2] can we posit here an identity of concerns, but even in such a case the philosophy of law would restrict us inappropriately. The Bavli, though obviously concerned with law, is concerned with many other subjects as well. Moreover, it often analyzes legal and nonlegal matters using precisely the same vocabulary and methods, suggesting that these areas are not as distinct as is often imagined. Rather, because its subject is God's will, we may more properly characterize the Bavli's concern as truth in the broadest sense. Only when conceived broadly, therefore, will this review do justice.

Second, in both philosophy and religion law is a subset of larger systems. Philosophy properly treats law as a category, but it is merely one category of many, all of which are necessary for one to speak of the larger, unified truth. It may be that law is distinct in nature from metaphysics, for example, requiring, as a result, a distinct epistemology. But even if this is the case in certain systems, that will not be relevant to the law of the Bavli, which is a religious law. Again, where law is a divine command, as in Judaism or Islam, law must be equated with the single, all-encompassing truth. In view of this conception of law, it is only appropriate to define our question openly, speaking of truth as the truth of all being.

Before embarking on this inquiry, though, it is essential to precisely define "truth." We will see that, with some differences, the philosophers, following Aristotle, are in virtual agreement in their use of this term.

Aristotle's definition of truth is this: "To say of what is that it is not, or of what is not that it is, is false, while to say of what is that it is, and of what is not that it is not, is true" (*Metaphysics* 4.7). Truth and falsehood seem, in this definition, to be a characteristic of language, truth being obtained by the conformity of language with the thing "as it is" (see also Plato *Sophist* 263a–d). But since, for Aristotle, "spoken words are the symbols of mental experience" (*De interpretatione,* ch. 1), the conformity spoken of here must be understood to pertain to intellect and perception as well.

By understanding words as "symbols of mental experience," we see that Aristotle's basic definition is followed by Augustine and Aquinas as well. Augustine writes: "That is true which is in reality as it is seen by the one perceiving" (*Soliloquies,* bk. 2, ch. 5). Truth, then, is the conformity of perception with things as they actually are. Aquinas, with a slightly different nuance, supports the same basic definition, saying: *"True* expresses the correspondence of being to the knowing power. . . . This agreement is called 'the conformity of thing and intellect.' In this conformity is fulfilled the formal constituent of the true" (*De veritate,* question 1, art. 1). Anselm returns more precisely to Aristotle's definition, writing: "When is a proposition true? When what it affirms to exist does exist, and when what it denies to exist does not exist" (*De veritate,* ch. 2).

Admittedly, there are important differences in these definitions. Language, perception, and intellect are plagued by distinct philosophical difficulties, making these definitions subject to independent critiques and defenses and preventing a complete reconciliation among them. Nevertheless, it is crucial to note that these philosophers all conceive of "truth" as the conformity of some aspect of mental experience (language, perception, intellect) with "what is." This agreement allows us to affirm, as a general definition, a second definition proposed by Augustine, that is, "the 'true' is that which exists," (ibid.). Notably, even despite the difficulty of moving from conformity to essence (and despite the redundancy of the statement "truth is what is"), Tillich is willing to express a similar judgment: "Truth, therefore, is the essence of things as well as the cognitive act in which their essence is grasped."[3] And other recent writers on epistemology, even while describing the variety of approaches to truth in the history of philosophy, endorse the broad characterization of truth as *"how things are."*[4]

The question, therefore, is whether a given philosophical or religious tradition assumes the possibility of knowing things "as they actually are." Do we have access to the fundamental structure of reality or is existence, in its fullness and its detail, ultimately inaccessible to full comprehension by the human mind?

Truth in the Classical Philosophical Tradition

Beginning with Plato, most major figures in classical and Western philosophy assumed that truth could be discovered through rational inquiry.[5] In particular Aristotle, whose influence on later medieval philosophy was most profound, affirmed this position with utmost confidence.

Relevant comments of Plato are not consistent with respect to the question of human access to truth. The early dialogues in particular, perhaps because they are the most genuinely "Socratic" of the dialogues, maintain that such knowledge is largely inaccessible.[6] The difficulty of isolating a definitive view is also compounded by virtue of the fact that several relevant dialogues, early and late, arrive at no particular conclusion, being content with refuting opinions that cannot be accepted. Still, it seems to me that Plato's preferred position affirms that truth may be determined.[7]

In the *Phaedo,* Plato's position on truth (or perhaps that of Socrates, which, we will see shortly, Plato later apparently abandons) appears at its most pessimistic. His dialogue finds Socrates arguing that death should not be feared, and to defend this position Socrates is represented as claiming that the body is an unavoidable hindrance to the acquisition of knowledge. The dialogue progresses in this way:

> [SOCRATES:] Now take the acquisition of knowledge. Is the body a hindrance or not . . . ? What I mean is this. Is there any certainty in human sight and hearing . . . ? . . . Then when is it that the soul attains to truth? When it tries to investigate anything with the help of the body it is obviously led astray.
> [SIMMIAS:] Quite so.
> [SOCRATES:] Is it not in the course of reflection, if at all, that the soul gets a clear view of facts?
> [SIMMIAS:] Yes.
> [SOCRATES:] Surely the soul can best reflect when it is free of all distractions . . . when it ignores the body and becomes as far as possible independent. . . . *So long as we keep to the body and our soul is contaminated with this imperfection, there is no chance of our ever attaining satisfactorily to our object, which we assert to be truth* . . . the body provides us with innumerable distractions . . . preventing us from getting a glimpse of the truth. . . . *[E]ither it is entirely impossible to acquire knowledge, or it is only possible after death.*[8] (*Phaedo* 65a–67b; emphasis added)

To make his peace with death, the philosopher is forced to deny that his most cherished possession—knowledge or truth—can be acquired during life. The body and its needs hinder the pursuit of knowledge and pollute one's perceptions. Only a pursuit that is restricted to the realm of pure ideas—in the mind and without distraction by the body—will arrive at the truth. True knowledge must therefore wait until after death.

But Plato elsewhere expresses contrary opinions, admitting that even before death truth is accessible to some. In his critique of Protagoras, who had argued that "man is the measure of all things," Plato has Socrates argue in this way:

> I am delighted with his [Protagoras's] statement that what seems to anyone also is, but I am surprised that he did not begin his *Truth* with the words, The measure of all things is the pig, or the baboon. . . . If what every man believes as a result of perception is indeed to be true for him; if . . . no one is better entitled to consider whether what another thinks is true or false, and . . . every man is to have his own beliefs for himself alone and they are all right and true—then, my friend, where is the wisdom of Protagoras, to justify his setting up to teach others . . . ? (*Theaetetus* 161c–d)

There follows a lengthy rebuttal of Protagoras's position.

Clearly, Plato denies that truth resides in individual perception. This accords with his notion, evident in the *Phaedo,* that there is a truth of pure ideas.[9] But contrary to his position expressed there, here Plato's rhetoric suggests that Socrates, unlike Protagoras, can be expected to speak *the* truth. For that reason, evidently, he (again, in contrast to Protagoras) is to "be preferred to the place of wisdom and instruction."

What is here merely suggested is made explicit in *The Republic.* In the well-known parable of the cave, Plato, through Socrates, likens humans in general to men who, since their childhood, were kept prisoner in a cave, unable to move their heads, thinking that shadows are real and knowing no other reality. The philosopher, in contrast, is likened to one who has been released from this prison and is able to look upon reality directly. The philosopher, properly trained, will be able to look upon "the region of the known [= the ideal forms] . . . the idea of the good" (bk. 7, 517b) and thereby become responsible, Plato argues, for sharing this "enlightenment" with society as a whole (through his leadership). "Philosophers," he states explicitly, "are capable of apprehending that which is eternal and unchanging" (bk. 6, 484b) and therefore ought to stand at the helm of Plato's ideal, but otherwise very this-worldly, republic; access to truth might be limited to a very small class, but at least some humans may, in their lifetime, acquire that truth through philosophical inquiry (see also Plato's *Seventh Letter,* 344a–b).[10]

If Plato's statements on truth are not consistent, Aristotle's position is clear: assuming that the subject of inquiry is such that it admits of single truths, that truth may be determined. Aristotle's caveat that the degree of attainable truth is dependent on the nature of the thing being investigated is spelled out in *Nicomachean Ethics* (1.3): "We must be content, then, in speaking of . . . subjects [such as politics] . . . to indicate the truth roughly and in outline, and in speaking about things which are only for the most part true . . . it is the mark of an educated man to look for *precision in each class of things just so far as the nature of the subject admits.*"[11] This is an important qualification. If the truths of such matters as "fine and just actions," which "exist only by convention, and not by nature" (ibid.), can be outlined only roughly, but not determined specifically and with clarity, then a system such as the rabbinic halakha— whose concern is precisely "fine and just actions"—should not be expected to yield precise truths. Aristotle would thus seem to be in agreement with the Talmudic views suggested in our earlier analysis.

But this conclusion would be a mistake. The simple fact, as noted earlier, is that halakha—derived from God's divine law—is not thought by the rabbis to "exist only by convention." On the contrary, halakha is ideally an expression of the divine will. More relevant to the present consideration, therefore, are Aristotle's statements that relate to metaphysics or other such subjects.

In connection with matters of this nature, Aristotle's opinion that truth might be determined is perfectly clear. This is stated unambiguously in *Posterior Analytics* (2.19): "Now *of the thinking states by which we grasp truth, some are unfailingly true,* others admit of error—opinion, for instance, and calculation, *whereas scientific knowledge and intuition are always true"* (emphasis added). Aristotle goes on to argue that intuition is more accurate than scientific knowledge and that intuition therefore must be the "originative source of scientific knowledge." It would appear, in fact, that the means of attaining this knowledge are less demanding, in Aristotle's scheme, than they were for Plato.

Aristotle makes this explicit in his *Metaphysics* (2.1):

> No one is able to attain the truth adequately . . . but every one says something true about the nature of things, and while individually we contribute little or nothing to the truth, by the union of all, a considerable amount is amassed. . . . We should [accordingly] be grateful, not only to those with whose views we may agree, but also to those who have expressed more superficial views; for these also contribute something, by developing before us the powers of thought.

Again, truth is available to the human mind. No single mind can determine the truth fully, but in combination, all minds can discover a considerable amount of the truth. Moreover, the truth is not the exclusive territory of philosophers; all minds can say something of the truth, and even the more "superficial" mind should therefore be heard. Obviously, Aristotle assumes that some minds will contribute more to the truth than other, more superficial minds, and he clearly includes himself among those who will contribute a great deal. Still, some element of the truth will be uncovered by even the ignoramus.

Aristotle's formulation may be relevant to this study because it recognizes the value of many views in developing "before us the powers of thought." This statement is reminiscent of the gemara at Eruvin 13b (see p. 142), which praises R. Meir for being able to argue in favor of even patently incorrect positions (= Aristotle's "superficial" positions), sharpening thereby the minds of his students. On a broader level, Aristotle's argument in support of multiple positions may be understood to relate to the gemara's insistence on the inclusion of multiple opinions. Superficially, at least, the two approaches have much in common.

But there is an important difference. Aristotle's recognition of the value of alternative views here is condescending—he assumes that the other views are essentially "superficial." In contrast, there is no evidence that when the Bavli includes multiple opinions, as it so often does, it condescends to one or the other. On the contrary, all views often find equal support and no view, certainly, is assumed to be superficial. If one argues, as I have suggested, that the gemara includes multiple views because each might include some element of the truth, then here we may find something that the Bavli and Aristotle hold in common. But this is not Aristotle's explicit defense for the inclusion of multiple opinions, and though it is suggested in his analysis, it is clearly secondary. Perhaps this is because Aristotle assumes, as he makes clear, that the truth can often be determined; beginning with such an assumption, one view among many will have to be preferred. In the Bavli, on the other hand, where single truths will not be determined, the reason for including multiple opinions cannot be only "to develop the power of thought."

In contrast to Plato and Aristotle, the Sophists, following Protagoras, and the Skeptics denied the determinability of truth. The Sophists, because of the ambiguities and contradictions of sense perception, were led to subjectivism.[12] The Skeptics, as their name has come to imply, professed a dogmatic doubt and claimed (Timon, Sextus Empiricus) that all arguments are either circular or an endless chain hanging from nothing.[13] But notwithstanding these (and other more minor) exceptions, the view that continued to predominate was that of Aristotle.

The affirmation of attainable truth is evidenced throughout medieval philosophy. This is true of Christian (Augustine and Aquinas), Muslim (Avicenna and Averroës), and Jewish (Saadiah, Maimonides) philosophers. (Because these individuals reckoned with both philosophical and revealed religious traditions, though, detailed discussion of their opinions will follow our review of religious traditions as such.) It is true, also, even with the earliest and some of the most critical modern philosophers. Descartes, for example, writes that "the power of judging well and distinguishing truth from falsehood . . . is naturally equal in all men."[14] And despite his promise "never to accept anything as true if I had not evident knowledge of it being so,"[15] he argues that "whatever we conceive very clearly and very distinctly is true"[16]—a considerable leap, indeed, from "I think, therefore I exist." Leibniz, less critically, assumes the existence of "eternal truths" and declares that knowledge of these truths is what distinguishes us from the animals.[17]

Evidently, the common philosophical assumption that truth was accessible to human inquiry continued to be current even into modernity. In fact, Aristotle's definition of philosophy as "the knowledge of the truth" (*Metaphysics* 2.1) so remained an accurate description of basic assumptions throughout the history of philosophy that Russell was able to comment that "every philosopher appears to himself to be engaged in the pursuit of something which may be called 'truth.' "[18] Philosophy's confident assertion of the power of human reason was uncompromised in the thought of many of its practitioners and, though different truths might have competed one with the other at any given time, the professors of those truths clearly imagined that it was "truth" that they in fact professed.

Religious Traditions and Truth

Most religious traditions have also assumed that their scriptures or doctrines describe the world "as it really is." Possessing the divine message and knowing that the world and its design are in accord with the divine will, they assert with confidence that their tradition holds *the* truth and, with equal confidence, claim that conflicting traditions are riddled with falsehood. Only the rare religious tradition is truly pluralistic.

Scriptures, beginning with the Hebrew Bible and including the New Testament, the Zend Avesta, and the Quran, speak with utmost faith in the truth of their own messages. Most often, perhaps, this is evident in the form by which they communicate their teachings. The Torah offers many examples of this position: "I am the Lord your God who brought you out of the land of Egypt" (Exod. 20:2); "You shall be holy, because I, the Lord your God, am holy" (Lev. 19:2); "Hear, O Israel, the Lord our God, the Lord is One" (Deut. 6:4); and so forth. Elsewhere, the Hebrew Bible speaks with equal lack of ambiguity; the prophetic texts, in particular, could virtually all demonstrate this common scriptural position.

The New Testament, close in spirit to the earlier prophetic books, communicates its message with similar clarity and confidence, often stating explicitly its claim for truth: "The true light that enlightens every man was coming into the world. . . . And the Word became flesh, and dwelt among us, full of grace and truth" (John 1:9–14); "I am writing you a new commandment, which is true in him and in you, because the darkness is passing away and the true light is already shining" (1 John 2:8); in implicit but no less forceful terms, ". . . go to the lost sheep of the house of Israel. And preach as you go, saying, 'The kingdom of heaven is at hand' " (Matt. 10:6–7); and so on. Speaking the word of God in Heaven, these texts exhibit clearly their certainty in the truth of their message.

The same assurance can be heard in the Zend Avesta. In the Gathas of Zarathustra, the claim to be speaking for truth is widespread. For example, we read in Yasna 30 (7–11):

> But to this world He [Ahura Mazda] came with the rule of good thinking and of truth, and (our) enduring piety gave body and breath (to it). . . .
>
> (to the wise Lord) And thus, when the punishment of these sinners shall come to pass, then, for Thee, Wise One, shall the rule of good thinking be at hand, in order to be announced to those, Lord, who shall deliver deceit into the hands of truth. . . .
>
> Wise One, and ye other Lords, be present to me with support and truth. . . .
>
> (to the adherents) Men, when ye learn those commandments which the Wise One has posed; when ye learn . . . salvation for the truthful, then each one (of you) shall abide by (all) these commandments.[19]

Similar confidence in the truth of the scriptural message, either explicit or implicit, can be heard in other legal and liturgical Avestan texts.

Quranic pronouncements are likewise confident of their truth. Some are explicit: "God has caused the Book to come down with the truth. Those who differ as to the Book surely are in total schism" (Surah 2:171). Others make the claim implicitly but no less clearly: "By the star when it sets your kinsman [= Muhammad] here is not astray nor does he err. He is not speaking out of whims. His word is nothing but an inspired revelation" (Surah 53:1–3). The scripture is the word of God and, being so, its words are the complete and unimpeachable truth.

Of course, those who follow these scriptures have well understood their claim. Witness the many Catholic treatises, for example, that profess the truth of that faith (Augustine's *De vera religione*, Aquinas's *De veritate*, Anselm's *De veritate*, etc.). Augustine's affirmations are particularly eloquent:

> The way of the good and blessed life is to be found entirely in the true religion wherein one God is worshipped and acknowledged . . . to be the beginning of all existing things, originating, perfecting and containing the universe. Thus it becomes easy to detect the error of the peoples who have preferred to worship many Gods rather than the true God. (*De vera religione*, 1.1)

> In Christian times there can be no doubt at all as to which religion is to be received and held fast, and as to where is the way that leads to truth and beatitude. (Ibid., 3.3)

> This is truth, the Word that was in the beginning, the divine Word that was with God. (Ibid., 36.66, cf. John 1)

A statement attributed to the ninth-century Muslim theologian Ahmad ibn Hanbal makes the case for his scripture in a way that is highly reminiscent of Augustine's last statement: "The Quran is the speech of God. He has spoken by it. It was not created."[20] The word, that is, is eternal; it *is* things as they actually are. Reality, in a basic sense, is in no way distinct from it and its conformity with "the way things are" may therefore be said to be absolute.

Eastern faiths profess a starkly different approach to knowledge than those of the Western scriptural faiths but, despite such differences, truth in those traditions is no more elusive. According to Samkhya Yoga, for example, "knowledge is a simple 'awakening' that unveils the essence of the Self." This knowledge is disclosed in a kind of revelation to the individual of the "ultimate reality."[21] In Hinduism, too, true knowledge, taught in the Veda ("knowledge"), is deemed accessible. The Veda, transmitted orally in tradition from generation to generation, was first received by individuals called *rishi* ("seer" or "knower"), who, after obtaining a vision of the truth, passed it on to their disciples.[22] The truth of this tradition is available to adherents in all generations.

Similarly, in Buddhism it is assumed that the individual can ascertain "the nature of things as they are." This knowledge must be in conformity with the "four Noble Truths," truths that constitute the heart of Buddha's teachings. These truths declare that (1) all is suffering, (2) the origin of suffering is desire, (3) by abolishing one's appetites one is delivered from pain, and (4) there are ways, taught in Buddhism, to eliminate one's desire and thus to cause an end to suffering. By meditating on these truths, the adherent is led to understand the truth of existence and is, as a consequence, relieved of suffering.[23]

Many other examples, scriptural and liturgical, could be presented as evidence, but the point is already clear: religious traditions as a whole—like classical philosophy in its major elements—assume that truth is accessible and claim, in fact, to possess and teach the truth. The major difference distinguishing religious and philosophical claims to truth is the source of that truth. In pure philosophy, truth is discovered by the efforts of the human mind; there is no source, independent of the intellect, from which the truth will emerge. In religion, on the other hand, truth is more often thought to originate in some kind of revelation. Truth may be claimed by both, but the different sources of that truth establish a potential for conflict that has been felt by practitioners of both throughout the centuries.

The potential for conflict lies not merely in the possibility that reason and revelation may lead to different conclusions. Also troubling, at least to those who begin with a commitment to revelation, is the fact that another source of truth, independent of revelation, is necessary or possible at all. Tertullian articulated this difficulty simply. "What indeed," he wrote, "has Athens [= philosophy] to do with Jerusalem [= scripture]? What concord is there between the academy and the Church? What between heretics and Christians?"[24] Christians accept revelation. There is not only no need for philosophy, therefore, but—in his view—there can be no peace between the two. A good Christian will shun philosophy; and one who does not do so is a heretic. There can be, it may reasonably be concluded, only one source of truth, and if this source is to be found in scripture (or in some other revelation), then the claims of philosophy must be viewed as downright dangerous.

In view of this possible conflict, it is particularly noteworthy that the major philosophers of the Middle Ages, following the classical tradition, were all also men of religion. Despite their commitment to a revealed scripture, they defended the propriety of philosophy and claimed that it too was a viable source of truth—one that did not undermine the teachings of scripture. Accordingly, we will consider the proposed resolutions of this possible conflict, as spelled out in the writings of the major figures of medieval philosophy.

Philosophy Meets Scripture

As Aristotle came to be known by the medievals—Muslims, Christians, and Jews—it was understood, almost as a matter of course, that some resolution between his teachings and those of each respective revelation had to be discovered. There are some important differences among the proposed resolutions, but striking—in view of the number of thinkers who addressed this problem and the variety of backgrounds from which they emerged—is the similarity in approaches that often unites them.

The case for accommodation between philosophy and Islam is made most directly by Averroës (twelfth century). In a brief treatise, *On the Harmony of Religion and Philosophy*,[25] the author argues, first, that according to Islamic law the study of philosophy is not merely permitted but is enjoined upon the individual who is capable of such study. Recognizing, though, that not all minds are prepared for such a discipline, Averroës admits that the lessons of philosophy and its consequences for religion (discussed later) should not be shared with all believers.[26] Following this, the author speaks directly to the problem of potential conflict. "Since this religion is true," he writes, "and summons to the study which leads to knowledge of the Truth, we the Muslim community know definitely that *demonstrative study does not lead to [conclusions] conflicting with what Scripture has given us; for truth does not oppose truth.*"[27] What, then, should one do if the conclusions of philosophical inquiry do appear to conflict with scripture? "If [demonstrative study] conflicts [with scripture,] there is a call for allegorical interpretation of it. . . . We affirm definitely that whenever the conclusion of a demonstration is in conflict with the apparent meaning of Scripture, that apparent meaning admits of allegorical interpretation according to the rules for such interpretation in Arabic."[28] There is no real conflict, in other words, and apparent conflict should be taken as an indication that scripture has been understood incorrectly.

What is remarkable about Averroës's resolution is that he assumes that philosophy (meaning, for him, Aristotle) will always reveal the truth and, as a consequence, it is the plain meaning of the Quran that must always yield to reason. Scripture, ever more pliable because of the possibility of allegorical interpretation, must give way to the conclusions of demonstrative study and, curiously, the revealed truth of the Quran will never—at least according to his present argument—point out an error in the philosophical method.

Though much influenced by Averroës, Aquinas (thirteenth century) nevertheless resolves the conflict between philosophy and, in his case, Catholicism by granting primacy to revelation. Aquinas's primary argument is that human reason is limited and insufficient to discover some of the most essential truths. He writes: "Some truths about God exceed all the ability of the human reason. . . . But there are some truths which the natural reason also is able to reach." [29] Again, "the human intellect is not able to reach a comprehension of the divine substance through its natural power." [30] So human reason has its realm, but its limitations must be recognized. There is no problem, therefore, if prophecy sometimes reveals what reason could also have revealed because, Aquinas argues, included in prophetic revelation are some crucial truths that reason could *not* have revealed. The whole of revelation is essential because of these otherwise unknowable parts and for these elements, at least, revelation is an indispensable independent source of truth. But what of the fact that philosophy, as Aquinas knows it, in any case, doesn't admit this limitation? "It is the acme of stupidity for a man to suspect as false what is divinely revealed through the ministry of the angels simply because it cannot be investigated by reason." [31] Revelation is primary, that is, and if there must be compromise, it is reason that must yield. Averroës, reflecting the Muslim tradition in which works are as primary as faith, sees no problem granting priority to reason and allegorical interpretation. For the believing Christian, Aquinas, faith remains primary and revelation's claim for truth must be respected.

Despite their obvious difference, these philosophers share a basic common premise. Note the echo of Averroës's assumption in Aquinas's statement: "Although the truth of the Christian faith which we have discussed surpasses the capacity of the reason, nevertheless that truth that the human reason is naturally endowed to know cannot be opposed to the truth of the Christian faith." [32] So for Aquinas, too, both reason and revelation are sources of truth—though their relative values are different than they were for Averroës—and, most crucially, in his understanding, as well, the truth of reason and the truth of revelation cannot be in conflict. When conflict does appear, Aquinas argues, we should conclude that we have identified one of the limitations of reason and grant priority to the truth of scripture.

Saadiah, a Jewish philosopher of the tenth century, approaches this problem in a manner far closer to Averroës than to Aquinas. Saadiah unequivocally states his confidence in human perception and reason: "Blessed be the Lord, God of Israel, to whom truth is known with absolute certainty; who confirmith to men the certainty of the truths which their souls experience—finding as they do through their souls their sense perception to be trustworthy; and knowing as they do through their souls their rational knowledge to be correct."[33] There are, Saadiah explains, three sources of truth that are available to all mankind: (1) the knowledge given by sense perception, (2) the knowledge given by reason, and (3) inferential knowledge.[34] These, as suggested previously, are absolutely trustworthy under the proper conditions, and Saadiah's estimation of philosophy as a reliable source of truth may be said to be essentially unconditional. But, Saadiah explains, "We, the Congregation of the Believers in the Unity of God, accept the truth of all the three sources of knowledge, and we add a fourth source . . . the truth of reliable Tradition."[35] So, in addition to the three sources of truth that are available to all mankind, Jews possess reliable Tradition, meaning scripture and other unwritten traditions. This, too, must be a perfect source of truth, and so we return to the problem that we saw earlier.

Saadiah states the problem simply: "If the doctrines of religion can be discovered by rational inquiry and speculation, as God has told us, how can it be reconciled with His wisdom that He announced them to us by way of prophetic Revelation and verified them by proofs and signs of a visible character, and not by rational arguments?"[36] In other words, if the truth, through rational inquiry, is available to all, then what is the use of the unique revelation to Israel? Why should God waste time on revelations and miracles if the same end is available, more universally, through other means? Saadiah's answer:

> God knew in His wisdom that the final propositions which result from the labour of speculation can only be attained in a certain measure of time. Had He, therefore, made us depend on speculation for religious knowledge, we should have existed without religion for some time. . . . Perhaps many of us would never have finished their labour. . . . From all these troubles God . . . saved us quickly by sending us His Messenger, announcing through him the Tradition, and allowing us to see with our own eyes signs in support of it.[37]

Reason, as Averroës had also argued, is difficult and not accessible to all. Philosophical inquiry takes patience and time; had we been left with it alone as a source of truth, we might have lived without truth for many generations. To prevent this possibility, God gave us the Law and Tradition. At the same time, it was still worthwhile to engage in philosophical speculation because, Saadiah explains, it is worth our discovering truth independently for ourselves and it is only through the path of philosophy that we can refute nonbelievers who attack our religion.[38]

Thus Saadiah justifies both revelation and reason as sources of truth and compromises neither. He declares, with utter confidence, that both will yield the same truth and, in his opinion, they stand as twin pillars upon each of which, independently, the truth may rest.

Maimonides (twelfth century) is less direct in his response to this problem, but his solution is perfectly evident from the general approach he takes in his *Guide for the Perplexed*. To begin with, it is clear from his methodology and from his explicit statements that Maimonides has faith in the ability of reason to yield truth. He speaks of "those who have apprehended the true realities."[39] He notes that "the fourth species [of human perfection] is the true human perfection; it consists in the acquisition of the rational virtues—I refer to the conception of the intelligibles, which teach true opinions concerning the divine things."[40] So the true philosopher, in any case, will, through his intellect alone, discover the truth. Once again, therefore, the question arises: What is to be done if the dictates of reason conflict with revelation?

Maimonides' answer to this problem is found, in practical terms, throughout the first book of the *Guide,* where he methodically reinterprets all apparent anthropomorphic references to God in scripture in a way that denies this sense. His solution, in other words, is the same as the one we saw in Averroës; when revelation appears to conflict with reason, revelation must be reinterpreted. In his discussion of creation *ex nihilo* and Aristotle's doctrine of the eternity of the world (i.e., that the world existed from eternity and was not created at a point in time), Maimonides discusses this solution directly. He explains that the reason for his denial of Aristotle's doctrine is *not* because Genesis seems to contradict it: "Know that our shunning the affirmation of the eternity of the world is not due to a text figuring in the Torah according to which the world has been produced in time. . . . Nor are the gates of figurative interpretation shut in our faces. . . . [This is] responsible for our not [interpreting the text figuratively] . . . [T]he eternity of the world has not been demonstrated."[41] The number of texts that speak of God in anthropomorphic terms is far more numerous, Maimonides notes, than those that speak of the world as being created in time, and yet that fact did not prevent him from interpreting *those* texts figuratively. The reason that he does not reinterpret in this case is simply because he believes that Aristotle's arguments for the eternity of the world are inconclusive. (In fact, Maimonides claims that Aristotle knew this and that it is only his followers who insist that this is one of the basic conclusions of his *Physics*.) Had they been conclusive, he would also have interpreted the texts about creation in a way that is not obvious according to their simple meaning.

Once again, for Maimonides—as for Averroës and Saadiah—speculative reasoning is an independent and reliable source of truth; his confidence in it is uncompromised. And also for Maimonides reason and revelation, both sources of the truth, cannot conflict. His solution, therefore—the same as Averroës's—is to use the power of interpretation to make scripture accord with the conclusions of philosophy.[42] Properly understood, then, both will remain the full truth.

For the medievals, then, the meeting of scripture and philosophy neither created a crisis nor, for the most part, resulted in compromise. From religion they inherited a confidence in the truth of revelation and from the philosophers they inherited a confidence in the truth emergent from reason. For Aquinas, philosophy was forced to admit some limitations, but these were relatively modest and, in fact, even in his system philosophy yielded little ground. In general, it was believed that apparent conflicts could be resolved, and no evident sobriety resulted from the introduction of philosophy and religion to one another—at least not in the minds of those who recognized the value of each. Truth not only could be discerned, therefore, but it could be approached from two directions, each acting as a guarantee for the other.

In contrast, as we saw, when the Bavli admitted the value of the contributions of both reason and revelation, *both* were compromised. Scripture could not reveal the single definitive truth because its meaning was dependent on the application of human reason. But reason, being human and therefore fallible, could also not generally be trusted to yield definitive truth. Nevertheless, reason was affirmed and the human contribution—whether interpretive or legislative—also became Torah. In consequence thereof—as the form of the discourse in the Bavli reveals—truth had to be understood as indeterminable. In light of the conclusions of others, why does it perceive necessary limitations where others do not?

In Conclusion: Why the Bavli?

When comparing the Bavli to the variety of classical philosophical systems reviewed in this chapter, it immediately becomes clear that in the Bavli the same centrality of reason is never approached. In philosophy, reason is the primary, if not the exclusive, source for discovering truth. Not so in the Bavli—at least not in an explicit, self-conscious way. In the Bavli, reason is not a *system* but a *participant,* a partner or player in a total system in which alternative authoritative sources of truth are always present and often primary. The perceived meaning of those authoritative sources—scripture or Mishnah, in particular—may be *dependent* on the application of human reason but, in contrast with philosophy, reason is rarely the originating *source* in the Bavli. Reason may be the midwife of truth in the Bavli's system, but it is not the mother of that truth.

Consequently, the Bavli never explicitly expresses, as does philosophy, a definitive confidence in the capabilities of human reason, independently applied. Reason may, from time to time, be a source of instruction by the side of scripture or some other authoritative source but, explicitly, that's as far as the Bavli will go. To be sure, the place of reason is more central in fact than the Bavli admits, as discussed in previous chapters, but that doesn't affect the system's self-perception. Clearly, then, if the Bavli never has the confidence in reason that is typical in philosophy, it will not—and does not—imagine that reason might yield the definitive truth that philosophy often claims.

At the same time, when we contrast the Bavli with other religious systems, it is clear that the Bavli admits the necessary dependence of its system on human reason, a recognition that has crucial consequences. Though other religious systems understand that revelation can yield alternative interpretations, they generally do not translate that fundamental fact into a doctrinal expression; even in the presence of multiple interpretations they still claim to teach the whole truth.[43] The Bavli, in contrast, makes such alternatives a programmatic expression of its doctrine. Alternatives are so often suggested because different interpretations are nearly always possible. Human reason, the vehicle by which scripture or Mishnah must be understood, can never claim full, definitive comprehension. Any interpretation thus is necessarily imperfect, and for this reason alternatives are always to be considered. Of course, if authoritative sources can communicate their truths only by means of an encounter with human reason, the truths of those sources can never emerge fully.

In the Bavli, then, in contrast to many other religious systems, there is little willingness to declare the definitive meaning of revelation. Almost any source can—and is—made to yield multiple meanings. In one sense, each of these alternatives is a truth in a community of truths. But no statement can claim that it speaks *the* truth. Being dependent on interpretation, the revelation, by definition, always remains partly hidden; thus those who teach the revelation (written and later oral) are not able to speak in the name of a pure and uncompromised truth.

Not surprisingly, if both of the poles from which truth can emerge are in the Bavli judged to be imperfect, then the conflict that medieval philosopher–theologians felt in the meeting of these realms is not necessary in the Bavli. In a sense, the Bavli does occasionally admit this conflict when it suggests that if a certain conclusion could be taught by ''reason,'' the same teaching would be unnecessary in scripture. But generally it would be more nearly correct to say that the Bavli understands there to be not a conflict but a tension between reason and revelation. This tension is evident, in particular, in the earlier amoraic hesitancy to challenge opinions using reason alone; at the earliest stage objections were to be based on authoritative sources. Even as a willingness to employ reason in this way developed, it remained clear that sources were generally preferred (see p. 36). Still, as we saw, Reason ultimately emerges to claim a well-earned place in the center of the system, and even to become ''Torah.'' As it does, any possible conflict between revelation and reason is eliminated by definition, because, having been included in Torah, reason too is now part of revelation. The two poles become, in the Bavli, complete partners in the promulgation of a much compromised truth.

For the rabbis, truth is ideally to be found in scripture. In Susan Handelman's formulation, ''In the contingent world of [rabbinic] thought, one must not look to nature for ultimate reality, but to the divine creative word which simultaneously reveals and conceals the hidden God.''[44] Truth is present in scripture, to be sure, but scripture, by its nature, both reveals and hides. To the extent that it reveals, we have access to the truth. But to the extent that it hides the divine, making discovery difficult and leaving understanding to the frailty of the human intellect, truth is irreversibly distanced from us. Because scripture reveals its truth only through interpretation, truth, like interpretation, is always insecure. When faced with the immensity of Torah, the Talmudic rabbis conclude that their limitations are in some degree insurmountable.

Nevertheless, because there can be no alternative to this condition, the product of the rabbinic application of reason is affirmed. Though both reason and revelation are imperfect sources of truth, this does not mean that Torah is to be abandoned; it means, instead, that imperfection, too, is to be made Torah. Consequently, the Bavli makes the imperfect and imperfectible pursuit of divine truth the very center of its enterprise. It concerns itself and its students with multiple interpretations of scripture, with multiple opinions in the law, that is, with multiple approaches (but only approaches) to the truth. Even when it renders decisions or favors particular interpretations, the Bavli makes it clear that the process, and not the conclusion, is its utmost concern. It makes a mitzvah out of studying study (talmud torah) and admits thereby that the human encounter with the divine will—however human, and therefore imperfect, that encounter is in fact—is itself of equal value with the divine will itself.

Notes

Introduction

1. Among many statements of this position, see especially Jacob Neusner, "Talmudic History: Retrospect and Prospect," in *A History of the Jews in Babylonia.* Vol. 1. *The Parthian Period,* 3rd printing (Chico, Calif. 1984), pp. xxviii–xxxv.

2. Among the most outstanding such works, see especially David Halivni, *Midrash, Mishnah and Gemara: The Jewish Predilection for Justified Law* (Cambridge, Mass., 1986), Jacob Neusner, *Judaism in Society: The Evidence of the Yerushalmi* (Chicago, 1983), and Neusner, *Judaism: The Classical Statement* (Chicago, 1986).

3. The range admitted by present scholarship extends from the beginning of the sixth century to the early part of the seventh. The former is the view of Halivni; see his *Midrash, Mishnah and Gemara,* p. 76. The latter limit recognizes that the closure of the Bavli was certainly accomplished by the time of the Islamic conquest of Persia.

4. Neusner is an exception, though his conclusions in this matter are nowhere defended; he merely describes what in his view is the uniqueness of the Bavli and claims that it is the reason for the Bavli's final triumph. See his *Judaism: The Classical Statement,* pp. 223 and 233. Contesting his conclusions, see my "Scripture Commentary in the Babylonian Talmud: Primary or Secondary Phenomenon?," *AJS Review,* 14, no. 1 (March 1989): 1–15.

5. See pp. 66–68.

6. The pluralistic nature of the rabbinic community in Babylonia may also be a factor. But even in the face of this varied community, the authors of the Bavli could have editorially excluded alternatives, censoring the reality of the community and offering an opposing ideal. Their failure to do so must therefore be interpreted as an ideologically significant choice.

7. A noteworthy exception is the *Arba'a Turim* of R. Yehiel b. Asher, which often records several opinions and is generally less definitive in its presentation of any particular opinion. This document, though a law code, is closer in spirit to the Bavli than other documents of the same genre.

Chapter 1

1. For a brief discussion of several applications of this assumption, see René Wellek and Austin Warren, *Theory of Literature* (San Diego, 1977), pp. 118, 183–84.

2. For a discussion, at greater length, of the relationship of literature and society, see Wellek and Warren, *Theory of Literature,* pp. 94–109.

3. Leo Strauss, *The City and Man* (Chicago, 1964), p. 52.

4. Ibid., p. 50.

5. Ibid., p. 59.

6. Ibid., p. 53.

7. Ibid., p. 61.

8. Ibid., p. 50.

9. See also Hans-Georg Gadamer's interpretation of Plato's dialogues in *Dialogue and Dialectic,* trans. P. Christopher Smith (New Haven, 1980), pp. 93–123, esp. p. 95; and Drew A. Highland, "Why Plato Wrote Dialogues," *Philosophy and Rhetoric,* 1, 1 (Winter 1968): 38–50.

10. David Halivni, *Midrash, Mishnah, and Gemara: The Jewish Predilection for Justified Law* (Cambridge, Mass., 1986).

11. See Richard Kalmin's critique in his review of Halivni's work, *Conservative Judaism,* 39, no. 4 (Summer 1987): 81.

12. Halivni, *Midrash, Mishnah and Gemara,* pp. 40, 54.

13. Ibid., p. 52.

14. Jacob Neusner, *Judaism: The Evidence of the Mishnah* (Chicago, 1981).

15. Ibid., pp. 217–23. This quotation is from p. 223.

16. See the pages referred to previously and, in addition, "Ways Not Taken," pp. 25–44.

17. Scholars, based on the testimony of m. Yadaim 3:5, have long assumed that Hebrew scripture came to a definitive close at Yavne in the late first century C.E. Sid Z. Leiman, in *The Canonization of Hebrew Scripture: The Talmudic and Midrashic Evidence* (Hamden, Conn., 1976), argues that Jews thought scripture effectively to have been closed long before this (see pp. 129–35). Even if Leiman is correct for most biblical books, there was clearly room for limited dispute in the first century. Moreover, Leiman takes full regard only of explicit testimony with respect to this issue and does not adequately account for the implications of the *form* of documents promulgated by Jews in the centuries before Jesus.

18. Neusner, *Judaism,* p. 224.

19. Ibid., p. 226.

20. Ibid., pp. 224–29.

21. Ibid., pp. 244–45.

22. Ibid., p. 245.

23. See the excellent article by E. Y. Kutscher in the *Encyclopedia Judaica,* vol. 16, pp. 1590–93.

24. Zechariah Frankel, *Mevo ha-Yerushalmi (Introduction to the Yerushalmi)* (Breslau, 1870; rpt. Jerusalem, 1967). Cf. Baruch Bokser, "The Palestinian Talmud," in *The Study of Ancient Judaism II,* ed. Jacob Neusner (Hoboken, N.J., 1981), pp. 50–53.

25. Frankel, *Mevo ha-Yerushalmi,* pp. 28b–36b.

26. Ibid., p. 35b.

27. Ibid., p. 36a.

28. See Jacob Neusner, *Judaism: The Classical Statement* (Chicago, 1986), pp. 94–114, and cf. David Kraemer, "Scripture Commentary in the Babylonian Talmud: Primary or Secondary Phenomenon?," *AJS Review,* 14, no. 1 (March 1989): 1–15.

29. Though Yerushalmi deliberations might, on rare occasions, go on at great length. The longest that I found was at Ned. 6:8 III (using Neusner's notation), which extended for 95 steps. The longest I found in the Bavli, at San. 9:6 XII, is 102 steps. It should be noted that far less of the Bavli translation is presently available.

30. See Gherardo Gnoli, "Avesta," in *The Encyclopedia of Religion,* vol. 2, p. 16. Convenient editions of the texts include *The Sacred Books of the East.* Vol. 3. *The Zend-Avesta,* trans. James Darmesteter (New York, 1898), and Stanley Insler, *The Gathas of Zarathustra* (Leiden, 1975).

31. See Hans Julius Wolff, *Roman Law* (Norman, Okla., 1976), pp. 166–67.

32. See Baruch Bokser, *Post Mishnaic Judaism in Transition* (Chico, Calif., 1980), pp. 429–50, for a comparison of Samuel's commentary with several possible precedents. Bokser's concern is amoraic commentary in particular (in its earliest forms), whereas ours is the form of the Bavli as a whole.

33. For an excellent general observation on the concern for truth—or the absence thereof—in ancient historians, see M. I. Finley, *Ancient History: Evidence and Models* (New York, 1986), p. 18.

34. See David Kraemer, "Tannaim," in *The Encyclopedia of Religion,* vol. 14, pp. 271–72, and, at greater length, Saul Lieberman, *Hellenism in Jewish Palestine* (New York, 1950; rpt. New York, 1962), pp. 83–99.

35. Jacob Neusner, *The Rabbinic Traditions About the Pharisees Before 70* (Leiden, 1971), vol. 3, p. 180.

36. See J. N. Epstein, *Mevo'ot lesifrut ha-amoraim* (Jerusalem, 1962), pp. 290–92, L. Greenwald, *Ha-ra'u mesadrei ha-bavli et ha-yerushalmi?* (New York, 1954), pp. 56–70, and more generally, Bokser, "The Palestinian Talmud," pp. 49–53. Martin Jaffee, in "The Babylonian Appropriation of the Talmud Yerushalmi: Redactional Studies in the Horayot Tractates," in *New Perspectives on Ancient Judaism.* Vol. 4. *The Literature of Early Rabbinic Judaism: Issues in*

Talmudic Redaction and Interpretation, ed. Alan J. Avery-Peck (Lanham, N.Y., 1989), pp. 3–27, has noted certain striking redactional similarities between Yerushalmi and Bavli tractates Horayot and suggests that the latter document may have been influenced by the former in its redactional choices. However, he makes the claim for influence only on the level of redaction, that is, the level of overall arrangement and ordering of the text, and *not* for the content of the two documents; see p. 6, n. 9, and pp. 7–18. Whatever the merit of his particular argument, therefore, it does not affect our present discussion. If the authors of the Bavli were, in fact, familiar with the Yerushalmi, the fact that they did not emend their Palestinian traditions on the basis of the Yerushalmi only strengthens the conclusion that they possessed their own earlier, independent tradition to which they were willing to give priority.

37. Jacob Neusner, *The Bavli and Its Sources: The Question of Tradition in the Case of Tractate Sukkah* (Atlanta, 1987), p. 50.

38. Jacob Neusner, *Judaism in Society: The Evidence of the Yerushalmi* (Chicago, 1983), p. 31; emphasis added.

39. See Chanoch Albeck, *Mevo la-talmudim* (Tel-Aviv, 1969), pp. 452–504.

40. For a lengthier and more detailed discussion of this problem, see David Kraemer, "On the Reliability of Attributions in the Bavli," *Hebrew Union College Annual,* 60 (1989), pp. 175–90.

41. Ibid., pp. 178–82.

Chapter 2

1. Two generations of less significant amoraim continued to produce traditions until the end of the fifth century.

2. See Richard Kalmin, *The Redaction of the Babylonian Talmud: Amoraic or Saboraic?* (Cincinnati, 1989), pp. 54–55 and 123–25.

3. See C. Y. Kasovsky, *Otzar leshon ha-Mishnah,* 4 vols. (Tel-Aviv, 1957, 1967), vol. 2, p. 576.

4. Baruch Bokser, in *Post Mishnaic Judaism in Transition* (Chico, Calif., 1980), chapter 5, categorizes Samuel's traditions that relate to m. Ber. His chart (p. 291) lists the following types of comments:

A. Definitions of a word	9	(15.3%)
B. Definitions of a case	9	(15.3%)
C. Textual notes	1	(1.7%)
D. Reasons	3	(5.1%)
E. Decisions	10	(16.9%)
F. Related rulings	8	(13.6%)
G. Additional cases	19	(32.2%)

In his immediate analysis of these data (pp. 290 and 292) Bokser argues that all of these categories can be expected to appear in a commentary on the Mishnah, where "commentary" is understood, in the broadest sense, as virtually any response to the text that is being commented upon. As far as it goes, this is correct. But if we instead ask which traditions are halakhic and which interpretive, we will see that these data yield very different conclusions.

The first four categories (A–D) are clearly interpretive. Granting, for present purposes, that Bokser's evaluation of which traditions may be appropriately assigned to these categories (though I disagree with some of his specific evaluations), we will have a total of 22 cases (37%) in which the primary purpose of the comment is the illumination of the Mishnah. In such cases the tradition generally depends directly on the Mishnaic text, and it is often incomprehensible without its referent. The last three categories (E–G), on the other hand, are declarations of halakha, as I describe in the text. This means that, in terms of the distinctions that are important here, at least 37 (63%) of the cases in Bokser's sample are halakhic.

5. The page references in this chapter, where not otherwise indicated, refer to my Ph.D. dissertation, "Stylistic Characteristics of Amoraic Literature" (henceforth SCAL), Jewish Theological Seminary of America, 1984.

6. To make this determination I counted all brief traditions attributed to Rav and subsequently to Rabba and Abbaye. I found in these countings that the proportion of Hebrew to Aramaic for each sage did not change significantly over the whole (i.e., from tractate to tractate). For other sages, therefore, I used a sample that was less than the total body of their brief (nonargumentational) traditions but in no case less than half of the available traditions. For Samuel I counted through Seder Nashim, a total of approximately 450 traditions.

7. In numbering these sequences, I am speaking only of those arguments that are attributed, either explicitly or with strong contextual support, to amoraim. Sequences where a tradition of a named sage generates a longer discussion by the anonymous gemara are obviously not relevant here.

8. For examples of these and other such phenomena, see SCAL, pp. 70–71.

9. Cf. Michael Chernick, *Leheqer ha-middot "khlal ufrat ukhlal" v' "ribui umiut" bemidrashim u'vetalmudim* (Lod, Israel, 1984), esp. pp. 127–29, on development in the methods of midrash halakha from the tannaitic period through the period of the amoraim and beyond. The development that I describe would parallel what he has discovered and would suggest that there might be a relationship between these phenomena.

10. Some versions have "Rava" of the next generation. Rabbinovicz prefers Rabba, for reasons that I find convincing. I therefore consider this example pertinent here. See *Diqduqei soferim,* ad loc., n. *"resh."*

11. "Presumably" because by means of creative interpretation an amora could virtually always differ with a tannaitic opinion. For example, the claim that a particular ruling applied in only very specific circumstances (*"lo shanu 'ela"*) could effectively nullify the ruling. See also Judith Hauptman's conclusions in *Development of the Talmudic Sugya: Relationship Between Tannaitic and Amoraic Sources* (Lanham, N.Y., 1988), p. 217.

12. J. N. Epstein, *Mevo Ienusaḥ ha-Mishnah,* 2 vols. (Jerusalem, 1948), pp. 175–76.

13. See note 9.

14. Several variants collected in *Talmud Bavli: Masekhet Yevamot* (Jerusalem, 1983), p. 122, make this perfectly explicit.

15. See Bokser, *Post Mishnaic Judaism,* pp. 461–62.

16. This statement is found in the Bavli at Eruv. 50b, Ket. 8a, B.B. 42a, San. 83b, and, in a slightly different form, at Hul. 122b. Only in the last mentioned case is the statement associated with a named amora. In all of the other instances the observation is made by the anonymous gemara and it is justified, it appears, only because the gemara on those occasions has irrefutable evidence that Rav did dispute the Mishnah.

17. George W. E. Nickelsburg, *Jewish Literature Between the Bible and the Mishnah* (Philadelphia, 1981), pp. 73–80.

18. I do not mean to suggest that the Hebrew of the amoraim was identical with that of the Mishnah. The differences between the two are today widely recognized; see E. Y. Kutscher's "Hebrew Language" in *The Encyclopedia Judaica,* vol. 16, p. 1591. I mean merely to point out that Middle (or rabbinic) Hebrew was common to the Mishnah and the earlier amoraim and grew gradually less so in the middle amoraic generations.

19. Cf. b. A.Z. 35a: "When they issue a decree in the West [Palestine] they do not reveal its reason for twelve months lest there be a person who doesn't agree [with the reason] and come to deal lightly with it."

Chapter 3

1. It should be recalled that by argumentation I mean record (actual or fictitious) of give-and-take between two or more parties. The mere record of differences of opinion, so common in the Mishnah and gemara, is not, by itself, argumentation.

2. *Midrash, Mishnah, and Gemara: The Jewish Predilection for Justified Law* (Cambridge, 1986), p. 2.

3. Ibid., p. 70.

4. Ibid.

5. Ibid., p. 77.

6. Ibid., p. 78.

7. See chapter 1, n. 34, and add Jacob Neusner, *The Pharisees: Rabbinic Perspectives* (Hoboken, N.J., 1973), pp. 255–57.

8. Halivni, *Midrash, Mishnah, and Gemara,* p. 77; emphasis added.

9. Ibid., p. 86; emphasis added.

10. Which is not identical to four steps. Where three steps of dialogue are supplemented by a follow-up by the last of the participants, I count this as "three and one-half" steps, and I do consider such sequences later.

11. See David Kraemer, "Stylistic Characteristics of Amoraic Literature," Ph.D. diss., Jewish Theological Seminary of America, 1984 (henceforth SCAL). Page references in this chapter, where sources are not otherwise indicated, refer to SCAL.

12. By "genuine" I do not intend literal records of actual argumentation. I intend, rather, near-contemporary literary formulations in the argumentational form.

13. "R. Yosef" is missing in MS Munich. I make references to variants from the printed text only when they affect the present analysis.

14. See SCAL, p. 126, n. 22. It should be evident that I have changed my mind with respect to certain steps of the overall analysis there.

15. For a discussion of the relationship between so-called unusual tractates, including Nazir, and the rest of the gemara, see David Goodblatt, "The Babylonian Talmud," in *The Study of Ancient Judaism II,* ed. Jacob Neusner (Hoboken, N.J., 1981), pp. 167–70.

16. See David Halivni, *Meqorot umesorot* (Jerusalem, 1982), p. 409.

17. For a record of all of these cases, see SCAL, chapters 5 and 7, and to those add Shab. 99b, Eruv. 17a, 93b, and 103a, and Git. 29b.

18. See note 7.

Chapter 4

1. "R. Naḥman" is missing in manuscripts. It is clear, in any case, that this response is being assigned to him.

2. MSS Munich and Rome do not include this phrase.

3. For a more detailed analysis of some parts of this text, see David Kraemer, "Stylistic Characteristics of Amoraic Literature," Ph.D. diss., Jewish Theological Seminary of America, 1984 (henceforth SCAL), pp. 262–69.

4. By "this specific type" I mean argumentational sequences using *eitivei* that also employ literary conventions such as, most commonly, tripartite structuring. One such objection (but *only* one) that appears alone, out of a more formal literary context, is paralleled in the Yerushalmi. For a detailed analysis of these cases, see SCAL, chapter 6.

5. Yaakov Spiegel, in his "Hosafot me'uḥarot (saborai'ot) beTalmud Bavli," Ph.D. diss., Tel-Aviv University, 1976, demonstrates that many nonattributed legal decisions in the Bavli, employing the term *hilkheta* or related forms, are in fact later additions to the original Talmudic text. The same is true, he shows elsewhere ["'Amar Rava hilkheta—piskei halakha me'uḥarim," in *'Iyyunim besifrut hz'l bemiqrah uvetoledot yisrael,* ed. Y. D. Gilat, C. Levine, and Z. M. Rabinowitz (Ramat-Gan, Israel, 1982), pp. 206–14], of some attributed decisions. In particular, of some twenty-two cases of decisions attributed to Rava using the term *hilkheta,* he demonstrates that eight are actually later additions to the Talmud. Other instances, employing different terminology but also attributed to Rava, are also shown to be late. B. M. Lewin, in *Rabbanan sabora'i vetal-*

mudam (Jerusalem, 1937), pp. 47–53, also suggests that unattributed legal decisions of this sort are commonly later additions to the original text.

6. C. Y. Kasovsky, *Otzar leshon ha-Talmud* (Jerusalem, 1958), vol. 3, pp. 1531–32, 1560, and (1968) vol. 19, pp. 802–6.

7. See C. Y. Kasovsky, *Otzar leshon ha-Yerushalmi* (Jerusalem, 1982), vol. 2, pp. 931–32. To make this assessment, I have examined those occasions when the respective documents use the form "scripture should say" and related forms.

8. Jacob Neusner, *Judaism in Society: The Evidence of the Yerushalmi* (Chicago, 1983), pp. 110–11; emphasis added.

9. For the Bavli, see *Otzar leshon ha-Talmud,* vol. 3, pp. 633–40. The listing for the Yerushalmi can be found in *Otzar leshon ha-Yerushalmi,* vol. 1, pp. 417–18.

10. The fact that the Bavli is longer than the Yerushalmi, and might for that reason record so many more such cases, should not be thought to present a problem for the argument that I have made. For we must consider *why* the Bavli is so much longer than the Yerushalmi. It is not because the Bavli comments on more of the Mishnah than the Yerushalmi—that is not the case. Both of the talmuds comment on major parts of four orders of the Mishnah. Rather, the Bavli is so much longer than the Yerushalmi—in ways that will be discussed later—in large part because of the very fact that it is willing to consider such alternatives so consistently. This factor, therefore, has widespread compositional implications and is the crucial difference between the two documents.

11. Some are found on rare occasions in the name of amoraim, but their very rarity renders such occurrences suspect; in any case, their full creative expression awaits the anonymous usage.

12. See Adin Steinsaltz, "The Relationship Between Babylonia and the Land of Israel," *Talpiot,* 9 (1965): 294–306. Steinsaltz suggests that the "deterioration" was due to ideological differences connected with academic method. I do not find his argument convincing but I am not in a position to offer an alternative explanation.

13. Zechariah Frankel, *Mevo ha-Yerushalmi (Introduction to the Yerushalmi)* (Breslau, 1870; rpt. Jerusalem, 1967), pp. 28b–36b.

14. There are rare exceptions to these rules. See Martin Jaffee, "The Babylonian Appropriation of the Talmud Yerushalmi: Redactional Studies in the Horayot Tractates." In *New Perspectives on Ancient Judaism.* Vol. 4. *The Literature of Early Rabbinic Judaism: Issues in Talmudic Redaction and Interpretation,* ed. Alan J. Avery-Peck (Lanham, N.Y., 1989).

15. On the inclusion of scripture commentaries, see Jacob Neusner, *Judaism: The Classical Statement* (Chicago, 1986), pp. 94–114, 222–40, but cf. David Kraemer, "Scripture Commentary in the Babylonian Talmud: Primary or Secondary Phenomenon?," *AJS Review,* 14, no. 1 (March 1989): 1–15. On other large literary blocs, see Abraham Weiss, *'al ha-yetzirah ha-sirfrutit shel ha-'amoraim* (New York, 1962), pp. 264–75.

16. *Judaism: The Classical Statement,* pp. 48–76. Specific quotations in this paragraph are from pp. 64, 67, and 75.

Chapter 5

1. See Jacob Neusner's definition of these forms in *The Rabbinic Traditions About the Pharisees Before 70* (Leiden, 1971), vol. 3, pp. 5–6, 16–17.

2. See Huntington Cairn's introduction in *Plato: The Collected Dialogues,* eds. Edith Hamilton and H. Cairn (Princeton, 1961), pp. xiv–xv.

3. See Hans-Georg Gadamer, *Dialogue and Dialectic,* trans. P. Christopher Smith (New Haven, 1980), p. 122, and idem, *the Idea of the Good in Platonic–Aristotelian Philosophy,* trans. P. Christopher Smith (New Haven, 1986), pp. 23, 24, 28.

4. Chaim Perelman and L. Olbrechs-Tyteca, *The New Rhetoric: A Treatise on Argumentation* (Notre Dame, 1969), p. 4; their emphasis (henceforth TNR).

5. David Kraemer, "Composition and Meaning in the Bavli," *Prooftexts,* 8 (1988):271–91.

6. For a general review of Perelman's work, see Sonja K. Foss, Karen A. Foss, and Robert Trapp, *Contemporary Perspectives on Rhetoric* (Prospect Heights, Ill., 1985), pp. 101–23. On *The New Rhetoric* in particular, see the review by Carroll C. Arnold in *The Quarterly Journal of Speech,* 56 (February 1970): 87–92, and by John Kozy, Jr., in *Philosophy and Rhetoric,* 3, no. 4 (Fall 1970); 249–54.

7. For a more formal definition of "truth," see the beginning of chapter 7.

8. Borrowing the words of Susan Handelman, *The Slayers of Moses* (Albany, 1982), p. 30. Whether or not Handelman's characterization pertains to "Hebrew thought," as she claims [cf. David Stern, "Moses-cide: Midrash and Contemporary Literary Criticism," *Prooftexts* 4 (1984): 195], it is certainly appropriate for the rabbis at large.

9. Of course, this is not to suggest that the Mishnah is uninterested in persuading its readers. I am merely noting here the tenor of its form, in contrast with that of the Bavli.

10. *The Karaite Anthology,* ed. and trans. Leon Nemoy (New Haven, 1952), p. 78; emphasis added.

11. This point has been observed previously, in particular by Louis Jacobs. See especially *The Talmudic Argument* (Cambridge, 1984).

12. See chapter 7.

13. David Goodblatt, "The Babylonian Talmud," in *The Study of Ancient Judaism* II, ed. Jacob Neusner (Hoboken, N.J., 1981), pp. 177–81.

14. Jacob Neusner, *A History of the Jews in Babylonia* (Leiden, 1970), vol. 5, pp. 60–69, 72.

15. Ibid., pp. 95–105, esp. pp. 104–5.

16. See Neusner, *History* (1966), vol. 2, p. 16 and n. 3; (1968), vol. 4, p. 19; and esp. (1969), vol. 5, pp. 90–91 and 90, n. 4.

17. Walter Ong, *Orality and Literacy: The Technologizing of the Word* (London, 1982), pp. 9, 105. Cf. C. Mackenzie Brown, "Purana as Scripture: From Sound to Image of the Holy Word in the Hindu Tradition," *History of Religions,* 26, no. 1 (August 1986): 85. Despite his specific critique, Brown agrees that writing has the power that Ong describes; see n. 69 there.

18. George A. Kennedy, *New Testament Interpretation Through Rhetorical Criticism* (Chapel Hill, N.C., 1984), p. 64.

19. *Orality and Literacy,* p. 119, emphasis added.

20. TNR, p. 106.

21. Jacob Neusner, *Midrash in Context: Exegesis in Formative Judaism* (Philadelphia, 1983), pp. 2–12.

22. See, at length, Neusner, ibid., pp. 2–65.

23. Jacob Neusner, *Torah: From Scroll to Symbol in Formative Judaism* (Philadelphia, 1985), pp. 26, 32, 53, 54–56, 61; and Martin Jaffee, "Oral Torah in Theory and Practice: Aspects of Mishnah-Exegesis in the Palestinian Talmud," *Religion,* 15 (1985): 390.

24. The fact that the designation "Torah" is not explicitly applied to the rabbinic tradition in the earlier period—at least not with any currency—is probative. It may safely be assumed that the absence of the term is indicative of the absence of the concept in any significant sense. For a discussion of this connection, see Ernst Cassirer, *The Philosophy of Symbolic Forms.* Vol. 1. *Language,* trans. Ralph Manheim (New Haven, 1955), pp. 86–90.

25. Neusner, *Torah,* p. 145.

26. See David Kraemer, "On the Reliability of Attributions in the Bavli," *Hebrew Union College Annual,* 60 (1990): 186–87.

27. See Adin Steinsaltz, "The Relationship Between Babylonia and the Land of Israel," *Talpiot,* 9 (1965): 300ff. Whatever the explanation of the absence of the Babylonian materials in the Yerushalmi—and Steinsaltz's analysis is problematic—it is clear that there is no influence of third- to fourth-generation Babylonian masters in the Palestinian document.

28. On the influence of such "distances" on the developing tradition, see Baruch Bokser, "Ma'al and Blessings over Food: Rabbinic Transformation of Cultic Terminology and Alternative Modes of Piety," *Journal of Biblical Literature,* 100, no. 4 (1981), esp. pp. 567–72. See also my proposal in "The Scientific Study of Talmud," *Judaism,* 36, no. 4 (Fall 1987): 477.

29. See Neusner, *History,* vol. 2, pp. 255–58, vol. 4, p. 127, and vol. 5, pp. 217–43, 322–24.

30. For a discussion of the extent of the rabbis' power in the Babylonian Jewish community, see Neusner, *History,* vol. 2, pp. 252–87, vol. 3, pp. 220–338, vol. 4, pp. 125–278, and vol. 5, pp. 244–329, summarized in *There We Sat Down* (Nashville, Tenn., 1972), esp. pp. 108–28.

31. See E. E. Urbach, "When Did Prophecy Cease?," *Tarbiz*, 1946: 1–11, recently reprinted in Urbach, *The World of the Sages* (Jerusalem, 1988), pp. 9–20. Urbach reviews the ongoing assumption of the possibility of prophecy in various Jewish sources of the late second Temple period and beyond, but he fails to take proper note of the fact that the denial of this possibility is a rabbinic innovation. If my analysis is correct, this innovation radically transformed the nature of the perceived rabbinic interface with the divine.

32. See E. E. Urbach, "Halakha and Prophecy," *Tarbiz*, 18 (1947): 9–10, rpt. *The World of the Sages*, pp. 29–30.

33. Note Hans Kelsen's comment, regarding the application of law in general, that "the higher norm cannot bind . . . the act by which it is applied"; see *Pure Theory of Law,* trans. Max Knight (Berkeley, 1967) p. 349. But see my reservations expressed on p. 173, concerning the incomparability of halakha and conventional legal systems.

34. Although manuscripts vary in the precise wording of this section, they agree that the response was joyful. See R. Rabbinowicz, *Diqduqei soferim,* ad loc.

35. David Halivni, *Meqorot umesorot: yoma-ḥagigah* (Jerusalem, 1975), p. 9 (introduction).

36. See David Stern's recent comments on this matter in "Midrash and Indeterminacy," *Critical Inquiry,* 15, no. 1 (Autumn 1988): 146.

37. A similar conclusion, in this case with reference to the Yerushalmi's use of the Mishnah, is suggested by Martin S. Jaffee. See his "Oral Torah in Theory and Practice: Aspects of Mishnah-Exegesis in the Palestinian Talmud," *Religion,* 15 (1985): 387–410.

38. Manuscript variants affect the precise mechanisms of the midrash at this and other points; see *Diqduqei soferim,* ad. loc. None of the variants affect the text as it serves as an example here.

39. This, for slightly different reasons, is Jacob Neusner's conclusion in *The Bavli and Its Sources: The Question of Tradition in the Case of Tractate Sukkah* (Atlanta, 1987). Also, I do not mean to suggest that change is untraditional; see Edward Shils, *Tradition* (Chicago, 1981), pp. 213–86, and note, especially, p. 216. I use "untraditional" here in the popular sense of that term.

40. To do so one would merely have to review cases that employ the challenge "it is obvious!" (*"peshita!"*) or, in fewer numbers, the solution "it is the opinion of an individual" (*"yeḥida'a hi"*), as identified in the concordance.

41. This judgment is supported by Maimonides in his *Mishneh Torah,* Laws of Prohibited Sexual Relations, 13:3.

42. See my discussion of "logic" in "Stylistic Characteristics in Amoraic Literature," Ph.D. diss., Jewish Theological Seminary of America, 1984, pp. 94–96.

43. Francis Brown, S. R. Driver, and Charles A. Briggs, *Hebrew and English Lexicon of the Old Testament* (Boston, 1907), p. 873, *piel* form, 4. b.

44. See tosafot, s.v. *"v'Rabbi Yehoshua . . ."*; their solutions to the problem include the possibility that "the women may not have been included in that sprinkling," as though women were not part of "the people."

45. This alternative version of the tradition is not found in MS Munich. However, although it is possible to explain its omission on the basis of scribal error, it is difficult to explain its inclusion if it is not an original part of the text. For that reason, and based on its presence in other manuscripts and versions, I treat it as an essential part of this deliberation.

46. This gemara can be outlined as follows:

I. Initial presentation of views
  A. (a–b)
  B. (c–e)
  C. (f–s)
    1. (h–i) ⎫
    2. (j–k) ⎪
    3. (l–m) ⎬ Attempted solutions
    4. (n–o) ⎪
    5. (p–q) ⎪
    6. (r–s) ⎭

II. Related question (t–dd)
  A. (y–z) ⎫
  B. (aa–bb) ⎬ Attempted solutions
  C. (cc–dd) ⎭

47. Other medieval rabbinic authorities also recognize the effect of this question and the thrust of the gemara as a whole. One authority who wants to claim, unlike this gemara, that burial has definitive scriptural support suggests as a source a verse (Gen. 3:19) that the gemara doesn't even consider; see *Otzar ha-geonim* (Jerusalem, n.d.), p. 361, par. 516. R. Hananel recognized what my analysis reveals and admitted that the requirement to bury is only rabbinic.

48. Shamma Friedman, *Pereq ha-isha rabba bebavli* (Jerusalem, 1978), pp. 47–48.

Chapter 6

1. See also the appendix to chapter 5.

2. For a more detailed analysis of this text, see David Kraemer, "Composition and Meaning in the Bavli," *Prooftexts,* 8 (1988): 275–81.

3. The exceptions to this rule number perhaps a half a dozen; see the comment of tosafot, s.v. *"d'amar lakh,"* Suk. 3a.

4. Other reasons may be suggested for the inclusion of Shammaite positions at an earlier stage; see Jacob Neusner, *The Rabbinic Traditions About the*

Pharisees Before 70 (Leiden, 1971), vol. 2, pp. 3–4. These reasons would not explain, however, why the Bavli, centuries later, would have given serious attention to Shammaite views. It is this latter phenomenon that I seek to explain here.

5. An Aramaic word that, like "Meir," derives from the root for "light." Alt: Meisha; see *Diqduqei soferim,* ad loc.

6. That is, R. Judah the Patriarch. Alt.: Rav; see *Diqduqei soferim,* ad loc.

7. Alt.: Rav or Rava; cf. San. 17a and *Diqduqei soferim* here.

8. See *Diqduqei soferim,* ad loc.

9. Again, this explanation does not contradict Neusner's suggestion that Shammaite views were included, and even given priority, because they predominated before 70; see note 4. Whatever the historical explanation of the earlier phenomenon, what concerns us here is the Bavli's later attitude.

10. Neusner argues, in fact, that there is a conscious polemic against this position in, at least, the Sifra. See *Sifra: An Analytical Translation* (Atlanta, 1988), vol. 1, pp. 46–52.

11. The cases are as follows: Ber. 4b, Yev. 35b, Kid. 35b, B.B. 8b (2), B.B. 9a, San. 30a (2), Shev. 22b, A.Z. 34b = Temurah 30b, Zev. 2a = Zev. 7b = Men. 2a, Men. 13b, Men. 73b, Hul. 118b.

12. See *Otzar leshon ha-Talmud,* vol. 3, pp. 1531–32, 1560, and vol. 19, pp. 802–6.

13. See Git. 48a, Kid. 4a, B.Q. 64b, A.Z. 8a, Tem. 9a, Zev. 50a, Zev. 107a and b, Men. 75a, Tem. 3b, Tem. 30b, and Ker. 11a.

14. This particular derivation (up to "shall be") is not present in manuscripts.

15. See, e.g., Taan. 3a, Zev. 97b, and Men. 17b.

16. For a broader consideration of the phenomenon described here, that being limitation in canon followed by ingenious extension, see Jonathan Smith, *Imagining Religion* (Chicago, 1982), pp. 36–52.

17. See, e.g., Yerushalmi Pes. 7:13 (35b), Yom. 8:3 (45a), Yev. 2:10 (4a), and Ket. 3:6 (27d).

18. For the earliest use of this phrase, see Sifrei Bamidbar 112 (ed. Horovitz [Jerusalem, 1966], p. 121). See also Burton L. Visotzky, "Jots and Tittles: On Scriptural Interpretation in Rabbinic and Patristic Literatures," *Prooftexts,* 8, no. 3 (1988): 257–69.

19. For one dating of Avot d'Rabbi Nathan, see M. B. Lerner, "The External Tractates," in *The Literature of the Sages,* pt. 1, ed. Shmuel Safrai (Philadelphia, 1987), pp. 376–77.

20. See Schechter's edition (Vienna, 1887), pp. 61 (31a)–62.

21. Affirming the priority of the Bavli's version of this story, see Burton L. Visotzky, "Hillel, Hieronymous and Praetextatus," *Journal of the Ancient Near Eastern Society,* 16–17 (1984–85): 223 n. 35, and J. Neusner, *The Rabbinic Traditions About the Pharisees,* vol. 1, p. 322.

22. J. Neusner, *Torah: From Scroll to Symbol in Formative Judaism* (Philadelphia, 1985), p. 145.

23. *Mechilta D'Rabbi Ismael,* ed. H.S. Horovitz and I. A. Rabin, (Jerusalem, 1970), p. 61.

24. See *Diqduqei soferim,* ad loc., n. 4.

25. The text in the latter part of Kid. 4:14 is not part of the Mishnah at all. See J. N. Epstein, *Mevo lenusaḥ ha-Mishnah* (Jerusalem, 1948) vol. 2, p. 977.

26. *Sifre on Deuteronomy,* L. Finkelstein, (New York, 1969), pp. 84–85 (emphasis added).

27. Note that this is precisely the way that the Bavli understood this text; see B.Q. 17a.

28. I omit from consideration here the first Mishnah of the so-called sixth chapter of Avot. As the language of that text indicates, it is not actually a part of the Mishnah, having been added much later as a consequence of its inclusion in that connection in the Siddur liturgy. Its source seems to be in one of the so-called minor tractates and its redaction is, in any case, post-Talmudic. There is certainly no reason to believe on the basis of its evidence, which is contradicted by all other available information, that this usage was known in the Mishnaic period. On this text, see Shimon Sharvit, "Textual Variants and Language of the Treatise Abot," Ph.D. diss. Bar-Ilan University, 1976, pp. 310–13.

29. In its only other usage in the Yerushalmi, at Hag. 2:1 (77c), someone who studies *torah lishma* is contrasted with one who studies "not for the sake of Heaven." The concern, therefore, is motives, and *lishma* apparently describes a pious intent, directed toward the fulfillment of God's commandments.

30. See also David Halivni's history of talmud torah in *Midrash, Mishnah, and Gemara: The Jewish Predilection for Justified Law* (Cambridge, Mass., 1986), pp. 108–11, and Norman Lamm, *Torah lishma bemishnat R. Hayim mi-Volozhin* (Jerusalem, 1972), pp. 77–158.

Chapter 7

1. See De Lacy O'Leary, *How Greek Science Passed to the Arabs* (London, 1951), pp. 28–29, 68–70, and F. E. Peters, *Aristotle and the Arabs* (New York, 1968), pp. 45–49.

2. See W. Friedmann, *Legal Theory* (New York, 1967), p. 109.

3. P. Tillich, *Systematic Theology* (Chicago, 1951), vol. 1, p. 102.

4. Paul K. Moser and Arnold Vander Nat, *Human Knowledge: Classical and Contemporary Approaches* (New York, 1987), p. 11; their emphasis.

5. Cf. Chaim Perelman, *The Idea of Justice and the Problem of Argument* (London, 1963), p. 128.

6. See Bertrand Russell, *A History of Western Philosophy* (New York, 1945), pp. 91–92.

7. I venture this proposal mindful of Strauss's methodological caution in *The City and Man,* pp. 50ff. And in contradistinction to my tentative conclusion, it is also necessary to recall that Gadamer interprets the dialectical form of Plato's

dialogues to suggest that truth is assumed to be ultimately indeterminate in his philosophy; see *Dialogue and Dialectic,* pp. 93–123, esp. p. 122, and pp. 154–55.

8. All translations of Plato are taken from *The Collected Dialogues of Plato,* eds. Edith Hamilton and Huntington Cairns (Princeton, 1961).

9. See Francis M. Cornford, *Plato's Theory of Knowledge* (New York, 1957), pp. 162–93.

10. Gadamer (*The Idea of the Good in Platonic–Aristotelian Philosophy,* p. 28) reads the parable of the cave to suggest that the idea of good, like the sun, cannot be viewed directly but can be grasped only through its effects. It seems to me, though, that the bulk of what Plato has to say in this context, both explicitly (as quoted here) and implicitly, allows for the possibility of more direct, definitive knowledge.

11. Emphasis added. All translations of Aristotle are taken from *The Basic Works of Aristotle,* ed. Richard McKeon, (New York, 1941).

12. See Russell, *A History of Western Philosophy,* p. 233.

13. Ibid., p. 234, and Sextus Empiricus, *Outlines of Pyrrhonism,* bk. 1, 14:112–17.

14. "Discourse on Method," in *Philosophical Writings* (Indianapolis, 1971), p. 7.

15. Ibid., p. 20.

16. Ibid., p. 32.

17. *Monadology,* pars. 29 and 45.

18. Russell, *A History of Western Philosophy,* p. 785. See also idem., *Philosophical Essays* (New York, 1966), p. 114.

19. *The Gathas of Zarathustra,* trans. Stanley Insler (Leiden, 1975), p. 35.

20. Quoted in Kenneth Cragg and Marston Speight, eds., *Islam from Within* (Belmont, Calif., 1980), p. 125.

21. Mircea Eliade, *A History of Religious Ideas* (Chicago, 1982), vol. 2, p. 58.

22. See Frederick M. Denny and Rodney L. Taylor, eds., *The Holy Book in Comparative Perspective* (Columbia, S.C., 1985), pp. 126–27.

23. See Eliade, *A History of Religious Ideas,* vol. 2, pp. 93–95, and Denny and Taylor, *Holy Book,* pp. 156–57.

24. Tertullian, *On Prescription Against Heretics,* quoted in Etienne Gilson, *Reason and Revelation in the Middle Ages* (New York, 1938), p. 8.

25. Averroës, *On the Harmony of Religion and Philosophy,* trans. George F. Hourani (London, 1961).

26. Ibid., pp. 44–49.

27. Ibid., p. 50, emphasis added.

28. Ibid., pp. 50–51.

29. Thomas Aquinas, *On the Truth of the Catholic Faith (Summa Contra Gentiles),* Book 1: *God,* trans. Anton C. Pegis (Garden City, N.Y., 1955), 3 [2], p. 63.

30. Ibid., 3 [3], p. 64.

31. Ibid., 3 [4], p. 65.

32. Ibid., 7 [1], p. 74.

33. Hans Lewy, Alexander Altmann, and Isaak Heinemann, eds., *Three Jewish Philosophers* (New York, 1969), p. 25, and see also pp. 38–39.

34. Ibid., p. 36.

35. Ibid., p. 37.

36. Ibid., p. 45.

37. Ibid., p. 45.

38. Ibid.

39. Maimonides, *Guide for the Perplexed,* trans. Shlomo Pines (Chicago, 1963), p. 620.

40. Ibid., p. 635.

41. Ibid., pp. 327–38.

42. In theory; in fact, he also sometimes interprets Aristotle to make his doctrine accord with the truth of scripture.

43. In connection with religious traditions and truth, see also Hendrick M. Vroom, *Religions and the Truth* (Grand Rapids, Mich., 1989). Regrettably, this work appeared when it was no longer possible for me to include specific references to Vroom's discussion in the present book.

44. *The Slayers of Moses* (Albany, 1982), p. 30.

Bibliography

Albeck, Chanoch. *Mavo la-talmudim*. Tel-Aviv: Dvir, 1969.

Aquinas, Thomas. *On the Truth of the Catholic Faith (Summa Contra Gentiles)*. Book 1, *God*. Trans. Anton C. Pegis. Garden City, N.Y.: Hanover House, 1955.

Aristotle. *The Basic Works of Aristotle*. Ed. Richard McKeon. New York: Random House, 1941.

Averroës. *On the Harmony of Religion and Philosophy*. Trans. George F. Hourani. London: UNESCO, 1961.

Bokser, Baruch. *"Ma'al* and Blessings over Food: Rabbinic Transformation of Cultic Terminology and Alternative Modes of Piety." *Journal of Biblical Literature*, 100, no. 4 (1981): 557–74.

———. "The Palestinian Talmud." In *Austeig und Niedergang der römischen Welt II*. Vol. 19, no. 2, pp. 139–256. Rpt. in *The Study of Ancient Judaism II*. Ed. Jacob Neusner. Hoboken, N.J.: Ktav, 1981.

———. *Post Mishnaic Judaism in Transition: Samuel on Berakhot and the Beginnings of Gemara*. Chico, Calif.: Scholars Press, 1980.

———. *Samuel's Commentary on the Mishnah. Part One: Mishnayot in the Order of Zera'im*. Leiden: Brill, 1975.

Chernick, Michael. *Leheqer ha-middot "khlal ufrat ukhlal" v' "ribui umiut" bemidrashim uvetalmudim*. Lod, Israel: Haberman Institute, 1984.

Cornford, Francis M. *Plato's Theory of Knowledge*. New York: Liberal Arts Press, 1957.

Cragg, Kenneth, and Speight, Marston, eds. *Islam from Within*. Belmont, Calif.: Wadsworth, 1980.

Denny, Frederick M., and Taylor, Rodney L., eds. *The Holy Book in Comparative Perspective*. Columbia: University of South Carolina Press, 1985.

Eliade, Mircea. *A History of Religious Ideas.* 3 vols. Chicago: University of Chicago Press, 1978–1985.

Encyclopedia Judaica, s.v. "Hebrew Language," by E. Y. Kutscher.

The Encyclopedia of Religion, s.v. "Avesta," by Gherardo Gnoli.

————, s.v. "Tannaim," by David Kraemer.

Epstein, J. N. *Mevo lenusaḥ ha-Mishnah.* 2 vols. Jerusalem: J. N. Epstein, 1948.

————. *Mevo'ot lesifrut ha-amoraim.* Jerusalem: Magnes Press, 1962.

Finley, M.I. *Ancient History: Evidence and Models.* New York: Elisabeth Sifton Books and Penguin Books, 1986.

Foss, Sonja K., Foss, Karen A., and Trapp, Robert. *Contemporary Perspectives on Rhetoric.* Prospect Heights, Ill.: Waveland Press, 1985.

Frankel, Zechariah. *Mevo ha-Yerushalmi.* Breslau, 1870. Repr. Jerusalem, 1967.

Gadamer, Hans-Georg. *Dialogue and Dialectic.* Trans. P. Christopher Smith. New Haven: Yale University Press, 1980.

————. *The Idea of the Good in Platonic–Aristotelian Philosophy.* Trans. P. Christopher Smith. New Haven: Yale University Press, 1986.

The Gathas of Zarathustra. Trans. Stanley Insler. Acta Iranica. Leiden: Brill, 1975.

Gilson, Etienne. *Reason and Revelation in the Middle Ages.* New York: Scribner, 1938.

Goodblatt, David. "The Babylonian Talmud." In *Aufsteig und Niedergang der römischen Welt II.* Vol. 19, no. 2. Rpt. in *The Study of Ancient Judaism II.* Ed. Jacob Neusner. Hoboken, N.J.: Ktav, 1981.

Greenwald, L. *Ha-ra'u mesadrei ha-bavli et ha-yerushalmi.* New York: Hamakhon lemeḥqar ulemad'a ha-Yerushalmi, 1954.

Halivni, David. *Meqorot umesorot.* Jerusalem: Jewish Theological Seminary of America, 1982.

————. *Meqorot umesorot: yoma-ḥagiga.* Jerusalem: Jewish Theological Seminary of America, 1975.

————. *Midrash, Mishnah, and Gemara: The Jewish Predilection for Justified Law.* Cambridge, Mass.: Harvard University Press, 1986.

Handelman, Susan. *The Slayers of Moses.* Albany: SUNY Press, 1982.

Hauptman, Judith. *Development of the Talmudic Sugya: Relationship Between Tannaitic and Amoraic Sources.* Lanham, N.Y.: University Press of America, 1988.

Jaffee, Martin. "The Babylonian Appropriation of the Talmud Yerushalmi: Redactional Studies in the Horayot Tractates." In *New Perspectives on Ancient Judaism.* Vol. 4. *The Literature of Early Rabbinic Judaism: Issues in Talmudic Redaction and Interpretation.* Studies in Judaism. Ed. Alan J. Avery-Peck. Lanham, N.Y.: University Press of America, 1989.

————. "Oral Torah in Theory and Practice: Aspects of Mishnah-Exegesis in the Palestinian Talmud." *Religion,* 15 (1985): 387–410.

Kalmin, Richard. *The Redaction of the Babylonian Talmud: Amoraic or Saboraic?* Cincinnati, Ohio: Hebrew Union College Press, 1989.

————- "Review of 'Midrash, Mishnah and Gemara: The Jewish Predilection for Justified Law,' by David Halivni." *Conservative Judaism,* 39, no. 4 (Summer 1987): 78–84.

The Karaite Anthology. Ed. and trans. Leon Nemoy. New Haven: Yale University Press, 1952.

Kasovsky, C. Y. *Otzar leshon ha-Mishnah.* 4 vols. Tel-Aviv: Massadah, 1957, 1967.

————. *Otzar leshon ha-Talmud.* 41 vols. Jerusalem: Ministry of Education and Culture of the Government of Israel and The Jewish Theological Seminary, 1954–82.

————. *Otzar leshon ha-Yerushalmi.* 3 vols. Jerusalem: Israel Academy of Sciences and Humanities and The Jewish Theological Seminary of America, 1979–84.

Kennedy, George A. *New Testament Interpretation Through Rhetorical Criticism.* Chapel Hill: University of North Carolina Press, 1984.

Kraemer, David. "Composition and Meaning in the Bavli." *Prooftexts,* 8 (1988): 271–91.

————. "On the Reliability of Attributions in the Bavli." *Hebrew Union College Annual,* 60 (1989):175–90.

————. "The Scientific Study of Talmud." *Judaism,* 36, no. 4 (Fall 1987): 471–78.

————. "Scripture Commentary in the Babylonian Talmud: Primary or Secondary Phenomenon?" *AJS Review,* 14, no. 1 (March 1989): 1–15.

————. "Stylistic Characteristics of Amoraic Literature." Ph.D. dissertation, Jewish Theological Seminary of America, 1984. University Microfilms International.

Lamm, Norman. *Torah lishma bemishnat R. Hayim mi-Volozhin.* Jerusalem: Mossad Harav Kook, 1972.

Leiman, Sid Z. *The Canonization of Hebrew Scripture: The Talmudic and Midrashic Evidence.* Hamden, Conn.: Published for the Connecticut Academy of Arts and Sciences by Archon Books, 1976.

Lerner, M. B. "The External Tractates." In *The Literature of the Sages.* Part 1. Ed. Shmuel Safrai. Philadelphia: Fortress Press, 1987.

Lewin, B. M. *Rabbanan sabora'i vetalmudam.* Jerusalem: Ahiever, 1937.

Lewy, Hans, Altmann, Alexander, and Heinemann, Isaak, eds. *Three Jewish Philosophers.* New York: Atheneum, 1969.

Lieberman, Saul. *Hellenism in Jewish Palestine.* New York: Jewish Theological Seminary of America, 1950. Rpt., 1962.

Maimonides. *Guide for the Perplexed.* Trans. Shlomo Pines. Chicago: University of Chicago Press, 1963.

Moser, Paul K., and Vander Nat, Arnold. *Human Knowledge: Classical and Contemporary Approaches.* New York: Oxford University Press, 1987.

Neusner, Jacob. *The Bavli and Its Sources: The Question of Tradition in the Case of Tractate Sukkah.* Atlanta: Scholars Press, 1987.

————. *A History of the Jews in Babylonia.* 5 vols. Leiden: Brill, 1965–70.

————. *A History of the Jews in Babylonia.* Vol. 1. *The Parthian Period.* 3rd printing. Chico, Calif.: Scholars Press, 1984.

————. *Judaism: The Classical Statement.* Chicago: University of Chicago Press, 1986.

————. *Judaism: The Evidence of the Mishnah.* Chicago: University of Chicago Press, 1981.

————. *Judaism in Society: The Evidence of the Yerushalmi.* Chicago: University of Chicago Press, 1983.

————. *Midrash in Context: Exegesis in Formative Judaism.* Philadelphia: Fortress Press, 1983.

————. *The Pharisees: Rabbinic Perspectives.* Hoboken, N.J.: Ktav, 1973.

————. *The Rabbinic Traditions About the Pharisees Before 70.* 3 vols. Leiden: Brill, 1971.

————. *Sifra: An Analytical Translation.* Vol. 1. Atlanta: Scholars Press, 1988.

————. *There We Sat Down.* Nashville, Tenn.: Abingdon Press, 1972.

————. *Torah: From Scroll to Symbol in Formative Judaism.* Philadelphia: Fortress Press, 1985.

Nickelsburg, George W. E. *Jewish Literature Between the Bible and the Mishnah.* Philadelphia: Fortress Press, 1981.

Ong, Walter. *Orality and Literacy: The Technologizing of the Word.* London: Methuen, 1982.

Perelman, Chaim. *The Idea of Justice and the Problem of Argument.* London: Routledge and Kegan Paul, 1963.

Perelman, Chaim, and Olbrechts-Tyteca, L. *The New Rhetoric: A Treatise on Argumentation.* Notre Dame and London: University of Notre Dame Press, 1969.

Plato: The Collected Dialogues. Ed. Edith Hamilton and H. Cairns. Princeton: Princeton University Press, 1961.

Rabbinovicz, R. *Diqduqei soferim.* 2 vols. New York: M.P. Press, 1976.

Russell, Bertrand. *A History of Western Philosophy.* New York: Simon and Schuster, 1945.

————. *Philosophical Essays.* New York: Simon and Schuster, 1966.

Sharvit, Shimon. "Textual Variants and Language of the Treatise Abot." Ph.D. dissertation, Bar-Ilan University, 1976. (in Hebrew)

Shils, Edward. *Tradition.* Chicago: University of Chicago Press, 1981.

Smith, Jonathan. *Imagining Religion.* Chicago: University of Chicago Press, 1982.

Spiegel, Yaakov. "'Amar Rava hilkheta—piskei halakha me'uḥarim." In *'Iyyunim besifrut hz''l bemiqrah uvetoledot yisrael.* Ed. Y. D. Gilat, C. Levine, and Z. M. Rabinowitz. Ramat Gan, Israel: Bar-Ilan University, 1982, pp. 206–14.

————. "Hosafot me'uḥarot (saborai'ot) beTalmud Bavli." Ph.D. diss. Tel-Aviv University, 1976. (in Hebrew)

Steinsaltz, Adin. "The Relationship Between Babylonia and the Land of Israel." *Talpiot,* 9 (1965): 298–307. (in Hebrew)

Stern, David. "Midrash and Indeterminacy." *Critical Inquiry,* 15, no. 1 (Autumn 1988): 132–61.

Strauss, Leo. *The City and Man.* Chicago: University of Chicago Press, 1964.

Tillich, Paul. *Systematic Theology.* Vol. 1. Chicago: University of Chicago Press, 1951.

Urbach, E. E. "Halakha and Prophecy." *Tarbiẓ,* 18 (1947): 1–27. Rpt. in E. E. Urbach. *The World of the Sages.* Jerusalem: Magnes Press, 1988. (in Hebrew)

———. "When Did Prophecy Cease?," *Tarbiẓ,* 17 (1946): 1–11. Rpt. in E. E. Urbach, *The World of the Sages.* Jerusalem: Magnes Press, 1988. (in Hebrew)

Visotzky, Burton L. "Hillel, Hieronymous and Praetextatus." *Journal of the Ancient Near Eastern Society,* 16–17 (1984–85): 217–24.

———. "Jots and Tittles: On Scriptural Interpretation in Rabbinic and Patristic Literatures." *Prooftexts,* 8, no. 3 (1988): 257–69.

Vroom, Hendrik M. *Religions and the Truth: Philosophical Reflections and Perspectives.* Grand Rapids, Mich.: William B. Eerdmans, 1989.

Weiss, Avraham. *'al ha-yetzirah ha-sifrutit shel ha-'amoraim.* New York: Horeb Yeshivah University, 1962.

Wellek, René, and Warren, Austin. *Theory of Literature.* San Diego: Harcourt Brace Jovanovich, 1977.

Wolff, Hans Julius. *Roman Law.* Norman: University of Oklahoma Press, 1976.

General Index

Index to Primary
Rabbinic Sources

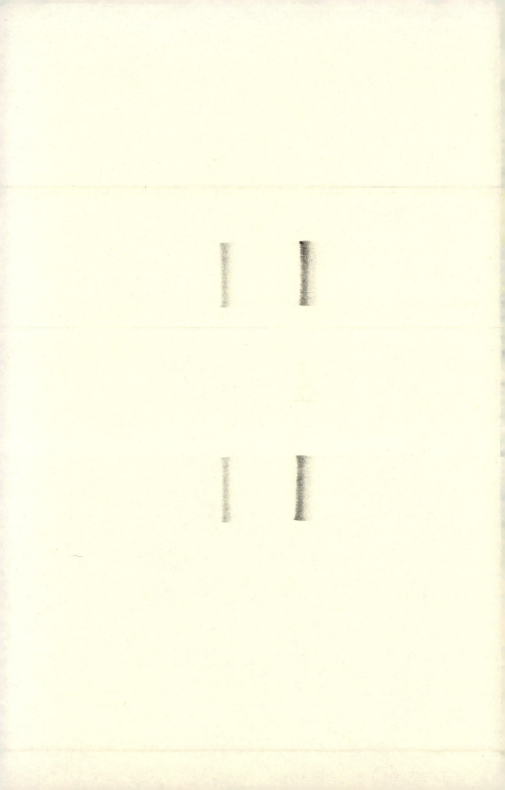